CONCORDIA UNIVERSITY
HQ682.B55
LOVE MATCH AND ARRANGE

3 4211 000042245

WITHDRAWN

WITHDRAWN

W9-DIT-996

DATE DUE

OC2 3'96		
FE1 3'97		
JE31'97		
JY01'97		
NO23'02		
NO2 8 00		
DE29'01		
APR 2 3 2005		

DEMCO 38-297

ATCH

RANGED MARRIAGE

Love Match
and
Arranged Marriage

A TOKYO-DETROIT COMPARISON

Robert O. Blood, Jr.

University of Michigan, Ann Arbor

KLINCK MEMORIAL LIBRARY
Concordia Teachers College
River Forest, Illinois

THE FREE PRESS, *New York*
COLLIER-MACMILLAN LIMITED, *London* $\boxed{Fp}$

Copyright © 1967 by Robert O. Blood, Jr.

Printed in the United States of America

All rights reserved. No part of this book may be reproduced or transmitted in any form or by any means, electronic or mechanical, including photocopying, recording, or by any information storage and retrieval system, without permission in writing from the Publisher.

Collier-Macmillan Canada, Ltd., Toronto, Ontario

Library of Congress Catalog Card Number: 67-12511

First Printing

25261

PREFACE

IN 1955 I directed the Detroit Area Study of the University of Michigan in interviewing a representative cross-section of married couples in the Detroit metropolitan area. The results of this study appear in a Free Press monograph (now reissued in paperback) entitled *Husbands and Wives: the Dynamics of Married Living* (with Donald M. Wolfe).

In 1958–59 I spent ten months in Japan on sabbatical leave from the University of Michigan. A Fulbright Research Fellowship enabled me to devote the year to research through the facilities of the Department of Sociology of Tokyo Educational University. My sponsor was Professor Yuzuru Okada, chairman of the department. Professor Kiyomi Morioka shared his office with me and served as my chief consultant on the details of the study. Also helpful in the planning stage were Professor Ezra Vogel of Harvard University and Professor Takashi Koyama of Toyo University (President of the Japan Sociological Society and chairman of the Ninth International Seminar on Family Research). Professor Eiichi Isomura of Tokyo Metropolitan University provided access to the government housing projects where the interviews were conducted.

Mr. Mitsuru Shimpo, a graduate of International Christian University in Tokyo, served as my research assistant, training and supervising women who interviewed 444 wives and collected questionnaires from their husbands.

A grant from the National Science Foundation (G-23493) supported the analysis of the data. George Jarvis (now teaching at the University of Western Ontario) was the principal analyst of the Japanese data. Fred Campbell (who has joined the faculty of the University of Washington) reanalyzed the American data to match the Japanese sample.

The draft manuscript was read by Professor Morioka, Professor Hiroshi Wagatsuma of the University of Hawaii, and Dr. William Caudill of the

v

National Institute of Mental Health (Bethesda). Their painstaking critiques caught errors in interpretation and supplied comments which I have often added as footnotes identified by name with no date attached.

Needless to say, there were numerous others whose assistance was invaluable. As a newcomer to Japan, I needed more than the usual orientation to a foreign country and devoted several months to exploratory interviews with English-speaking Japanese before developing my interview schedule. Successive versions were pretested with patient respondents who helped me find both the right Japanese expressions and the right English translations.

The final product answers two questions. (1) What are the differential consequences after marriage of the new and old systems of mate-selection in Japan? (2) Are the effects of internal and external forces on marriage the same in Tokyo as they are in Detroit? The latter investigation provides an international replication of my *Husbands and Wives* monograph. Similar efforts have been undertaken by scholars in various other countries, notably by Dr. Reuben Hill in Louvain, Belgium, Dr. André Michel in Paris and Bordeaux, and Dr. Constantina Safilios-Rothschild in Athens. These several replications of the original Detroit research promise increasing development of scientific generalizations about marital interaction patterns in modern communities.

The tentativeness of generalizations in this book is symbolized by the non-use of tests of statistical significance of differences. Difficult problems of translation across language barriers and of achieving "equality" between sample populations in very different societies render my findings preliminary at best. I hope not so much that this book will *prove* scientific propositions as that it will suggest lines of inquiry to be pursued more rigorously in the future.

ROBERT O. BLOOD, JR.

Ann Arbor

CONTENTS

APPENDIXES

TABLES

APPENDIXES

FIGURES

Part 1

Japanese Mate-Selection and Courtship and Their Marital Consequences

JAPAN is a postfeudal country emerging from a hierarchical, authoritarian past into greater equality between parents and children, women and men. One facet of this revolutionary transition is the appearance of a new system of mate-selection alongside the old system of marriage arrangement, and the gradual transformation of the latter even while it retains its old name.

The Japanese term for arranged marriage is *miai kekkon* (literally, "interview marriage") from the formal meeting at which the prospective bride and groom are introduced to each other by the matchmaker. Because the couple are then free to date and to make up their own minds whether to get married, the marriage is no longer definitively arranged by the parents. Nevertheless, even modernized *miai* marriages are still more old-fashioned than self-initiated love matches.

The first half of this book traces these ways of choosing marriage partners in a very old country. Then we ask, "So what? Do husbands and wives treat each other any differently after choosing one another than after having their partners chosen for them?" Finally, we explore the marital consequences of courtship activities, regardless of how the courtship happened to start.

1

LOVE MATCH

AND ARRANGED MARRIAGE–

CONTRASTING CONCEPTS OF

MATE-SELECTION

O<small>NE</small> afternoon in the spring of 1959, my wife and I rode a commuter train to a Tokyo suburb for dinner with our friends, the Kondos. Because Japanese addresses are hard to find, the young newlyweds met us at the station and escorted us to their home. Knowing of my interest in Japanese matchmaking, they described their experience to us as we walked along the quiet residential streets.

They met in 1955 at an open-house reception at a Quaker neighborhood center. Their common interests in world peace and religion attracted them to each other. In addition, Masako pumped Tsuneo with questions about the four years he had spent abroad because she, too, hoped to go to America soon. This chance encounter led to their attending other functions of mutual interest. As friendship ripened, dates at coffeehouses were added. Then Masako went off to America for two long years bridged by correspondence. On her return, she and Tsuneo were so glad to see each other that they soon decided to get married.

Their wedding differed from an American one only in using a foreigner (an American Quaker) for advice and the customary ceremonial speech of moral instruction at the reception. Technically, this speech-maker was a so-called "go-between," but he had nothing to do with arranging the marriage. That was done by the couple themselves in consultation with their parents.

love story

For the past year they had been living with Tsuneo's parents—not because it was their duty, but because of the Tokyo housing shortage. As far as duty was concerned, Masako had been expected to stay with *her* family and have Tsuneo adopt *her* last name. As an only child, she could thus carry on the family name. But neither partner felt bound by old-fashioned reasoning. Although living under the same roof with one set of parents, they were already functioning quite independently and planned to move shortly to the southern island of Kyushu, where they would be completely on their own.

After a delicious dinner of sukiyaki, Tsuneo said, "Now I want you to hear what marriage was like in the old days." His father told us first about *his* father's marriage:

In those days (the 1850's), marriage was a contract between families, not between individuals. My grandparents carefully investigated my mother's family background before choosing her to be my father's wife. They wanted to be sure that her family was of the same rank, was of good financial reputation, and had no hereditary diseases that might be transmitted to later generations of Kondos. After they decided she was suitable, they went around and got the approval of all their close relatives before entering into negotiations with the other family, using a relative as a go-between. The wedding was followed by a series of drinking parties lasting several days, first at the groom's home and then at the bride's home. The women attended these festivities, but only the men did any drinking. Every year after that, the two families got together at every festival occasion.

My father and mother were from villages ten miles apart in an age when sedan chairs were the only means of transportation. They never met until the wedding ceremony. My own marriage was unusual in that my wife and I didn't meet even then. I was away from home at the Imperial University and studying hard for the civil service exam. Since I was the eldest son, my parents were anxious to have me get married. My father's uncle and my mother's uncle were good friends and made the arrangements on behalf of the two families. My wife was 17 years old at the time of the wedding, and I was 27. She had seen my picture, but I had never seen hers—I was too busy studying to be disturbed. The wedding was unusual because I was represented by proxy. After the ceremony, the main relatives on both sides brought my wife to Tokyo to meet me, completed the formalities, and then left us to begin living together. In those days love affairs were unheard of except in the lower class.

The Kondos illustrate dramatically the change which has occurred in Japanese mate-selection. Prior to the opening of Japan to the West in 1868, mate-selection was a family affair for the middle and upper classes.[1] Parents took the initiative in deciding when and whom their child should marry. The criteria for choice were family-oriented, since marriages established bonds between families. Wives were chosen with special care for oldest sons because they were expected to move into the husband's household and become dutiful servants

---

1. Professor Yuzuru Okada reports that before 1868 there was no word for "marrying" in Japanese, only "getting a wife" for one's son or "giving away" one's daughter or "disposing of her." The latter was the more humble expression and has the same "cleaning up" implications as in English.

of his parents. The wife's absorption into her husband's family line was symbolized by ceremonially erasing her name from her family's registration book at the city or town hall and adding it to the husband's family registry. Marriage was less the symmetrical linking of two family lines than the recruitment of women into a male line which could not continue without women to bear sons in each generation. Unbroken family lines preserved the family land intact in an agrarian society, provided financial and personal care for aged parents, and preserved their memory after death through "ancestor worship."

The importance of continuity created a biological emphasis in mate-selection. Brides were selected for their presumed ability to bear healthy children (preferably sons, but one had to take one's chances on that). The eugenic calculus considered the young woman's health, prizing vigor and robustness. It examined her family tree for rotten fruit such as criminal acts and mental or physical illnesses presumed to be hereditary and likely to introduce weakness into the husband's genetic line. The final danger to be avoided was the potential "racial" taint if a prospect's ancestors turned out to be outcasts (*Eta* or *Burakumin*, see DeVos and Wagatsuma, 1966).

Parents, then, used both short-run and long-run considerations in choosing a daughter-in-law. In the short run, she should be compatible with her new family. This required willingness to conform to the family pattern of living. She came a stranger into a pre-existing household. She could expect neither concessions nor compromises from a way of life so long established. Her task was to obey her mother-in-law, to submit, to conform, to serve.

For the long run, parents sought a firm link in the chain of generations.

To train daughters for such a future, parents taught them to be submissive and obedient. Nevertheless, the parents sought to minimize the hardships suffered by many young wives by marrying their daughters into good families. Since parents lost their daughters after marriage and could hardly intervene on their behalf in case of trouble, they were almost as concerned with their daughters' marriages as with their sons'.

Such concern on both sides created a bargaining situation in which each party exaggerated its assets and hid its liabilities, worrying lest the antagonist succeed in doing the same. For families who knew each other, the danger of being trapped in a disadvantageous bargain was minimized—but the danger of creating a feud should the negotiations go wrong was maximized. Relying on matchmakers as literal "go-betweens" saved rejected parties from the loss of face felt by jilted American suitors. It also protected the family who broke off negotiations from the consequences of openly offending a family that—by virtue of its social status—was important to them.

For families who did not know a suitable prospect, the matchmaker was even more indispensable. She broadened the range of acquaintance of the prospecting family to include her own circle of friends. It was also her responsibility to cut through the double-edged strategy of boasting and concealment employed by both sides. As an intermediary, she could be counted on to be dispassionate, independent, and objective, negotiating a mutually satisfactory liaison.

We have described the three active parties to the negotiations—the two sets of parents and the go-between. To increase the probability of success in these delicate transactions, they preferred not to involve the young people until the contract was ready to be sealed in a betrothal ceremony, exchanging gifts between the families. To inform children prematurely would risk the intrusion of extraneous factors such as personal wishes and sentiments.[2] The authority and interests of the extended families could be safeguarded best when young people were excluded from the selection process (Goode, 1959).

Once the couple were betrothed, there remained the task of arranging the wedding ceremony. This also was the parents' responsibility. Contacts between the betrothed were considered indecent. Each still belonged to his respective family. Only after the wedding did the bride move to the groom's household, beginning interaction between partners.

If there were no interaction prior to marriage, there could be no sentiment either (Homans, 1950). In this sense, such marriages started out "cold." As I lectured to public audiences throughout Japan, I was often told by members of the older generation that "arranged marriages start out cold and get hot, whereas love matches start out hot and grow cold." In Chapter 3 we will test this epigram empirically.

In arranged marriages, love might be expected to increase as long as the interaction of husband and wife was mutually satisfactory. However, three-generation households de-emphasized the husband-wife relationship. Eldest sons never "left home," but continued their childhood dependence on their mothers. Wives focused their attention on the children. For sexual satisfaction and affection, men often turned to mistresses less submissive than their wives. Hence we cannot assume that the average marriage grew more than lukewarm in feudal Japan.

The belief that love matches grow cold reflects the traditional link in Japanese literature between love and tragedy. Extramarital love for a mistress was tolerated by the Japanese family system with equanimity since it did not threaten the system. Filial duty and child-rearing responsibility could be carried on undisturbed by the existence of an extra household of mistress and children on the other side of town, provided financial resources were sufficiently lush.

Sometimes extramarital love was even incorporated into the family system. If the legal wife were barren, she might be divorced. Alternatively, the husband could acquire a mistress to give birth to a son who would become his heir and carry on the family line. Thus Confucian ethics sometimes defined extramarital love as a form of filial duty (Wagatsuma).

Extramarital relationships also served as status symbols in certain circles. One Japanese informant told of a lawyer who wanted to run for the national Diet but was advised against it because, "You don't have the guts to have a concubine." According to this informant, "People *expect* a prominent politician

2. This discussion portrays the classical ideal more than the historic reality. Kiyomi Morioka writes: "In general, the children were informed of their prospective spouse and their reactions were more or less seriously taken into consideration."

or businessman to have a concubine" and wonder what is wrong if he doesn't. In her own family:

> My father made a fortune in the stock market and needed to be notified of business emergencies, so he always told my mother where he was going when he went to be with his concubine. My mother says she never felt any jealousy. Of course, hers was not a love match. She was interested only in her parents and her children. Her husband was only a source of money for her to use for her children. She is a perfect Japanese wife, uncomplaining, and spoiling her husband.

Premarital love was another matter. If a boy and girl fell in love and wanted to marry, parental authority and the arranged marriage system were challenged. Moreover, people generally assumed that lovers were unsuited for each other (by the usual familistic criteria). The girl was assumed to be socially inferior— and she usually was! The segregation of the sexes saw to that. High-status boys and girls were prevented from falling in love with each other by lack of contact. Therefore, most love affairs crossed class lines, involving household servants and other nonsegregated inferiors. This made marriage doubly impossible. The only escape from the dilemma was the ubiquitous fiery volcano. Double suicides were the expected denouement of love in real life as well as in fiction.[3]

Breakdown of the Traditional System

Paradoxically, the first phase of the modernization of Japan extended the arranged marriage system downward into the peasantry and urban working class. Feudal Japan had been rigidly stratified, and familistic mate-selection had been one of the badges of elite status. But the Meiji reform government of the late nineteenth century promulgated the Confucian family ethic of the aristocracy as a code for the whole nation, taught through ethics classes in the public schools. So, for a time, the old system became more firmly established (Ariga, 1955).

But this extension was imposed from above. Below the formal surface of Japanese manners, other aspects of the modernization process weakened the system at its roots. Youthful acceptance of parental dictation had relied on respect for parental authority and lack of contact with alternative systems. Parental authority was gradually undermined by an increasing tempo of social change which made parents seem no longer wise but old-fashioned. Loss of respect for parents not only lessened children's willingness to let their parents choose their partners, but undermined the three-generation household which had necessitated parental mate-selection in the first place.

3. Wagatsuma and DeVos (1962) suggest that feudal Japan "considered a love marriage as something improper, indecent, 'egoistic,' or something similar to an extramarital affair in Western Christian moral codes." Thus Japan traditionally viewed extramarital love with a tolerance and premarital love with a horror which are reversed in the Western tradition.

As three-generation households became less common, the husband-wife relationship was freed from subordination to filial responsibility. In neolocal households, marital relations were no longer overshadowed by relations with the husband's parents. Husband and wife had to depend on each other for support and nurture.

Emphasizing the marital bond altered the criteria for a good wife. No longer were submissiveness and fertility important. Rather, the ability to assume household responsibility and to replace the mother in the life of the husband were required. A new pattern of intimate, affectionate interaction with the husband became possible.

Spousal intimacy was spurred by changes in the life of women. Modernization brought more education to women, making them the intellectual peers of their husbands. It brought vocational opportunities—before marriage and even after. Peasant women had always worked alongside their husbands in the rice paddies but industrial and commercial development gave women jobs independent of their families.

Such changes introduce new complexities into the mate-selection process. No longer can carbon-copy conformity be expected of all prospective brides. Greater variability in attitudes, values, experiences, and perhaps even temperament develops among women. The new emphasis on love and intimacy raises problems of rapport which can hardly be judged by parents or matchmakers. Indeed, they can hardly be judged by young people themselves short of a trial period of interaction. These changes shift responsibility from the older to the younger generation, who must rely not on information obtainable by objective investigation, but on subjective reactions to interactive experience.

Forces at work within Japan have been reinforced by influences from abroad. The Meiji government hoped to modernize the economic system without changing the family system. It was a futile hope. Not only did industrialization set in motion social processes which modernized the family system, but the contact with Western culture necessary to master the complexities of its technology brought contact with Western family ideals. After World War II, the occupation of Japan by American soldiers and the control of the country by an American governmental bureaucracy produced a massive injection of formal and informal Western influence. Before and after the war, international travelers to and from Japan, Western books devoured by one of the most literate peoples on earth, and Western movies and television (with or without dubbed-in Japanese dialogue) exposed the Japanese people to Western individualism and equalitarianism. (In the 1950's, *Father Knows Best* was a Tokyo TV favorite.)

Individualism and equalitarianism appealed to those who had previously been subordinate—the younger generation. So pervasive was this invasion of Western ideals that love matches became the preferred system of mate-selection for the younger generation. In 1955, three quarters of 5,000 high school and college students said they considered the love-match method the ideal way of choosing a spouse (Baber, 1958).

These influences culminated in dramatic legal changes in the Family Code of

1948. Encouraged by the American occupation forces but readily adopted by the postwar Japanese government itself, the Code guaranteed the right of young people to choose their own marriage partners.

The fact that love matches became normative both legally and attitudinally did not mean, however, that they predominated in actual practice. Studies in several parts of Japan in the postwar years found love matches in the minority (e.g. Norbeck, 1954: none in Takashima, a fishing village; Smith, 1956: "the only true love match having been made some forty years ago under unusual circumstances" in rural Kurusu; Ministry of Labor, 1957: 25 per cent of urban marriages and half as many rural marriages; Steiner, 1950: 38–40 per cent of two Tokyo areas after the war; Dore, 1958: 50 per cent of another Tokyo neighborhood, 1946–51).

The chief reason for the relatively small number of love matches in contemporary Japan is not parental opposition but lack of opportunity. Japan is an extraordinarily segregated society by Western standards: "Beginning with adolescence, the mixing of the sexes is discouraged. Admonition seems never to be necessary, as the proper behavior has become the preferred pattern by the time adolescence is reached. In recent years there has been some mixing on special occasions, such as the playing of ping-pong in the meeting hall on festival days. Dating . . . is known to Takashima boys and girls, but it is considered too bold and daring" (Norbeck, 1954). Dating shyness is also described by my colleagues at Tokyo Educational University: "Japanese young people don't like to make appointments for a date. If a boy wants to see a girl, he will continue to meet her 'accidentally' on the street without her knowing it was deliberate. Or he will call on her and her family, saying he 'just happened to be in the neighborhood' and thought he would 'drop in.' This is partly a reflection of the absence of telephones but mostly a defense against seeming too presumptuous as dating would be."

Although coeducation is standard in the primary schools and middle schools, at the high school level it was an American export which conservatives in many communities tried to abolish after the Peace Treaty was signed. In higher education, segregation of the sexes was even more complete. Before the war, coeducation at the college level was practically unheard of. After the war, the Imperial Universities were theoretically thrown open to women on an equal footing with men. But after an initial flurry of applications the supply of feminists decreased and one institution after another regressed toward masculinity. In 1959, women's colleges still enrolled most of the women students, the chief exceptions being the coeducational Christian colleges serving a tiny minority of the total population.[4]

Under segregation, dating begins late if it begins at all. A study of one Tokyo women's college and of six Nagoya colleges, conducted for me in 1959 by

4. The modernization and westernization of Japan involve forces that are bound to decrease the segregation of the sexes in the future. Wagatsuma reports that since 1959 the number of women students attending universities previously closed to them has risen until they now dominate some departments of Literature and Humanities. As student bodies become increasingly coeducational, opportunities for college dating increase correspondingly.

Professors Ernest Shinozaki and Tsuneo Yamane, respectively, found that most students had never had a single date. In contrast to the United States (where dating typically begins in junior high school), dating for Japanese college students seldom began before graduation.[5]

When dating begins in college it does not lead so smoothly to marriage as in the United States. Student couples are too closely matched in age to be considered good prospects by traditional Japanese standards:

> Personally I know only a handful of student marriages which have occurred since the war. One deterrent is the similar age of students. Parents often object to close age. Since the Japanese wife is a kind of servant whom the husband couldn't afford to have die first or grow senile when he does, the Japanese man hates to be a widower and prefers to marry a younger woman. Also an older wife is less easily dominated than a young one (Professor Ernest Shinozaki).

Even after graduation, opportunities for acquaintance with potential dating partners are limited. There is no general equivalent of the ubiquitous church youth group which brings so many American young people together.[6] Reacting to the shortage of opportunities, Professor and Mrs. Hidaka of Tokyo University and Mr. Takeda, an aristocratic architect, became famous for their "Hidaka parties" and "Takeda parties," thrown expressly to give young people opportunities to become acquainted. This was a new way of implementing the traditional Japanese belief that everyone should arrange three matches before he dies. Although she eventually married a man she met on the tennis courts, Michiko Shoda (now the Crown Princess) had previously sipped coffee and listened to classical music at a Takeda party.

The Takedas and Hidakas of Japan are rare enough to be newsworthy. Most young people have no sponsored social activity. Almost the only structured opportunity for contact between the sexes is the job. By no means universal (especially for middle-class girls), employment is one of the few bases for potential dating and therefore for potential matchmaking.

Sometimes potential dating partners are available but social pressure discourages taking advantage of them. Students enrolled in my Waseda Hoshien marriage seminar described the Japanese atmosphere as "hostile to dating. After just one date, everyone expects the couple to get married. The only circumstances under which people are encouraged to date is after engagement!"

Given such handicaps, no wonder so many young people reach the age of marriage empty-hearted and fall back on their parents to fill the gap. This

---

5. Similarly, Asayama (1957) finds strikingly less physical contact among Japanese teenagers than Kinsey (1953) found for Americans of the same age. At age 18, the proportion of boys and girls who had ever kissed was approximately 10 per cent in Japan, 90 per cent in the U.S.A.

6. Even where religious opportunities for acquaintance do exist, social pressure may discourage love matches. Members of a small congregation in Wakayama told me their church was "opposed to love matches and wouldn't want to get a reputation for being a matchmaking place." Consequently, their most active go-between always seeks partners in other congregations.

produces regret and wistfulness, but it has advantages. Particularly for girls unsure of their ability to exercise freedom wisely, there is a sense of relief in "passing the buck" to parents. Responsibility for making the right choice is, after all, one of the concomitants of freedom of choice.[7]

Parents traditionally have manipulated their children's lives in many ways. Professor Burton Martin of Waseda University (writing in the March 1965 *Dartmouth Alumni Magazine*) describes how parents groom their children for university entrance examinations: "They push, encourage, threaten, and push again; they push some children beyond their native abilities, they push most children beyond good health . . . ." And once a son passes his entrance exam, "Mother can begin, if she has not already begun, to find the right girl for the wedding, four or five years hence."

However, responsibility seldom reverts completely to parents. Indeed, arranged marriages in the traditionally authoritarian sense of the term have almost disappeared. The forces that enable more and more young people to abandon arrangement altogether have transformed what remains of that system into something radically different.

Whereas, traditionally, arrangements were initiated and negotiated by the parents before being announced to the child, today the two generations collaborate. Parents *may* still take the initiative, but young people may also ask their parents to help find a partner. If parents initiate the process, the child is no longer confronted with a *fait accompli* but given an explicit opportunity to veto the nominee before negotiations are pursued.

Parents vary in the pressure they exert, and sons and daughters (especially daughters) vary in their ability to resist. Nevertheless, both generations acknowledge that an arranged marriage should have the consent of both generations. In this veto power, the modern arranged marriage system fits the Family Code's requirement of freedom of choice of marriage partner.

The existence of the right to be discriminating does not guarantee that it will be exercised. One middle-aged man described how he allowed himself to be married by *miai*:

> I thought I was too young. (It was my first year out of the university at age 26 or 27.) But the girl's brothers pestered me so I thought I would give in and put an end to their pressure. I felt sorry for the girl because she was willing to marry me but I couldn't help it—I wanted to study in peace. Even today I have little idea what she was like then because I didn't look at her—I was careful not to!

Normally, the young person is consulted early in the selection process. He not only has the right to veto a choice proposed by his parents but may be

7. Wagatsuma comments: "Another reason why love matches are still not very common among young Japanese is that they are still emotionally dependent on their parents. In spite of their love of autonomy and their yearning toward love matches, they are still afraid of taking completely the responsibility for their marriage and they are still in favor of depending upon their parents even in such an important matter as mate-selection . . . the Japanese people [are] not quite psychologically weaned from their parents."

offered a range of choices from the very beginning. Rather than being confined to accepting or vetoing a single nominee, he may be offered a whole panel of eligibles to peruse jointly with his parents. In effect, therefore, Japanese matchmakers widen the "field of eligibles" for young people who lack contacts.

A variety of choices is particularly apt to be presented if the parents have no immediate acquaintances in the younger generation and must bring in a matchmaker. Contemporary matchmakers are sociable middle-aged women whom Americans would call "the club-woman type" (Vogel, 1961b). If they take their hobby seriously, they maintain a portfolio of ten or a dozen eligible young people. For each there is a one-page dossier giving the standard information—name, age, health, education, occupation, and marital status of all members of the individual's family—plus a photograph of the eligible person.

If a 27-year-old man wants to get married (or his parents think he should), his mother will approach a friend who is a matchmaker. The two of them may screen the matchmaker's portfolio to eliminate obviously inappropriate cases. The surviving candidates' dossiers, or at least their photographs, will then be taken home for Junior to scrutinize. Parents and son establish a priority list of prospects and ask the matchmaker or a private detective agency to find out more about their first choice and her family. If this investigation locates no "skeletons in the closet," the matchmaker will arrange an interview with the young lady.

Perhaps in her own home but more likely in a private room of a restaurant, the matchmaker will invite the two principals and their parents (especially their mothers) to come together for an introductory meeting. Refreshments will be served and the adults will attempt to draw the embarrassed young people into conversation. So great is the tension generated by the attempt to make a good impression that *faux pas* are often committed. Indeed such *miai* (as these meetings are called) are standard fare for slapstick movies in Japan.

Sometimes the elders withdraw to give the young strangers a chance to converse alone. More often, such opportunities arise through follow-up dates if the impression made in the *miai* is mutually favourable. If either side is dissatisfied, attention shifts to the next girl on the list and another *miai* is scheduled.

The term *miai* is important because *miai kekkon* (literally "interview marriage") is the Japanese term for arranged marriage. Japanese marriages are no longer arranged by parents on behalf of unknowing children, but arranged by matchmakers on behalf of participating families. "Arrangement" now means primarily the formal introduction of potential marriage partners to each other and secondarily the follow-up message-carrying which cements a promising relationship.[8]

8. Single young people without parents or other sponsors may turn to the city government *in loco parentis*. The Tokyo Municipal Marriage Bureau in the 1950's received approximately 50 applications per day from marital aspirants who searched the files for likely prospects. Staff counselors functioned as go-betweens, bringing interested parties together. The result: 1,000 marriages per year.

Contemporary Views of Mate Selection in Tokyo

Knowing that most research projects in Japan had discovered a majority of arranged marriages, I hoped to locate a segment of Japanese society with a 50/50 balance of love matches and arranged marriages. I had already chosen Tokyo as the site for my research, hoping that the largest city in Japan (and, incidentally, in the world) would have the largest proportion of love matches. Secondly, I assumed that love matches were progressively increasing among the younger generation. Therefore I put an upper age limit of 40 on wives to be interviewed. This had the added advantage of eliminating marriages contracted during the wartime chaos or the prewar conservatism.[9] Third, in order to be able to study how both types of marriages worked out unaffected by the presence of relatives, I ruled out three-generation households.[10] Lastly, in order to increase cooperation of wives with the interviewers and of husbands with their written questionnaires, I selected three government apartment house projects populated largely by white-collar workers accustomed to such verbal exercises.[11]

A total of 444 married couples met these specifications and completed the research instruments published in the Appendix.[12] When they were asked to

9. A Japanese government survey in 1956 showed a major loss below age 40 in popular support of traditional family patterns (succession of lineage, family name, estate, and occupation).

10. According to the Statistical Department of the Ministry of Health and Welfare, 30 per cent of all married couples in large cities in 1960 shared their homes with relatives. The remaining 70 per cent of couples lived alone or with their unmarried children, that is, were nuclear families of the sort studied here.

11. The sample population is typical of Japanese *danchi* apartment dwellers in the following respects: (1) nuclear families; (2) husbands employed by large corporations; (3) a large proportion of working wives; (4) a majority of the husbands college graduates; (5) young families with preadolescent children. See Hoshino, 1964.

12. Of the grand total of 1,220 familes living in the three housing projects, almost half (46 per cent) were ineligible for inclusion in this study. 19 per cent were over age 40, 15 per cent included relatives, and 12 per cent lacked one spouse. This left 646 young, nuclear, intact families eligible for interview. Interviews were completed with 76 per cent of the eligible wives and questionnaires secured from 69 per cent of the husbands.

A special analysis was made of the interview schedules of women whose husbands failed to complete their questionnaires. The proportion of *miai* marriages in the uncooperative group is the same as in the cooperative group, but the degree of love and of eagerness to marry felt by the wives is significantly lower. These are more often lukewarm love matches pushed by the mother or father.

The wives themselves are an ordinary group with respect to their preference for the female role and their utilization of husbands for therapeutic relief. In interactive situations their marriages differ only slightly with almost as much courtesy, joint decision-making, and companionship as usual.

The husbands are significantly less communicative on return home from work and in their therapeutic response, being characteristically passive or else active only to the point of dismissal or advice, not sharing through sympathy or cooperation. As a result, the wife tends after marriage as well as before to feel less love for her husband and to be less satisfied with his love for her, even though the marriage is not deficient in some of its objective characteristics.

A minority of the husbands seem to be authoritarian patriarchs, but their chief characteristic is psychological or emotional withholding, which is reciprocated by the wives. The label their own marriages, I found I had chosen almost too well. Less than a third of the couples had *miai* marriages (see Table 1–1).

Table 1–1—Classification of Marriage by Tokyo Husbands and Wives*

	Husband's Classification						
	LOVE MATCH		MIAI MARRIAGE		BOTH or	TOTAL	
WIFE'S CLASSIFICATION	Pure	Qualified	Qualified	Pure	NEITHER	N	%
Love Match							
Pure	202	20	2	3	1	228	51
Qualified	40	17	8	7	2	74	17
Miai Marriage							
Qualified	4	5	9	21	3	42	9
Pure	4	0	20	69	1	94	21
Both, neither	2	2	1	1	0	6	1
Total N	252	44	40	101	7	444	99%
Total %	57%	10%	9%	23%	2%	101%	

* "In general, would you classify your marriage as a *miai* marriage or a love match?" Verbatim comments were used to code the qualified responses. The tendency of wives to give qualified responses more often than husbands may reflect the greater ease of making oral rather than written comments as well as possible sex differences in response patterns.

I had assumed that people could tell me easily whether theirs was a love match or an arranged marriage. However, classification sometimes proved to be difficult. Only 72 per cent of the wives and 80 per cent of the husbands were willing to call their marriage unqualifiedly one or the other. An even smaller number of couples (61 per cent) agreed on the same type. By contrast, four husbands labeled as pure love matches marriages which their wives thought of as pure arranged marriages, and three other couples contradicted each other in the reverse direction.

All the other questions in our interview and questionnaire schedules were answered in fixed response categories. The one exception was this classification question. Here we recorded verbatim any comments the wives made and asked the husbands, "In addition to checking, please comment on the extent to which you feel the term chosen is appropriate." The hundreds of men and women who took the trouble to comment reflect the complexity of the issues involved and illuminate both the pure types and the mixed forms of *miai* and love marriages.

PURE MIAI MARRIAGES

Comments on pure *miai* marriages focus around four main themes: (1) observing traditional formalities, (2) relying on other people's initiative and judgment, (3) lack of premarital interaction, and (4) lack of love.

Formality—Marriage arrangement is the traditional system in Japan. The key activity is the *miai*, or formal introduction of the prospective partners to each other by a matchmaker. Those who are ceremonially introduced usually classify theirs as a *miai* marriage (as the name suggests).

---

unwillingness of the husband to fill out the questionnaire is symptomatic of his general marital uncooperativeness (since it is the wife herself who had the task of securing the husband's cooperation).

In one extreme case, a wife reports that "the process started with arrangements between the parents of us both." However, this old-fashioned parental contracting resulted from the geographical separation of parents and children and led subsequently to a truncated *miai* meeting of the two individuals with the blessing of the absent parents. Given the modern interpretation of the *miai* system, an actual confrontation of the young people was necessary before the parents' arrangements could be considered complete.

Although classically a *miai* introduces strangers to each other, in some cases it provides the "proper" starting point for marriage between childhood acquaintances who had not perceived each other as potential marriage partners:

> In my childhood, I knew him a little but had no feeling of affection for him. He called at my house at one time or another in my junior high school days, but did not leave an especially strong impression on my mind. After that, I regarded him for the first time as the object of marriage through a formal introduction. It may well be said, therefore, that our marriage was a pure *miai* marriage. Since we lived far apart (Tokyo and Osaka), we seldom had contact with each other.

The husband reports that it was his brother who made the formal introduction, setting the wheels in motion for this couple to marry.

In another extreme case, arrangement mechanisms were used even though the two individuals were living in the same house:

> It is hard to decide which my marriage belongs under, *miai* or love. My husband had bed and board at my house for five years, and so I knew him very well. My mother liked him, and started making arrangements. Being young at the time, I did not think about marriage seriously. Then friendly contacts gradually developed into affectionate association and finally into the marriage.

Apparently only after the proper formalities had been negotiated did this couple begin to fall in love. In that sense, they began on a *miai*-like basis even though not actually *introduced* to one another.

In both the previous cases, a love match could have occurred spontaneously. Since it didn't, the old system was invoked by relatives to encourage young people to regard each other as potential marriage partners. In this setting, a *miai* is not simply a permissive legitimation of courtship but a structured imperative to courtship. Once a *miai* occurs, one is supposed to pursue the matter to a conclusion: either marriage or a formal veto. Once young people allow themselves to be formally introduced, they can no longer regard themselves simply as friends or acquaintances. The *miai* redefines their relationship as one of eligibility for marriage, raising a question which must be answered. With both families formally posing the question, social pressure forces the couple to move rapidly toward a decision. The traditional American practice of "dallying" is out (Waller, 1938). Formality governs not simply the process of being introduced but the process of notifying the matchmaker (and through her the opposite family) of the results of the introduction.

However, to be a pure arranged marriage, more is needed than just a formal introduction. Indeed, the spirit of an arranged marriage can occur without the form. Table 1–2 shows that over a third of those who were formally introduced were unwilling to consider their marriage a pure *miai* type, and some of these who met via the other three channels considered their marriage purely *miai* despite the absence of a formal introduction.

Table 1–2—Wife's Classification of Marriage by Type of Introduction

| | | | Introduction* | |
| | | | AS A POSSIBLE MARRIAGE PARTNER | |
Classification	NONE	JUST AS A FRIEND	Informal	Formal
Pure love match	81%	62%	26%	3%
Qualified love match	15	31	17	12
Qualified arranged marriage	2	1	23	22
Pure arranged marriage	1	3	31	62
Both or neither	1	3	3	1
Total	100%	100%	100%	100%
N	212	70	35	127

* "When you first met your husband, did someone introduce you to each other, or not?"
If yes, "Was he introduced as a possible marriage partner or not?"
If yes, "Did you have a formal *miai*?"

One feature that determines whether a marriage is perceived as "arranged" is the presence of *other* traditional ceremonies. If the introduction is followed by exchange of traditional betrothal gifts (by way of the go-between) and if the wedding ceremony itself is presided over by a matchmaker (the same one or a more honorific one, such as the groom's employer), the *miai*-marriage label becomes more appropriate.

Reliance on others—The most frequently discussed characteristic of arranged marriages is precisely the fact that they are arranged. Whenever other people promote the marriage more actively than the young person himself, he is apt to classify the marriage as arranged (see Table 1–3).

Table 1–3—Wife's Classification of Marriage by Her Initiative in Promoting the Marriage

| | WIFE'S INITIATIVE IN PROMOTING MARRIAGE* | | |
Classification	Primary	Secondary	Neither
Pure love match	64%	22%	15%
Qualified love match	16	20	15
Qualified miai marriage	7	20	10
Pure miai marriage	11	36	60
Both or neither	1	3	0
Total	99%	101%	100%
N	316	76	52

* As for your father, your mother, and yourself, who would you say had the most influence in the decision that you would marry this boy? Who had the next most influence?"

Other people sometimes force an individual to participate in a *miai* against

his will. One woman commented that "when the matchmaker suggested a *miai*, both my parents and I had no intention at all. I was somehow forced to attend the *miai*." A note of passivity appears in many comments about *miai* marriages. Parents or matchmakers initiate the matchmaking process. Girls especially often approach the *miai* with a sense that marriage is a foregone conclusion. Because of such passivity, the marriage die may be cast in advance by other parties.[13]

Sometimes it is not other people but circumstances that force the individual to rely on the traditional method of finding a mate. This is particularly true of girls with no contacts outside the home: "Having no occupation outside, I had to have a marriage arranged. I was not so interested in marriage myself. It was pushed on me by those about me." The loss of men in the war reduced the chances of finding one's own partner and increased the necessity of getting help:

> My present husband was a cousin of my friend and I associated with him in my school days. Then I reached the marriageable age and had *miai* two or three times which all failed. Meeting with the war, I was doubtful of my marriage materializing. I tried in vain to deny marriage. Deprived of my parents by the war and being an only daughter, I accepted my aunt's advice to choose my present husband without having my own way.

Pure *miai* couples rely heavily on others' opinions in evaluating the partner's suitability. Sometimes the matchmaker is seen as particularly "trustworthy." More often, the immediate family's opinions are persuasive: "I respected the judgment of mature people. . . . My sister and her husband approved of the match." A husband felt that a *miai* marriage was "advantageous in that we were able to foster and examine our affection with our parents, relatives, and friends watching us." A wife reported that her brother-in-law "made an investigation" of her prospective husband.

Passivity is often caused by unreadiness to marry anyone, much less the particular individual: "Being young at the time, I had no intention of marrying. Offered for marriage by those about me, I dared to do so feeling as if it were other people's affairs."

In extreme cases passive respondents (particularly women) allow others to push them into marriage against their own better judgment. One wife reports:

> My opinion was disregarded. I was at the mercy of other people. My mother wanted to marry me off as soon as possible. When I got engaged, I felt little affection. In fact, I rather disliked him, but I thought I could manage to get along once we got married.

13. Wagatsuma and DeVos (1962) conclude from projective test responses of rural Japanese that inner passivity and "strong unresolved attachments to parents" produce a "lack of inner strength for independence or autonomy," leaving many young people (especially girls) incapable of resisting the promotion efforts of their parents.

In another case a band of conspirators "ganged up on" a couple: "The brothers of both of us and my teachers acting as go-betweens pushed on the arrangements, and we two were completely left behind."

When the groom's employer proposes a marriage it is particularly hard to resist. One husband was "almost forced to marry by a director of my company." In another case both partners worked for the same company: "We were introduced by our senior in the office. I think the matchmaker was very forcible in arrangement."

However, it would be wrong to assume that matchmaking is usually resented. On the contrary, outside intervention is explicitly appreciated in many cases. One husband, describing himself as "a prudent man who cannot become passionate about anything by nature," reported that "after exchanging our pictures and investigating each other, we had a *miai* because "we did not want to have an unpleasant feeling caused by an unsuccessful result." A wife felt that the old system guaranteed better results: "I made an arranged marriage as I thought things would go better when the parents arranged a marriage than if we did ourselves."

Despite the gulf between the generations created by rapid social change, many Japanese young people still want their parents' approval for their marriages. Such approval is guaranteed by the *miai* system but problematic in love matches.[14] Hence another man's preference for involving these "significant others" from the very beginning of the mate-selection process:

> I think there are two ways of uniting a man and a woman: one is *miai*, the other love match. In the case of *miai*, approval by families is easier to get. Besides, the opinion of the one getting married is highly respected nowadays. For these reasons, starting with a *miai* is the most desirable.

Most often, however, the intervention of others is neither praised nor deplored but simply narrated as history:

> I decided to marry my present husband as he was a friend of my brother, my family encouraged the marriage, and I thought it all right after the *miai*.

Sometimes a third party's needs eclipse the individual's. Indeed, the latter's main motivation for marriage may be a desire to please significant persons in the environment. Matters of duty and social obligation, described by Ruth Benedict (1946) as deeply rooted in the Japanese character structure, enter into this motivation:

> My wife's brother was a friend of mine from childhood. When he went to the battle-field, he asked me to marry her, his sister. I was inclined to do so.

14. Wagatsuma and DeVos (1962) deduce from their projective test exploration of Niiike villagers that "an arranged marriage is psychologically easier for many individuals. Free choice in marriage very often involves rebellious attitudes toward parents and guilt feelings may be aroused in making such an attempt."

A wife reports:

> I was the youngest among my brothers and sisters. They were all married and I was left alone as a single woman. My mother got high blood pressure from worry about my being unmarried. My family were anxious to arrange a marriage as soon as possible and showed my mother the picture of my prospective husband. I was thus in haste to marry. After the *miai* I did not love my partner but I married him. It was not for my sake but because I wanted to relieve my mother and my family of their anxiety that I decided to marry.

In a remarriage, children were the primary concern:

> I met my husband at the formal place for *miai*. It was my first marriage but he had four children. Through meeting him several times after the *miai*, I came to sympathize with him. The matter of children was our chief concern in our talk and I did not get to the place where I felt any affection toward him.

Lack of interaction—So far we have seen that pure *miai* marriages involve formal introductions and leave primary roles to others. A third feature is minimal contact between the partners. To fit the "ideal type," couples should both come to the *miai* as complete strangers and decide to get married without benefit of further interaction.

Remembering that the following are independent reports, note how one couple echo each other in justifying the pure *miai* label:

Husband: I had a *miai* with a person who was absolutely a stranger to me and so my case was literally a *miai* marriage.

Wife: It was a pure *miai* marriage, for I had known nothing of him before the introduction.

In an unusual case, a husband didn't even meet the girl at first: "My marriage was of such an old type as to have seen her parents first before seeing herself."

Some couples decide to marry after the single contact in the *miai* itself. Most rely heavily on first impressions and incomplete knowledge. The crucial interval is not from *miai* to marriage but from *miai* to the decision to marry. One wife went with her fiancé for six months before getting married, but felt it was a pure arranged marriage because she decided within a week after the *miai* that she was willing to marry him. One extraordinary couple were married three days after being formally introduced!

Several respondents admit that limited contact provides a precarious basis for personal judgment. Said one husband, "Whether one's judgment at one's *miai* party was right or not determines everything in one's married life." For another husband, the risk-taking element was explicit:

> One of my neighbors introduced me to my wife. I had the interview on February 17

and the wedding on April 29 in the same year. Since I had regarded a marriage as a game of gambling, I hastened in arrangement. I have somehow won in this gambling, I believe.

Lack of love—Lack of interaction inhibits the growth of love. Hence, a distinguishing characteristic of *miai* marriages is the absence of precisely what is denoted by the term "love match."

Sometimes one partner dislikes the other so much that the marriage is obviously *not* a love match. More commonly there is no emotion—either positive or negative—between comparative strangers. Usually an absence of dislike is the best one can hope for from a *miai* ceremony. If the reaction is negative, that normally ends the relationship. But if there are no qualms, the marriage can proceed under today's modified system:

Husband: I had many chances to see women both on official and private business, but I had never felt any likes or dislikes for any of them as my partner for marriage. I was living alone with my father and got married to one he had found. I am satisfied with my marriage.

Wife: I didn't have any man whom I particularly loved. I married my husband, as I was introduced to him by other people, everyone about me approved of the match, and I myself did not dislike him.

Another wife spoke similarly: "As I was advised to marry by those about me after the *miai*, and I myself had no particular reason to refuse the proposal, I got married to him."

In many cases phraseology shifts from "not disliking" to even more neutral terminology. The partner seems to be "all right"—a phrase typical of the matter-of-factness of *miai* marriages: "When I saw his picture once, the impression was not bad. Therefore I followed the suggestion to have a *miai*. Since my parents approved of the match, I thought it all right."

Some respondents see their lack of love as advantageous. Emotional involvement might cloud one's intellectual faculties. Mate-selection is too fateful a process to be left to the vagaries of feeling. The marriage is more likely to succeed if one decides in a detached and objective manner.

Ours was a pure *miai* marriage and a very rational one. I must confess that in the marriage decision there was, to a certain extent, a calculating, self-interested aspect. I thought that after the calculation, affection for her would naturally arise in me.

Another husband:

I took an objective attitude toward marriage at first, namely my wife was chosen among many as one who satisfied my requirements most.

Just as too little interaction prevents affection, so may too long an acquaintance. In several *miai* marriages the partners were close relatives or grew up in the same neighborhood. Long acquaintance produced the taken-for-granted feeling of old married couples instead of the excitement of newlyweds.

PURE LOVE MATCHES

Since *miai* marriages and love matches are polar opposites, the defining characteristics of love matches are the converse of those of the *miai* system: (1) formal ceremonies are replaced by informality, (2) reliance on others by self-reliance even in the face of opposition, and (3) lack of interaction and (4) lack of love by courtship and emotional involvement.

Informality—With rare exceptions (three cases out of 127), a marriage is never called a pure love match after a formal introduction. The general practice is to abandon not only the *miai* but all traditional ceremonies:

Wife: We followed not a bit of the traditional form of *miai* marriage.

Husband: My case may safely be called a pure love match. We knew each other without introduction, go-between, or exchanging betrothal presents. The wedding was presided over by ourselves. During the whole process of arrangements for marriage no interference broke in from the parents or friends.

Sometimes deceremonialization extends even to the wedding. Two couples drifted into cohabitation and only subsequently formalized their liaison. Love-match weddings are often simplified. We attended a wedding reception complete with champagne, but the couple confessed later that their "wedding" consisted simply of visiting a popular Shinto shrine, unaccompanied and unnoticed. Even this visit was evidently more romantic than religious, as the couple added that (like most Japanese young people) they were not religious.

Of all the forms dispensed with, the crucial omission is the matchmaker's mediation. Since matchmakers play three roles—introducing couples by means of the *miai*, negotiating and cementing the betrothal through the *yuino* (exchange of presents), and presiding over the wedding ceremony—their absence abolishes or de-formalizes a whole series of ceremonies. Twenty-one love-match couples explicitly pointed out their lack of a go-between.

Not only do love matches abandon formality, but they often occur accidentally, unlike deliberately contrived arranged marriages:

I knew him through sitting next to him in the train by chance. With his cooperation, I broke off an engagement I had previously made to another person. A marriage was thus arranged only by our own efforts.

Similarly, the desire to get married at all may develop spontaneously and unexpectedly, rather than by forethought and planning:

We knew each other with no intention of marrying but through a mere chance of working together. Then, we gradually came to love each other. Therefore our marriage may be called a 100 per cent love match.

Self-reliance—To dispense with formalities and especially to by-pass the services of a match maker requires relying on one's own devices. Self-reliance is a radical phenomenon in Japan, "where the individual has been historically *de-emphasized* . . . . Traditionally, the Japanese individual did not exist as a distinct personality with his own separate sphere of existence. In every aspect of his life, the individual was tightly bound to group life with little area for personal activity" (Matsumoto, 1960). Lifton (1962) reports that Japanese young people, despite their ideal of individuality, still have a powerful urge to collective identification:

> But beneath this ideal of selfhood, however strongly maintained, one can frequently detect an even more profound craving for renewed group life, for solidarity, even for the chance to "melt" completely into a small group, a professional organization, or a mass movement, and even at the cost of nearly all self-assertion.

Such inner collectivism makes the assertiveness of love-match self-reliance psychologically costly. Few young people have a sufficiently well-established sense of autonomy to be able to choose their own partner without trepidation.

Our pure love-match couples stressed how utterly responsible they were for what happened: "We married only by ourselves." "We arranged everything for ourselves for the marriage."

Sometimes the emphasis is not only positively on self-help but negatively on the fact that nobody else helped—neither matchmaker, parents, nor friends:

> *Husband:* I was the strongest driver in arrangement. We did all by ourselves without any help such as introduction by others or an effort of superiors in the office.

> *Wife:* I was a nurse at a hospital. A doctor knew my present husband and through him I knew my husband by chance. After it the process advanced in the form of a love marriage.

Outside intervention is sometimes called "interference": "We arranged for marriage by ourselves without any interference from others."

In extreme cases, no one could intervene because no one knew a match was in the making: "Ours was almost a pure love-match because we announced the marriage to everyone after our having made it." Intervention was similarly impossible for couples isolated from significant others, particularly from parents:

> I have no parents so the decision to marry was naturally made by myself. My husband, whose parents are still alive, was in the circumstance where he was quite estranged from them. We compassionated each other, and the lonely sentiment united the two of us.

In other cases, parents were too far away geographically to be involved.

Most couples in our sample are in touch with their parents. But to have a pure love match, they must exclude parents from the decision-making process. Our couples mentioned the nonparticipation of parents almost as often as the absence of matchmakers. Many couples made their decision and then approached their parents, hoping for concurrence: "We had no one who went between us. We engaged ourselves first and later the formal engagement was announced after consulting our families and friends." "We decided to marry ourselves and got approval from our parents."

If the approval of parents is not forthcoming, love is proven by determination to marry anyway. Fifteen couples volunteered parental opposition as evidence of true love:

Wife: His family evacuated from Tokyo to our village in Akita Prefecture when I was in grade school. He remembered that he took me fishing and swimming, though I didn't. Then he wanted to go to Tokyo so as to get higher education. I saw him once a year when he came home during summer vacation. Then he went to the war. I met him again in May 1951 after a lapse of several years.

I was brought up in a farm village where they expect a girl to get married to any guy her parents arrange for her. Since I was the eldest daughter, I was expected to stay home with the husband my parents would choose in order to carry on the family succession. When I fell in love with my present husband and wanted to get married to him, my parents strongly opposed. Breaking the custom rules, I ran away from my parents and came to him. They thought I was crazy to do such a thing.

Husband: I think ours was one of the best love marriages because when her parents opposed our marriage, my wife left her home and parents in order to marry me.

Another wife successfully thwarted parental attempts to arrange an old-fashioned marriage:

My father, being against the marriage, tried to arrange another match. The family members of my present husband were all Christians, while I was not. I intended to marry him even by having my name removed from the official family register.[15]

Although the opposition of friends is far less common than that of parents, it also tests true love: "We met on the S.S. *Cleveland* on our way home from the States. Since then we promoted our marriage in spite of the surrounding friends' opposition."

Self-reliance may be demonstrated at many points. Table 1–2 showed that the great majority of love-match couples were not introduced by anyone. Thus, their *association* was their own affair from the very beginning: "We met and knew each other by ourselves. Then we had no formal go-between."

Following the initial meeting, love-match couples avoid *consulting* others in making up their minds: "I did not consult anyone about the marriage and so

15. All women have their names removed *after* they marry (if they adopt the husband's family name and leave their own household). Apparently this woman contemplated resigning from her family *before* marriage in order to be free of parental control and able to marry the man she loved.

it was no other than a love match, I think." Nor do others volunteer suggestions, unasked: "Without any suggestion by others, we married in a very natural way." Rather than asking someone else to investigate the partner, the individual does his own investigating:

> I observed him from various aspects: his private life, official work, and his character. I found him to be a person I had long been looking for. We made arrangements steadily and entered into married life with great hope.

A third place where love-match couples dispense with others is in making the *decision* to get married. Ideally, they decide entirely on their own: "The decision was made only by ourselves without seeking for others' opinions." Couples boast that they decided to marry of their own free will: "Our case may be called a typical love marriage in that it was based on our will and that we two took the whole responsibility in arrangement of the marriage." And again:

> My wife's family all approved of the marriage. We arranged for ourselves everything for the marriage. I may say our success in the marriage was due to the penetration of our will to the end.

Their boldness contrasts with their perception of *miai* marriages: "I got married not under compulsion by parents or others but only by my judgment."

To be a true love match, the decision must be *mutual*, freely made by both partners. If the man pushes the girl into marriage, an element of the *miai* system enters in. Just as there must be no compulsion from third parties, there should be none between partners: "We, having worked at the same place, decided to marry by mutual agreement." Similarly, "We two reached an agreement in will and attitude."

To decide to marry is to assume total *responsibility* for the success of the marriage, a responsibility shared by parents and matchmaker under the *miai* system:

> We married through working together without any interference. We intended to lead our married life with our cooperation and responsibility.

> We married after confirming success in our marriage instead of entrusting it to other people.

To assume so much responsibility in spite of skeptical parents is unnerving, especially for daughters:

> We knew and understood each other through working together. Since our parents were not eager about the match, we resolved to take responsibility in the arrangements, setting aside our parents from the first step. Though being a little anxious, I was hopeful about the future, and married him.

The more opposed the parents, the greater the courage required. Couples faced with this dilemma often use the word "dare" in their comments:

Wife: We two agreed to the match but my parents were opposed to it. However, we dared to marry ignoring others' opinions.

Husband: We managed to get married by our cooperation with a little struggle.

and again,

At first my parents were opposed to the marriage but we two decided to push on. As my husband strongly wished, I dared to marry him ignoring my parents' opposition. Anyhow, he was a man of good character, which I thought highly of.[16]

Dating and courtship—If love-match couples meet neither through matchmakers nor through anyone else, where do they meet? Even though we did not ask specifically, more than a quarter of our respondents spontaneously mentioned where they met. While not all of them are pure love matches, this is essentially a non-*miai* group.

Table 1–4—Sources of Love Match Contact

Organizational propinquity	75%
73 colleagues	
6 other business contacts	
11 schoolmates	
1 churchmate	
Residential propinquity	11%
7 childhood playmates	
4 adult neighbors	
2 boarders	
Sociability networks	11%
7 friend's sibling	
4 friend's friend	
2 parties, reunions	
Chance contacts	3%
3 public transportation	
1 coffee shop	
Total 121 cases	100%

The overwhelming importance of integrated employment as a basis for heterosexual acquaintance is apparent from Table 1–4. Three-fifths of all love matches stem from this single source, in contrast to American studies showing only 7 per cent (Burgess and Locke, 1953: 353) and 13 per cent (Popenoe, 1932). Even in the Soviet Union, work is the original contact point for only 21 per cent of a Leningrad sample (Kharchev, 1963).

16. Wagatsuma and DeVos (1962) find in rural Niiike that Thematic Apperception Test stories about arranged marriages usually contain no tension, whereas stories about love marriages are filled with tension, conflict, and tragedy. DeVos also sees "opportunity anxiety" affecting mate-selection in Japan, often precipitating marital choices and preventing the rejection of bad choices.

The reason for the difference is not that employment is more common in Japan but that alternative sources of acquaintance are rare. Few couples meet in college or church or via informal sociability in the homes of friends and relatives. We have previously noted the scarcity of coeducational colleges and congregational churches in Japan. Domestic parties and household entertaining are also infrequent, so that a home is seldom a place of contact for unattached boys and girls.

If a love match is to occur, the office is almost the only place where it can get started. Even there marriages used to be discouraged (unless the employer himself sponsored the relationship through a *miai*). Regardless of the type of sponsorship, nepotism rules required the wife to quit the firm.[17] However, the ban on office romances has subsequently relaxed and the daily colleague relationship of men and women provides one of the few social structures within which strangers of the opposite sex get to know each other well enough to fall in love.

Because Japanese culture values proper introductions (not simply when boy meets girl, but in all contacts between strangers), contact must be prolonged if unsponsored acquaintance is to develop into friendship. Inexperienced in casual sociability, Japanese young people are timid, formal, and reserved in early contact, requiring extra time before relaxing their guard and allowing friendship to blossom. By contrast the open, easy way Americans greet strangers requires less association before friendship is generated.

Romance usually develops so gradually that in retrospect the process seems entirely "natural":

Wife: My husband happened to be the first man I saw when I got a job. Then I came to love him by and by, and finally reached a marriage.

Husband: Very natural.

Although acquaintance begins in the office, it seldom ends there. Couples date after work, especially on the way home. Those who meet in other circumstances also may "go steady":

We used to be intimate friends in our college days. We came to have time only for ourselves. Through frequent contacts after graduation we married.

If dating is to be not only steady but frequent, the couple must either work or live close together in the sprawling metropolis:

Wife: We were friends in elementary school days, and were apart for a long time until we began contacts as a grown-up man and woman. Since he lived in my neighborhood, we met frequently and had a love of each other.

Husband: I met her again at an alumni meeting, and married her after dating for a year.

17. Mitsuru Shimpo reports that the mammoth Mitsukoshi department store in Tokyo "was very strict about purging *both* partners if employees married (up to the end of the war), because love was considered sinful."

A dozen couples stress that the longer the courtship, the more it deserves to be called a love match, because of the contrast to the pressure for quick decisions in *miai* marriages: "I knew her through working together, and married her after eight years of contacts." "Ours was a perfect love match because we were in contact for three years before marriage."

Wife: We were both teachers, working at the same school. I hesitated a little because I was older than he, but found him trustworthy by observing his nature and ability. Through a long period of contacts with him, we came to know each other better and decided to marry.

Husband: Ours was a love match because it was made through contacts for a long time at the same school.

Love-match courtships are not only quantitatively long but qualitatively rich. Reserve breaks down as partners unbend and share their inner thoughts: "For a long period of the engagement, we revealed to each other everything, good or evil." Opinions are exchanged on many topics:

A husband: While working at the same place we exchanged our opinions. I found we had views in common to a great extent.

A wife: We lived in the neighborhood. Through exchanging our opinions on our life-plan we became so intimate as to think about our marriage.

One young man even visited his girl friend when she was ill:

My husband, a student then, and I, an office girl, became intimate friends at a coffee-shop. He made a trip to Sado Island on business and we corresponded with each other almost every day. When I was taken ill, he took the trouble to come to the city to see me.

A husband: Working at the same place, I observed carefully and found her very pleasant, healthy, and a well developed athlete. I also play and like various sports. Having tastes in common united us.

A wife: I dated men of various types. When I first met my present husband, I found that we two were congenial and felt affection toward him.

Nine couples emphasize how well they came to know each other through repeated interaction: "We knew each other through working together and married after fully understanding each other."

Love-match couples believe that knowledge provides a sound basis for marital choice:

A husband: A marriage is a very important matter in one's life. If chosen by oneself, one's partner can be understood better. After all, a love match is far better than the other, I believe.

Another husband: By understanding the nature, the good and bad points of the party, life can be enriched, a new home can be set up, unnecessary conflicts may be avoided, and trouble to other people may be eliminated.

Intense love—With continued association, acquaintance turns to friendship and friendship to love. Normally this is a slow process, but soon or late, a marriage cannot be called a love match if there is no love.

For some couples love has a spiritual quality. One wife refers to the "deep meaning" which the word "love" has for her. Suffering and tragedy bring some couples together:

> I was on speaking terms with her in our company. Suffering from TB I took a long leave, and she was also affected by the same disease. We sympathized with each other and our love did not weaken during eight years between the beginning of our contacts and the marriage.

Note the emphasis in the previous paragraph on love's ability to survive hazards and conquer obstacles. We mentioned earlier its ability to surmount parental opposition. Other hazards include long separations ("We lived apart in Tokyo and Osaka for six years, but our affection for each other did not weaken") and long illnesses ("During the engagement period, my wife fell ill. I got married after waiting for her recovery seven years."). Sometimes illness is miraculously cured by love:

> I was depressed in both body and mind, but I recovered from depression by falling in love so well that it was noticed by those about me. Of course the marriage made me very healthy.

The concept of the miraculous powers of love echoes the traditional European romantic complex:

> I loved her so much that I felt lonely when I had not seen her for a week. We revealed everything to each other. Our marriage was, as it were, romance as seen in the classics.

Another man felt he was "destined" to marry his wife (they met on a bus): "Considering our marriage as a sort of destiny, I thought we should marry by all means." Love sometimes occurs at first sight: "The two persons who had been strangers to each other had very strong affection for each other when they met for the first time. We then proceeded to the marriage."

Whether at first glance or not, love is seen as intensely passionate, striking suddenly with explosive force: "I would choose the term 'love match' if it expresses the most passionate love in marriage." "Having very strong affection for each other, we had most passionate contacts for a year. We married after getting approval from the parents, brothers, and sisters on both sides."

Although love may ignite spontaneously, it also burns itself out—not completely, perhaps, but a fever pitch is difficult to sustain:

I would call our case a love marriage because it was made with affection toward each other. Generally speaking, a love marriage tends to be regarded as a match made with momentary passionate love. It was not so in our case. We had been in contact for eleven years before our marriage, and so by that time we had entertained a somewhat serene affection.

Couples who know each other from childhood may never get excited and therefore hesitate to call their marriage either a love match or a *miai* marriage:

Wife: Being friends from childhood, we knew each other very well. Our marriage was not from passionate love.

Husband: Our case does not belong under either of the two terms.

In contrast with passionate love, another wife describes her relationship as "compassionate," saying "we were on intimate terms as if we were brother and sister."

If passion is the essence of love, love matches are dangerous business:

Love marriage is often accompanied with danger, for the persons who have fallen in love tend to give themselves up to it instead of judging the party with presence of mind. A love match will be successful when an objective observation of the partner is made in addition to the affection between the two.

Apparently this man practiced what he preached, as his wife reports they married only "after deliberate thought about marriage as our responsibility."

QUALIFIED LOVE MATCHES

Such words and deeds of caution bring us to couples who feel that enough alien elements have crept into their love affairs to prevent calling them pure love matches.

One husband approached his marriage so deliberately he robbed it of the impetuousness of love: "Mine was a love match in a word. However, considering that I had a period of time to think over the marriage calmly, I would say it was much the same as a *miai* marriage." For another man, love was not the *only* basis of his marriage: "During the period of three to four years after we fell in love, we gave serious consideration as to whether two persons so different in nature could possibly lead a married life. From this fact I do not think the marriage was based only on affection." If one *thinks*, can it be love?

Intrusive formality—Given a mixture of *miai* elements and love elements, couples find it hard to decide what to call their marriage. If there is a *miai* ceremony, the distinction may be very subtle and subjective:

A wife: We started with a *miai*—*but*[18] we did not arrive at marriage without love, because there was a long period of time before the wedding. My case after all belongs under "love match".

18. I have italicized the word "but" which appears in each of these quotations to emphasize the respondents' sense of conflicting themes.

This *miai* was eclipsed by a long courtship. In other cases, a *miai* started the courtship, but couples made their own decision to marry and therefore feel justified in calling it a quasi-love match:

A wife: The process started in the *miai* form, *but* after all I believe we made a love marriage because the decision was made by ourselves.

A husband: The process started in the form of a *miai, but* I was not by any means bound up by having had the *miai*. I had my own way in every aspect, and so I would rather call my case a love match.

A wife: We had a *miai, but* the marriage was decided by mutual agreement after contacts. Therefore, "love match" is the more suitable term for our case.

When a *miai* results in falling in love, choosing a label becomes especially difficult. The largest number of qualified love matches (eight cases) reflect this dilemma:

A husband: Our marriage was arranged through a *miai, but* it was rather a love marriage because of the fact that frequent meetings aroused love in both of us. Besides we did not assume that we would marry when we met for the first time.

A wife: We knew each other through a *miai, but* came to have a love of each other while going together. "Love match" is after all a more suitable term in our case.

In one case, the *miai* was superimposed on a love match as a means of legitimizing the courtship:

When I first met her by chance, she made a favorable impression upon me. I asked my friend who knew her well for an introduction. After getting the approval of her parents, I dated her and then married her. In my case, the marriage belongs under "love match" in feeling and under arranged marriage in form.

Using a matchmaker at any point introduces an alien element:

I chose my wife by my own free will, but when we announced our engagement, we paid respect to Japanese tradition and did so through a go-between.

In the sense that we have known each other for a long time it was not a *miai* marriage. However, at the marriage I was formally introduced by another church member, so it was not a [pure] love match.

Intrusion of others—Without being exactly go-betweens, third parties may nevertheless mar the love-match pattern. Employers and parents are the most frequent intruders, either initiating or negotiating the arrangement:

At work my husband loved me and asked his superior to introduce me. After that, I felt love to him. So it was not a pure arranged marriage. Rather I think the term "love match" is more appropriate.

I think my marriage was a love match, but it may not have been a pure type because behind us two there were seniors in the office trying to unite us.

It is difficult to choose either of the two terms. Ours may belong under "love match" because we had no *miai*. I used to teach my husband's sister in elementary school. The principal of the school I was transferred to happened to be a friend of my husband. I took care of his sister when she was promoted to high school, and became intimate with him. Before long his parents made a proposal of marriage through the principal, and contacts with him followed it. We married neither through *miai* nor through an ordinary love match.

Truncated courtship—If circumstances prevent a couple from carrying on the usual courtship, the love match pattern is disrupted:

Until we were five or six we played with each other. Since then I often went abroad with my family and had short encounters when I came back to Japan. My husband proposed to me. It was the end of the war and we couldn't see each other very often. I can hardly explain but I always answer just "the middle" [between love match and arranged marriage].

Incomplete love—If love is less than romantic, the classification is often qualified. When a marriage has neither love nor a *miai*, it is difficult to classify: "I hesitate, but as I didn't hate him, perhaps I can call it a love marriage." Sometimes the partners feel "trust and respect" or "understanding," but these do not seem intense enough.

Another problem is to distinguish between friendship and love:

Wife: Since he and I were in the same university, we had a thorough knowledge of each other.

Husband: My feeling was closer to friendship than to love.

Another wife felt her marriage was "Just in between [a love match and an arranged marriage]. So to speak a compassionate marriage. We were on intimate terms as if we were brother and sister."

In other cases the classification problem arises not from the quality but from the quantity (intensity) of love:

I was introduced to him not as his partner for marriage. I was in contact with him for quite a long period, during which we came to love each other. In our case, however, our love was not so passionate as one sees in ordinary love matches.

Love must be intense on both sides for a pure love match. In several cases the man's love was adequate but the girl's lukewarmness spoiled the picture:

In our case I was more passionate and forceful than my wife. Our marriage may be a sort of love match.

Not a perfect love marriage; about 80 per cent. We loved each other, but I was not so passionate as to fall in love by nature. He was a friend of mine in the office. We had views in common. While going together for a long time, we decided to marry.

If the girl doesn't love at all, the love match is even less complete:

I am not sure if I can call my marriage a love match because in my case I was loved and proposed to one-sidedly.

My husband was passionately eager about the marriage, while I was not much interested in it, being only nineteen at that time. I was entirely passive and largely influenced by my mother's opinions. A woman, a generation ago, was very modest.

QUALIFIED MIAI MARRIAGES

The preceding section suggests that quasi-arranged marriages will resemble quasi-love matches. The only clear-cut distinction is between the labels the respondents choose (in response to our forced-choice alternatives) before going on to qualify their choices.

Incomplete formality—A marriage may be arranged but the *miai* by-passed:

As my wife's parents lived in a remote region, I visited my wife-to-be at her lodging house with a letter of introduction. Our marriage, therefore, was not through a regular *miai* interview but through an informal meeting of ourselves.

Two girls were tricked into participating in *miai* without realizing that they were being interviewed for marriage purposes:

We had a one-sided *miai*; she did not realize it. Besides, the arrangements were completed before she felt any affection for me. I should say it was a one-sided love marriage. But in form it was a *miai* marriage because my decision was made when I first saw her at the place of the *miai*.

Several couples knew each other before being officially introduced by a *miai*. Advance knowledge runs counter to the general rule, but did not obviate the value of the *miai* in making them eligible to marry:

A husband: Our houses were located in the same neighborhood and we had known each other's face. However, we didn't talk even a word, so they arranged an opportunity to introduce us. We became friends, and so on.

Another husband: We were introduced by my wife's elder sister, who was living near our house. The sister's family and I were very close friends and as we were all living near we had known each other. We were formally introduced, but I suppose ours wouldn't be a pure *miai* marriage.

A wife: I knew him from childhood but had not regarded him as my partner for marriage until our cousins both went between us. We started afresh to contact and understand each other better.

Intrusive self-reliance—Individuals who make their own arrangements after the *miai* fail to exhibit the proper passivity:

> It was a *miai* marriage in form. However, the *miai* only gave us a chance to start the arrangements by ourselves. We were quite independent and free in deciding the marriage. Therefore our case stands just between *miai* and love.

A decision of one's own free will (uninfluenced by parents or matchmaker) is another deviation:

> *Wife:* I was formally introduced but I decided my marriage by my own will, so I don't think arranged marriage is the most appropriate term.

> *Husband:* We started by *miai* and for a year we tried to understand each other. So when we married, our union was almost similar to a love match.

> *Another wife:* With respect to the fact that other people introduced us to each other in the traditional way, the marriage was made in the form of a *miai* marriage. However, after the first meeting we two conducted ourselves with our own free will. Therefore it may be more appropriate to say my case lies just between *miai* and love.

Intrusive courtship—Next most often mentioned to love itself was the idea that long courtship after the *miai* dissolves the boundary line between the two types of marriage. Fifteen couples mention this complication:

> *A husband:* A *miai* marriage and a love match may be different in motives and meanings at the first two or three meetings. However, the process of time makes the distinction very unclear, because a *miai* interview is made on the assumption that two persons are to marry. At present the terms are quite inappropriate.

> *A wife:* There was a considerably long period between the engagement and the marriage, and so a bit of love match is mixed in.

> *Another wife:* The process was in the form of a *miai* marriage. However, the period between the interview and the wedding was so long that it may be called a love match. Anyhow, my case is absolutely different from the traditional arranged marriage.

> *Another husband:* I had a *miai* with a person who was absolutely a stranger to me, and so my case was literally a *miai* marriage. On the other hand, it may be called a love marriage from the fact that we had a six-month period for contacts.

The following individual emphasizes the thoroughness of knowledge gained rather than the length of courtship:

> In my case, if I have to choose one of the two, I must admit it was *miai*. However that term doesn't describe our situation very well. Through introduction we got acquainted and discussed our ways of thinking or views of life and realized we had enough common background. This led us into marriage, so I think it was not the traditional type of interview marriage.

Intrusive love—As might be expected from the dichotomy posed between love marriage and interview marriage, the most common dilemma (two dozen cases) involves couples who meet by *miai* and later fall in love. So common is this particular outcome of *miai* that many couples propose a third category, to be called "*miai*-plus-love."[19]

One couple even fell in love at the interview itself:

Wife: Formally it was an interview marriage, but substantially our marriage was the result of love at "first sight."

Husband: Formally it was a *miai* marriage, but more suitably it was rather a love match, which both families admitted from the beginning.

Another couple made a point of not getting engaged until they discovered whether they could love each other:

It may be more appropriate to call our case an interview marriage because we first met in the form of a *miai*. However, we did not exchange betrothal presents until we ascertained each other's affection through several contacts. For this reason, it was not so different from a love marriage in substance.

The interval between *miai* and wedding determines how the marriage will be classified:

A wife: My marriage was a *miai* marriage because it began through an introduction. However, I found my love for him deepened during the period between the introduction and the wedding.

A husband: From *miai* to friendship and from friendship to love. Ten months later we married. During this ten months I thoroughly experienced human sentiment and emotions. . . . During our engagement period we took long trips several times. Therefore I think I would propose to call our case a "*miai*-friendship-love" marriage rather than a traditional *miai* marriage.

Such comments suggest the flavor of the mate-selection systems in contemporary Tokyo, but they depend too heavily on the spontaneous creativity of the respondents to be a reliable basis for statistical analysis. The next chapter focuses on a more objective classification, depending on the actual method of introduction. Highly correlated with the self-classification of marriage (as we saw in Table 1–2), this provides a more systematic means of discovering how the two systems of mate-selection operate in practice.

19. Wagatsuma comments that "happily married couples who are aware of the value of 'democratic' love marriage in contemporary Japan and who idealize love marriages might have been led to believe retrospectively that love existed even in the beginning of their arranged marriage. When married couples talk about love marriage versus arranged marriage, those who are married according to arrangement often refer to their arranged marriage with an apologetic tone in their voices. Sometimes they voice rather frankly their wish that they could have been married out of love instead of according to arrangement. Especially when they are happy in their marriage I think it is a very natural human tendency to wish to believe that love existed from the beginning of their marriage."

LOVE MATCH
AND ARRANGED MARRIAGE—
HOW MARRIAGE PARTNERS ARE
ACTUALLY CHOSEN

2

So far we have examined people's ideas about mate-selection: old-fashioned ideas and modern ones, conservative and radical. Most people see personal selection and third-party arrangement as polar opposites. Yet these systems exist side by side in contemporary Japan. In a concrete and steel apartment house in Tokyo, one couple fell in love at the office, whereas their next door neighbors were introduced by a middle-aged matchmaker. What happens from that point on? Does it really matter how people meet? Do love-match couples treat each other any differently than formally introduced couples, before or after marriage?

This chapter traces the behavior of nonintroduced and variously introduced couples up to the point where the marriage contract is sealed in engagement to be married. To choose a marriage partner requires more than simply meeting or being introduced. Between first encounter and engagement, what happens? How often do couples get together? What do they talk about? How well do they get to know each other, their families, and friends? How much does love blossom?

Among our 444 Tokyo couples, almost half had met without benefit of introduction (Table 2–1). These we will treat as pure love-match cases. Another sixth were introduced as potential friends with no matchmaking

Table 2–1—Type of Introduction of Marriage Partner

	Number	Per cent
Not introduced	212	48%
Introduced just as a friend	70	16
Introduced informally as a potential marriage partner	35	8
Formally introduced through a miai	127	29
Total	444	101%

supposedly intended by the introducer. In the United States it makes little difference whether people happen to be introduced when they first meet, but in Japan introductions are more influential. Even a "friendly" introduction may "contaminate" an otherwise pure love match by lending an air of sponsorship to the relationship. When American young people are "fixed up" as blind dates, there is no compulsion to marry just because a "match maker" introduced them. American matchmaking brings together potential *dating* partners whose subsequent dates determine whether they will "get serious." In Japan, however, dating is too serious a business to be severed from marriage. Even the most casual introduction tends to launch a marriage-oriented process of interaction. As the tables in this chapter show, all introduced couples tend to differ from nonintroduced ones because of this latent personal and situational pressure toward marriage.

An additional twelfth of our couples were introduced as potential marriage partners without benefit of a formal *miai*. Since formality is a key element in the *miai* system, these are only quasi-*miai* marriages. Finally, there are the genuine *miai* marriages, less than a third of the total, in which a full-fledged *miai* initiated the mate-selection process.

The Demography of the Various Introduction Systems

What kinds of people get introduced in these various ways? And when—in Japanese history and in the life histories of individuals—do people resort to one system more than another?

TRENDS

Our sample is not very useful for answering the historical question. By definition, it is limited to the postwar era. By virtue of the newness and smallness of the apartments, it is further limited to newly married couples (typically married only four years). Given such clustered wedding dates, it is precarious to infer trends. At least we can say there is no evidence of a short-run trend toward the love-match system. If anything, the tendency is in the opposite direction.

Such a trend could result from the return of normal social conditions, which allow greater formality. It could also reflect the post-Occupation return from things American to traditional Japanese practices.

In any case, we have no evidence within our sample for a trend toward the love-match system. In Chapter 1 we assumed a long-range trend and documented it with data from more inclusive studies in Japan. In the future, the industrialization and urbanization of Japan, the emancipation of women, and so on seem bound to transform the *miai* system further and increase opportunities for young people to enter love matches. Although our sample shows no internal trends, its high proportion of love matches contrasts with the prewar dominance of arranged marriages. Hence we believe our data do not invalidate the long-run trend from arranged marriages to love matches.

SOCIAL STATUS

Our sample is equally unsatisfactory for comparing high- and low-status groups. Confined almost exclusively to the upper middle class, it offers little variation in social status. Perhaps for this reason there is little correlation between measures of status and the various introduction mechanisms.

Neither the man's income nor his occupation nor his education shows any systematic connection with his introduction. Our tentative conclusion therefore must be that the systems exist side by side, equally dispersed among the same strata of the male population.

EMANCIPATION

Women in Japan (as in most countries) have always been more controlled than men by their parents. Trained to be submissive, they feel especially deeply the duties of filial piety. For instance, Professor Kiyo Tamura quotes a student as follows:

> I cannot imagine how my parents could get along without me—especially in my mother's case—and so their warm consideration becomes a burden to me. My problem is, how can I leave my parents with least sacrifice or sorrow? The pain I feel in that my marriage makes my parents lonely and sad may be the cause of my regarding love between a young man and woman as a sort of sin.

Feelings of responsibility to parents make arranged marriages attractive. When parents promote marriages, daughters can be sure they are doing their duty by getting married.

Surrounded by traditional attitudes, Japanese girls must be quite emancipated to dare to marry on their own initiative. Life experiences such as attending college, which take girls away from home and expose them to modern ideas, help wean them from old ways.

College-educated and masculine-oriented women have more than the usual number of love matches, perhaps partly by choice and partly by opportunity. On ideological grounds such women would be expected to prefer modern ways. Emancipated women have too much self-esteem to be willing to be manipulated into marriage. In addition, the very fact of going to college longer than usual or acting in aggressive masculine ways may provide greater contact with men and therefore more opportunities to fall in love. Office romances are another example of an emancipated activity creating love-match opportunities. A masculine or uncertain sex role preference is indicative of general rejection of the traditionally submissive feminine role.

Table 2–2—Type of Introduction by Woman's Emancipation Experiences

	WOMAN'S EDUCATION		
Type of Introduction	No College	Some College	College Graduate
None	48%	41%	62%
Friendly	16	14	17
Informal	8	8	4
Formal	28	37	17
Total	100%	100%	100%
N	300	96	48

	WOMAN'S SEX ROLE PREFERENCE	
Type of Introduction	Feminine	Masculine or Uncertain
None	44%	55%
Friendly	17	13
Informal	8	7
Formal	30	25
Total	99%	100%
N*	293	150

	WOMAN'S CONTACT WITH WESTERN CULTURE	
Type of Introduction	Stayed Home	Visited Abroad
None	48%	44%
Friendly	15	31
Informal	8	6
Formal	29	19
Total	100%	100%
N*	427	16

* Plus one case in which role preference or foreign travel was not ascertained.

Whereas foreign travel increases the eligibility of Japanese men, its effect on women is quite the reverse. Japanese girls who have studied abroad are viewed with suspicion by matchmakers and potential partners alike (see Blood, forthcoming). They are by definition usually college graduates. Their exposure to higher education at home and abroad tends to alienate them from traditional ways of arranging marriages. Hence neither they nor anyone else is likely to see them as suitable candidates for a *miai*.

On the other hand, their sojourn abroad constitutes a temporary ecological barrier to finding their own marriage partner, removing them from contact with their field of eligibles at a crucial time in life. Hence love matches are less available to them than to classmates who remain in Japan and secure a job (with all the structured opportunities that provides).

Deprived of both extremes of the mate-selection system, girls rely primarily on friendly introductions after returning home. That these introductions are often to others who have studied abroad is suggested by the sizeable proportion (57 per cent) of all couples in which both partners had been abroad who were introduced "just as friends." Indeed it would be no exaggeration to say that the frequent postwar reunions in Tokyo of students who had studied abroad under the Fulbright program offered another structural basis for creating friendships capable of blossoming into love.

One other measure of emancipation applies to both women and men—an ideological question requiring them to rank ten aspects of marriage from most to least important.

Table 2–3—First Ranked Aspect of Marriage by Type of Introduction (extremes only)

First-Ranked Aspect of Marriage	Introduction			
	MEN		WOMEN	
	None	Formal	None	Formal
Love	36%	31%	35%	24%
Understanding	25	29	18	18
Courtesy and respect	12	13	10	9
Decision-making compatibility	9	4	8	19
Husband's income	—	—	14	17
Wife's financial management	2	2	—	—
Good parent	6	4	7	6
Good health	4	6	6	4
Sexual attractiveness	3	6	*	2
Home management	1	3	—	—
Helpfulness in the home	—	—	1	1
Companionship	*	0	*	0
N.A.	1	0	0	0
Total	100%	98%	99%	100%
N	212	127	212	127

* Less than 0.5%.

Table 2–3 shows that love-match men and even more their wives emphasize love—which is one reason they marry that way. They are also the only ones who stress companionship, another modernistic value.

By contrast, *miai* couples emphasize the husband's income and the wife's home management, the wife's sexual attractiveness, and her understanding of the husband's problems—all traditional roles. These values are strongly sex-linked and therefore asymmetrical, whereas love-match men and women accentuate values with mutual implications.

Decision-making compatibility is chosen equally often by love match men and women. It is noticeably ignored, however, by *miai* men and strikingly emphasized by their wives. Does this mean that *miai* men take patriarchalism for granted but that their wives are afraid of being dominated? If so, it constitutes a feminine exception to an otherwise consistently traditional pattern of values in the *miai* group. If our question had been asked *before* marriage, we could be more confident of its interpretation.

TIMING

The biggest demographic differences between mate-selection groups are differences in timing. By and large, the same kinds of people get married by either system, but *when* they do is another matter; see Table 2–4.

Table 2–4—Age of Meeting Spouse by Type of Introduction

	INTRODUCTION			
Median Age	None	Friendly	Informal	Formal
Woman	21	21	23	23
Man	24	24	28	28
N	212	70	35	127

In our sample the median age at marriage is 24 for women and 28 for men. Table 2–4 shows that love-match contact generally begins considerably earlier than formal introductions, which typically occur close to the median age of marriage. In part this reflects differences in the length of courtship in the two mate-selection systems. *Miai* couples march quickly from introduction to wedding ceremony, whereas love blooms more slowly. However, personal selection is also the preferred system in contemporary Japan and *miai* a last resort, utilized chiefly after love has passed by.

Since men are the usual initiators, the age difference between marriage systems is particularly great for them. Indeed, all eight men in our sample who did not meet their wives until over 33 were formally introduced to them.

If love strikes soon enough, it leads to marriage in due time. When it fails to arrive, the traditional system is resorted to by default. Men and women who pass the normal age of marriage can expect their friends and relatives to become increasingly active on their behalf. (Though the mechanisms are not the same, such "help" for eligible bachelors and single girls is not unknown in the West!)

One of my Japanese friends was in such a fix. There I was, 37 years old, married fourteen years and the father of four children, while he was only two years younger and still single. As a scientist he had studied abroad during the years when he normally would have gotten married. His parents were desperately trying to find him a wife. They arranged a *miai* with one girl whom he found "rather a nice girl." But just when a friendship was beginning to develop, the parents withdrew their sponsorship because further investigation disclosed that in her college years she had lived in a rooming house instead of properly chaperoned with relatives. This evidence of emancipated independence (and the possibility that she might have engaged in unknown misdemeanors) ruined her reputation as far as the parents were concerned. So they turned to another matchmaker's portfolio and began scanning other photographs.

Table 2–5—Type of Introduction by Man's Contact with Western Culture

	VISITED ABROAD	
TYPE OF INTRODUCTION	Yes	No
None	35%	49%
Friendly	27	15
Informal	3	8
Formal	35	28
Total	100%	100%
N	34	406

That my friend was not unusual in being left stranded by prolonged absence overseas is suggested by Table 2–5. Formal introductions are often used to select partners for men temporarily removed from the marriage market by foreign study. Stay-at-home men have more chances for falling in love without help. Even if a foreign school happens to be attended by Japanese women, the ratio of women to men is apt to be very low. Moreover, men abroad are handicapped by skepticism about foreign-educated girls as potential wives. Hence for men, foreign study is a double barrier to finding one's own marriage partner.

PAIR CHARACTERISTICS

So far we have explored the sources from which the mate-selection systems draw their recruits. Our next task is to examine the pairings which result. Are *miai* pairs traditionally skewed in form, the man high, the woman low? Are love matches more symmetrical? The ages and educational qualifications of the partners offer two ways of testing this hypothesis.

Table 2-6—Comparative Age and Education by Type of Introduction

	INTRODUCTION			
COMPARATIVE AGE	None	Friendly	Informal	Formal
Man older				
5+ years	23%	21%	46%	48%
3–4 years	25	24	34	31
1–2 years	29	27	17	18
Equal	15	19	3	2
Woman older	9	9	0	1
Total	101%	101%	100%	100%
COMPARATIVE EDUCATION				
Man more				
4+ years	34%	47%	43%	41%
1–3 years	32	27	40	35
Equal	27	17	14	20
Woman more	8	9	3	4
Total	101%	100%	100%	100%
N	212	70	35	127

When formal and informal matchmakers look for eligibly young wives for overaged men, they widen the age differential in arranged marriages. Conversely, it is only when Japanese men accidentally fall in love that they pair off with girls their own age, to say nothing of girls who are actually older.

Educational differences are similar but smaller, suggesting that age is more important than education in conservative Japanese circles. The modal pattern is a four-year difference (typically a college-educated man married to a high-school-educated bride). Deviant patterns of educational equality or wife superiority are more common among love matches unguided by conventional criteria.

By contrast, Americans typically marry their educational equals, reflecting both the prevalence of love matches and the greater education of women in an affluent society (Blood and Wolfe, 1960: 163). Age differences in America have not yet disappeared. Nevertheless, the U.S. Census reports that the median gap has narrowed since 1890 when it was four years (the contemporary Japanese pattern), to hardly more than two years. Presumably Japan, too, will gradually attain educational and age equality under rising standards of living.

The Introduction Process

Having seen what sorts of people get introduced in various ways, the next question is, who does the introducing?

The traditional introducer was a middle-aged matchmaker. In contemporary Tokyo, formal matchmaking is still a middle-aged activity (Vogel, 1961b). As the arranged marriage system changes we would expect the monopoly of elders to be broken. Peers should play increasingly active roles, especially in "friendly" introductions.

Table 2–7—Relationship of Introducer to Man by Type of Introduction

RELATIONSHIP OF INTRODUCER TO MAN	INTRODUCTION			
	Friendly	Informal	Formal	Total
Authoritative				
Parent	8%	23%	31%	24%
Older relative	10	13	17	15
Employer, teacher	8	13	17	14
Advisory				
Older sibling	4	23	6	8
Organization leader	4	10	3	4
Equalitarian				
Friend	50	13	13	22
Young relative, younger sibling	13	3	2	5
Ambiguous				
Neighbor	4	0	11	7
Total	101%	98%	100%	99%
N*	52	30	123	205

* The relationship is not ascertained in 18, 5, and 4 cases respectively, the declining numbers reflecting the decreasing ambiguity of the three types of introductions.

Table 2-7 shows that elders still do most of the introducing, and their introductions are heavily marriage-oriented. The most authoritative elders (parents, older relatives, and employers) prefer the formality of the *miai*. The only exception is that employers go to less trouble with their *women* employees, for whom an informal introduction typically suffices. Because of their shorter career span and lower occupational status, women merit less investment of company resources than men.

Elder brothers and sisters and organizational leaders with less control over their leisure-time charges also use formal means of promoting marriages.

Merely friendly introductions, on the other hand, occur in equalitarian settings, particularly among mutual friends. (Neighbors are difficult to classify because their age relationship is unknown.)

In general, the greater the status differential between the introducer and the introduced, the more formal and marriage-oriented the introduction. In the most authoritative relationships the maximum status differential combines with the maximum formality to put heavy pressure on the young people involved.

In many cases the introducer's relationship to the two partners is not symmetrical. For example, parents may introduce their child to a young friend, relative, or neighbor of the opposite sex. Or the introducer may be a sibling of one and a friend of the other, as when big brothers introduce their "kid sisters" to their pals, or little sisters introduce their girl friends to their big brothers. The examples just mentioned are the commonest asymmetrical types found in our sample. Barely half the introductions are symmetrical, such as an employer's introducing two employees to one another. Moreover, some symmetrical cases require collaboration to achieve this effect, as when two sets of parents introduce their children to each other. Matchmaking, then, is a role primarily for elders, but all sorts of relationships are utilized in recruiting young candidates.

Miai PARTICIPATION

Ideally, a full complement of elders participates in a *miai*. In the old days when a *miai* functioned primarily to introduce the man's parents to their prospective daughter-in-law and the woman's parents to their daughter's prospective parent surrogates, both sets of parents had good reason to participate. Boy plus girl plus four parents plus matchmaker presumably yielded a minimum of seven participants (with occasional additions of other significant elders from the two extended families).

Today, however, the modified *miai* system decreases the importance of the elders' judgment. The couple themselves are the crucial participants, plus someone to bring them together. Moreover, there is no longer any assurance that the first *miai* will be the last. As personal preferences become individuated and willingness to accept adult manipulation attenuated, the chances diminish that one *miai* will suffice. Both trends dilute the momentousness of the occasion for parents. Hence we would expect fewer parents to take the trouble to participate, especially if they are occupied elsewhere.

Among our 127 *miai*, only 18 per cent commanded their full complement of seven or more participants. For most (55 per cent), the total attendance was five or six, meaning that at least one parent was missing. Probably the modal *miai* involves only one parent for each candidate. Because matchmakers are feminine, mothers are especially interested in their children's marriages, and men have other interests to preoccupy them, it is safe to assume that the missing parent is usually the father.

More than one fourth of our *miai*, however, had fewer than the five participants that result if each partner is accompanied by a parent. Mothers are still so important that we can assume their absence was involuntary. In most cases this was probably due to geographical mobility. Since the war Tokyo has been invaded by a mass of young adults whose parents cannot always afford to travel to the capital to attend a *miai*.

Whatever the reason for parental absence, the *miai* system is profoundly altered when parents disappear altogether. This is not to suggest any trend toward parentless *miai* in the future, but to emphasize that even the traditional ceremony may lose the parental sponsorship which was once its essence. In such circumstances the differences between an "arranged" marriage and a love match may become very small.

MULTIPLE INTRODUCTIONS

If every man married the first girl he met, the youngsters' veto power would be nullified. Since the veto is often mentioned in contemporary Japan (see Chapter 1), some of the *miai* we have been analyzing must have been the last in a series. Introductions, after all, involve *proposed* marriage partners—and even though propositions "take" more often in Japan than in America, the matchmaker's batting average could not be 1,000 and still leave the younger generation the decision-making power it now demands. Many introductions are trial-and-error affairs. Table 2–8 shows that the majority wind up as errors.

Table 2–8—Previous Introductions by Type of Final Introduction

		FINAL INTRODUCTION		
PREVIOUS MIAI	None	Friendly	Informal	Formal
Incidence				
Men	22%	33%	59%	57%
Women	30%	41%	46%	67%
Mean number				
Men	0.6	0.9	1.8	1.8
Women	0.7	1.0	1.4	2.1
PREVIOUS DATING PARTNERS				
Incidence				
Men	84%	86%	86%	81%
Women	84%	87%	71%	74%
Mean number				
Men	5.0	5.3	4.5	4.4
Women	4.2	4.7	2.7	2.8
N	212	70	35	127

Previous miai—For the total sample, the average individual had one *miai* with a person he didn't marry. The grand total of 976 unsuccessful *miai* for the men and women combined when compared with the 127 successful *miai* reveals that hardly more than 10 per cent were successful. Even those who eventually married by this system were not much more successful, since they typically scored on the third round.

The *miai* system is surprisingly ubiquitous. Instead of being confined to the 30 per cent who eventually married this way, it was also tried by nearly half of those who did not. If we add successful to unsuccessful *miai* for the sample as a whole, almost half the husbands and over half the wives (49 and 54 per cent respectively) attended at least one *miai* during their mate-selecting years.

Previous dating partners—Dating is even more widespread. Not only did the great majority date at least one other person, but there is little relation between the proportion of daters and the type of introduction that finally results in marriage. In contrast to the greater use of the *miai* system by those who ultimately marry that way, dating is tried by almost as many from the *miai* group as from the love-match group. This datum reflects the penetration of the *miai* system by the dating custom (as we shall see later), so that formally introduced couples are apt to date a bit before vetoing a proposed match. However, the number of persons dated so far exceeds the number of *miai* that *most* dating partners were obviously secured elsewhere. Moreover, a subanalysis of those *miai* husbands and wives without any previous *miai* shows that they too had a substantial number of dating partners.

Despite the overlap, there is a positive correlation between the extent of a person's participation in a mate-selection system and his chances of marrying by that system. Those who marry without introduction date the most partners and those who marry by *miai* attend the most *miai*. To some extent, then, these are still *alternative* systems of mate-selection despite the overlap.

However, when we remove the nonintroduced and the formally introduced extremes, we do not find the expected inverse relationship between number of dating partners and number of *miai*. Rather, within both mate-selection groups, those with the most dating partners also have the most *miai*.

Apparently some general factor underlies both dating and *miai* participation. Either those individuals who date the most are extraordinarily choosy in selecting their marriage partner by the *miai* system or else they are extraordinarily ineligible and get vetoed remarkably often. In view of male initiative in the mate-selection process, it seems likely that men who date a lot are more critical in choosing a marriage partner and hence need multiple *miai* to find a wife who meets their complex specifications. Dating so many girls may alert them to personality factors and make them less willing to accept just any girl from the right family background. Japanese women, however, have less choice. Hence those with extensive dating experience may often be vetoed by the man (or perhaps by his family) before finally having a successful match. In any case, extensive dating does not take the place of extensive matchmaking for either men or women. Rather, dating has invaded the most traditional segment of our Tokyo sample. The positive correlation between frequency of dating and of *miai* also reminds us that dating is not identical with love nor any guarantee that love will occur. Marriage-oriented, sociability-oriented, or desperate men or women may try both systems more often in the hope that eventually one system or the other will yield them a prize (or at least a catch).[1]

In conclusion, the two systems of mate-selection overlap for large segments of the population. So many people participate in both that there can be few demographic differences between those who eventually marry by different systems. To some extent, the system one marries by is a matter of chance. The crucial variable is not how one is introduced but how the individual (and his parents) react to the prospective partner. Provided two people are attracted to each other, they will marry anyway, unaffected by the fact that they either were or were not formally introduced.

A second generalization is that the predominance of love matches in our total sample is matched by an equal predominance of dating as the chief means of exposure to potential marriage partners. *Miai* are not only a minority source of successful matches in this sample but an even smaller source of unsuccessful matches. By and large, therefore, the contacts which produce marriages in this Tokyo group are overwhelmingly dating contacts, not the' traditional introductions.

Despite the dominance of dating as a source of exposure, the probability of marriage resulting from a single *miai* is greater than that from a single date. Formal introductions are primarily for persons who want to get married. Even though dating is more closely linked with marriage in Japan than in the United States, it nevertheless may occur between partners ineligible for marriage because of age or other factors. Japanese dating is partly a means of recreation and only potentially a means of mate-selection. Its current popularity in Tokyo is apparent from our data. In the future, it will provide even more opportunities for falling in love.

Marriage Promotion—Self-Reliance vs. Reliance on Others

The *miai* is only part of the mate-selection sequence for those who adhere to Japanese tradition, and no part at all for those who by-pass it. Nevertheless, the contrasting sex roles illustrated by differential parental attendance at the *miai* reflect a larger pattern for marriages of all types.

1. In the opinion of one young wife, dating is apt to be more marriage-motivated than merely sociable:

> There is no place in Japan for a fellow to date several girls without getting a bad reputation as a playboy who will make a poor husband. If a fellow is dating, he should have serious intentions of marrying—it's not considered decent to date only for friendship. My husband dated several girls and would have had a hard time getting a *miai* because girls' parents wouldn't have approved.

Such parents consider dating successive partners promiscuous.

To find out who was most influential in the mate-selection process, we asked our respondents, "As for your father, your mother, or yourself, who would you say had the most influence in the decision that you would marry this boy (girl)?" A more literal translation would be, "Who was the chief promoting power?"

Table 2–9—Parental Promotion of Children's Marriages

	Son's Marriage	Daughter's Marriage
Chief promoter		
Father	4%	8%
Mother	6%	18%
Secondary promoter		
Father	24%	24%
Mother	44%	51%
N	444	444

Residual roles are played by the young person himself or by others such as an elder brother or matchmaker

Most of our respondents saw themselves as the chief promoters of their own marriages. However, when the roles of fathers and mothers are compared, the preoccupation of mothers with marrying off their children is again apparent. Roughly twice as many mothers as fathers play primary and secondary roles in promoting their children's marriages. Maternal activity is accentuated in the case of daughters, who are less apt to marry on their own initiative and whose marrying-off is the special concern of the parent of the same sex.

Parents are understandably active in promoting arranged marriages.[2] However, Table 2–10 shows that a majority of men feel that even in *miai* marriages

Table 2–10—Personal Promotion of Marriage by Type of Introduction

	INTRODUCTION			
	None	Friendly	Informal	Formal
Man's role				
Primary	98%	90%	83%	73%
Secondary	1	6	6	12
Neither	1	4	11	15
Total	100%	100%	100%	100%
Woman's role				
Primary	90%	71%	54%	45%
Secondary	8	20	14	31
Neither	2	9	31	24
Total	100%	100%	99%	100%
N	212	70	35	127

2. After marriage, parental activism creates more in-law problems in *miai* marriages than in love matches. In the marriage counseling cases of private practitioner Kenji Tamura (Tokyo), in-law troubles were the presenting problem in almost a third of the *miai* marriages but in none of the love marriages (Cox, 1966). In a study of 14,000 cases coming before family courts for conciliation or adjudication, the Ministry of Justice similarly found in-laws more frequently a source of difficulty in arranged marriages (1957).

they were responsible for the final decision to marry the girl. By contrast, only a minority of *miai* wives take primary responsibility for their own marriages.

We shall have many occasions to see that Japanese marriages are usually male-initiated if the initiative is not mutual. This masculine emphasis seems to contradict our previous point about the eagerness of mothers to marry off their daughters. But maternal anxiety stems precisely from the passive role of the girl. Hence, when opportunity presents itself in the form of a marriage proposal, mothers often pressure their daughters into accepting.

More surprising than "arranged" marriages that are self-engineered are nonintroduced couples who are *not* self-reliant. These cases are by definition not pure love matches and notably often involve passive wives rather than passive husbands. Perhaps if parents get desperate enough, they pressure their daughter into marrying even a man of her own choosing. Better the wrong husband than no husband at all!

PARENTAL ATTITUDES TOWARD THE MATCH

Generally speaking, a greater promoting role of parents in *miai* marriages coincides with their greater enthusiasm (and less enthusiasm on the part of the child). To discover these attitudes, we asked our respondents for their own feelings and those of each parent towards the match at the time of the engagement.

Table 2–11—Parental Attitudes to the Match at the Time of Betrothal

	MAN'S PARENTS		WOMAN'S PARENTS	
ATTITUDE	Father	Mother	Father	Mother
(5)* Eager, enthusiastic	15%	14%	10%	12%
(4) Happy	48	46	41	44
(3) Indecisive	10	14	13	19
(2) Indifferent	14	9	11	9
(1) Reluctant, hesitant	4	4	7	8
(0) Opposed	5	4	7	6
N.A.	4	9	11	2
Total	100%	100%	100%	100%
Mean	3.45	3.50	3.18	3.26

* Numbers in parentheses show the basis for computing means in this and later tables. N is 444.

Fathers and mothers usually view their child's marriage symmetrically (see Table 2–11). The chief difference is that mothers tend to be undecided, whereas fathers are more often simply indifferent.

Between the two sets of parents, however, there is considerable difference. The man's parents are more enthusiastic than the girl's. This reflects the patriarchal bias in mate-selection. Since the bride is usually chosen *by* the man (with or without his parents' collaboration), it is to be expected that attitudes will be more positive on his side and more uncertain on the girl's.

Table 2–12—Parental Attitudes to the Match by Type of Introduction

| | INTRODUCTION | | | |
	None	Friendly	Informal	Formal
Man's parents				
Father	3.08	3.30	4.17	3.92
Mother	3.16	3.34	4.15	3.98
Discrepancy	—0.08	—0.04	+0.02	—0.06
Woman's parents				
Father	2.93	2.90	3.60	3.62
Mother	3.16	3.00	3.47	3.54
Discrepancy	—0.23	—0.10	+0.13	+0.08
Mean discrepancy between man's and woman's parents	+0.08	+0.37	+0.63	+0.37
N	212	70	35	127

Note: Scoring system is shown in the preceding table.

Table 2–12 shows that the man's family is particularly enthusiastic in non-love-match cases. By contrast, in love matches the two sets of parents are equally unhappy. In general, all four parents are happier about matches where the partners were introduced for marriage purposes than in either type of nonarranged marriage.

Between fathers and mothers the discrepancies are small but patterned. With a single exception, fathers are more enthusiastic about informally or formally arranged marriages than their wives, whereas the reverse is true without exception for unsponsored matches. The largest discrepancy involves daughter's pure love matches, about which fathers are as glum as usual but mothers are relatively enthusiastic. Perhaps these mothers achieve vicarious gratification through their daughters' emancipated behavior.

Parental opposition—Although parents are less enthusiastic about marriages they have not helped to arrange, they seldom oppose such marriages outright. (At least, few of our respondents actually married under these circumstances.) In pure love matches less than 10 per cent of even the wives' fathers went so far as to oppose the match.

A few respondents volunteered the reasons for their parents' opposition. Two were questions of timing. One girl's parents thought she was too young when a fellow employee first asked to marry her, but they relented when he asked again several years later. Another was not too young herself but was expected to wait until after her elder brothers had been married off, since birth order determines eligibility for marriage in Japanese tradition.[3]

3. Wagatsuma reports that "when there are two or three girls in a family and the eldest daughter is rather unpopular in *miai* or unsuccessful in a series of interviews, the parents' worry is doubled. When the eldest daughter's marriage is delayed, the second and third girls (even if they are much more attractive than their sister and even though there are many marriage candidates already asking to marry them) cannot marry because it is against the custom to have a marriage take place against the birth order. Very often parents want to have a grandson by their eldest son, but if their daughter is older than he and not yet married it's not quite appropriate to marry a son when his elder sister is not yet married."

Three prospective husbands failed to meet parental requirements. One lacked the necessary means of supporting a family:

> While I was associating with him as a friend, he lost his job owing to bankruptcy of his company. For this reason my parents were opposed to my marriage to him. With the help of my brother, however, I got the approval of my parents on condition that he should get employment first.

Not so unusual an objection, that. But the other two cases were distinctively Japanese. Both involved girls who were eldest daughters in all-girl families:

> Since I was the eldest daughter, I was expected to stay home with the husband my parents would choose in order to succeed my family (*Ie*).

This garbled translation means the husband was supposed to move into the wife's home, take over the family farm, take her family name, and carry on the family line. The unwillingness of love-match husbands to be adopted is disappointing to son-less parents. In this case, the couple eloped. In the other, the parents eventually relented, perhaps because other daughters were available for whom they might recruit more compliant husbands.

In a hierarchically ordered country, parents cannot be defied lightly, even if they can sometimes be defied successfully. Two husbands confessed that the emotional strain caused by their parents' disapproval spoiled their happiness in getting married:

> An opposed marriage cannot give a sweet tender sentiment. I struggled against the stream of society in order to get married. I disputed several times about a divorce.

> I couldn't be optimistic about the possibility of getting married. I often wished at that time that ours were an arranged marriage. Since our parents opposed our love match, I couldn't enjoy our life.

Parental opposition may be the acid test of love, but it is apt to corrode that love in the process. Life is sweetest when love is uncontaminated by embittered parents.[4]

COMPARATIVE ATTITUDES OF PARENTS AND CHILDREN

How do parents' attitudes compare with those of the engaged couple themselves? We already know that parental enthusiasm is greater in arranged

4. DeVos (1960) found in a study of TAT responses of Japanese villagers that both men and women express self-blame and blame others for engaging in love marriages:

> Marriages which go counter to family considerations and are based on individual passion or love are particularly prone to disrupt the family structure; they are likely to be of rebellious origin, and any subsequent stresses of adjustment to partner and respective families tend to remind the participants of the rebellious tone of the marriage and, therefore, to elicit guilt feelings.

Wagatsuma adds that "parental opposition means that the young couple marry against their parental wishes and this makes lovers or young couples guilty about hurting their parents. This guilt often jeopardizes the happiness of their love marriage."

marriages. It is to be expected that children's enthusiasm would be greater in love matches. Does this mean that in arranged marriages the parents' enthusiasm actually outstrips the children's? If so, the forcefulness of parental marriage promotion becomes even more striking.

Table 2–13—Attitudes of Parents and Children Toward the Match by Type of Introduction

INTRODUCTION

	None	Friendly	Informal	Formal	TOTAL
Man's engagement					
Parent's attitudes	3.12	3.32	4.16	3.95	3.48
Own attitude	4.20	4.09	4.00	3.92	4.09
Discrepancy	—1.08	—0.77	+0.16	+0.03	—0.61
Woman's engagement					
Parents' attitudes	3.05	2.95	3.53	3.58	3.22
Own attitude	3.92	3.87	3.50	3.42	3.74
Discrepancy	—0.87	—0.92	+0.03	+0.16	—0.52
N	212	70	35	127	444

The Total column in Table 2–13 shows that parents are generally less enthusiastic than children. However, when the two systems of mate-selection are compared, this relationship is reversed. In love matches, parents are far less positive than their children. However, in arranged marriages, parental enthusiasm is so great that it outweighs their children's decreased endorsement. Whereas love matches are heavily weighted on the children's side, arranged marriages involve so great an intervention by parents that the balance tips slightly in the parents' direction. However, this does not mean so much the replacement of the children by their parents as cooperation of both generations in promoting *miai* marriages.

Love

Comparing the attitudes of men with those of women in Table 2–13, it can be seen that the men are generally more enthusiastic but that the gap is wider in arranged marriages. To put it another way, the type of introduction matters more to women than to men.

Since the man's family takes the primary initiative in arranged marriages but love matches involve a mutually growing relationship, we can see why this sex difference is accentuated in the case of *miai* brides. Picked out by the man's family and pushed into marriage by her own parents, the girl often feels ambivalent when the die is cast and she is engaged to be married.

Table 2–14—Love for Fiancé(e) at Engagement

INTENSITY	Man's Love	Woman's Love
(5)* Very intense, powerful	29%	17%
(4) Strong, firm	42	39
(3) Considerable	17	27
(2) A little	11	13
(1) Hardly any	1	3
(0) None	†	†
N.A.	1	1
Total	101%	100%
Mean	3.86	3.52

* Numbers in parentheses show the basis for computing means in this and later tables. N is 444.
† Less than 0.5%.

My friend Masako Numata (who had been a charter member of the Friends International Coop House at the University of Michigan) described masculine reactions as she had observed them back home in Japan:

> The man's side often demands an immediate answer from the girl's side after the *miai* and the man makes up his mind immediately too. The [typical] Japanese man doesn't want to waste his money and time on a girl who might not marry him—he's too egotistical and impatient that way. When a man sees a girl with a pretty face and a good family, he wants to marry her right away—that's all he needs to know about her. Not very choosy!

Another way of approaching the same issue is to ask couples how much they loved each other when they first got engaged.[5] Table 2–14 shows that the men were much more in love at that time than the women. However, when this general picture is broken down by type of introduction, women entering nonarranged marriages are just as much in love as the average Japanese man (but their fiancés are even more enthusiastic).

Table 2–15—Love for Fiancé(e) by Type of Introduction

	INTRODUCTION			
Love for fiancé(e)	None	Friendly	Informal	Formal
Man's	4.12	3.94	3.60	3.46
Woman's	3.89	3.84	3.06	2.84
Discrepancy	+0.23	+0.10	+0.54	+0.62
Comparative love				
Both	65%	57%	27%	22%
Neither	13	16	32	37
Man only	14	17	35	35
Woman only	7	10	6	6
Total	99%	100%	100%	100%
N	212	70	35	127

5. Ideally a longitudinal research design would ask this question at the time of engagement, rather than retrospectively several years later. We cannot rule out the possibility that distortions appear in retrospective accounts of premarital love.

With love for the fiancé as with attitudes toward the engagement, type of introduction is more highly correlated with the woman's feelings than with the man's. *Miai* men muster up considerable affection for their fiancées, but the latter are conspicuously cool. From this standpoint the old Japanese saying that arranged marriages "start out cold" applies especially to women.

The bottom half of Table 2–15 classifies couples according to the separate reports of both partners. This highlights the mutual love of love-match couples in contrast with the coolness of *miai* couples. However, cool couples are almost matched in number by one-sided couples in which only the man is in love. Nor is stronger male love found only in *miai* marriages. In informally arranged matches it is the modal category, and even in nonarranged matches unreciprocated masculine love is (by a small margin) the next-to-modal category. Generally speaking the two main patterns are reciprocated love by the time of engagement for love-match couples but coolness for at least the woman in arranged matches. What happens to these feelings after marriage we shall see in the next chapter.

Dating and Courtship

Courtship may be divided into two phases. The first begins with the introduction (or first encounter for love matches) and ends with the decision to marry, sealed by the betrothal. The remainder consists of the engagement period and involves preparation for the marriage, culminating in the wedding ceremony.

In a country like Japan where engagements are seldom broken, mate-selection effectively ends at engagement. Hence we can ignore the interval between engagement and marriage as "beyond the point of no return."

The time before engagement is crucial, because the couple is deciding whether to discontinue the relationship. To be sure, vetoing is easiest right after the *miai* or after the first date. First impressions are extraordinarily important. Moreover, the watching public usually assumes that once a couple gets beyond the introductory meeting, they intend to get married. From the traditional viewpoint, it is immoral to "love 'em and leave 'em." The American system of casual dating without serious intentions strikes conservative Japanese as a shocking form of exploitation. If a man takes up a girl's time (and thereby deprives her for the time being of alternative suitors), he should be willing to marry her, *provided* their relationship develops smoothly.

There is always that proviso, however. No matter how strong the social and inner pressures to continue a relationship, there is always a potential escape prior to the official public commitment in the betrothal. We have already seen that multiple *miai* and multiple dating sequences are the standard pattern in our sample; hence we know that many tentative matches are discontinued before engagement.

If tentativeness characterizes abortive relationships, we would expect a tentative phase in fruitful relationships also. Young people whose first encounters seem auspicious should require additional encounters before feeling ready to commit themselves irrevocably to marriage.

For love-match couples a period of courtship is intrinsically necessary. The idea of marrying emerges only gradually from pleasurable association. For *miai* couples the situation is different. From the very beginning the partner is defined as a potential spouse. Formerly, selection by the parents was conclusive. To introduce the couple, much less to allow them to associate, was unnecessary or even dangerous (raising possible doubts in the young people's minds). Today, however, young people rarely entrust such power to parents. Even when parents are the primary promoters, the child must concur in their judgment. And the *miai* by itself is rarely a sufficient basis for judgment. It is too brief, too stiffly formal, too dominated by elders to test a couple's willingness to marry each other. Hence, it is standard practice now for the *miai* to be followed by a period of dating.

Table 2–16—Pre-engagement Dating by Type of Introduction

	INTRODUCTION			
	None	Friendly	Informal	Formal
Mean number of dates*	41.2	30.6	20.0	9.7
Mean number of months	18.9	18.9	10.5	5.3
Mean monthly rate	2.2	1.6	1.9	1.8
N	212	70	35	127

* "How many times before your engagement did the two of you go out alone together?"

We expect dating and courtship to be less extensive in arranged marriages than in love matches. Parents and matchmakers play influental roles in arranged marriages, making it easier for young people to make up their minds. They launch the couple with an impetus and seriousness of purpose which love-match couples seldom acquire until they have had time to fall in love. Despite the "first sight" theme in love-match ideology, love usually takes time to generate. Therefore unsponsored courtships are more prolonged.

Table 2–16 shows that love-match courtships are indeed longer—more than three times as long as *miai*-launched courtships, to be exact. Nor is the brevity of the latter counterbalanced by greater intensity of personal contact. Rather, relatively few dates suffice when parents, matchmaker, and the definition of the situation conspire to orient the couple toward engagement as a predetermined goal.[6]

Perhaps, however, rather than stressing the contrast between types of introduction, we should emphasize the similarities. For example, the five-month

6. The greater length of love-match courtship and the emphasis on personal qualities in mate-selection do not necessarily guarantee marital success, but do tend to weed out cases in which personality differences develop after marriage. Among the Tamura marriage counseling cases, personality conflicts were much less common in love marriages than in *miai* marriages (Cox, 1966).

time lapse between *miai* and engagement contrasts sharply with rural Niiike, where "within five days from the *miai* when the two families first meet, the go-betweens look for a decision" (Beardsley, Hall, and Ward, 1959). Similarly, pre-engagement dating dots those five months in Tokyo almost as regularly as for couples in love. Averages, in the *miai* cases, are pulled up by cases of unusually intensive dating, but even the medians for this group show half a dozen dates spread over four months. At the other extreme, only 11 of the 127 *miai* couples by-passed dating entirely. Dating has thus become a standard part of marriage "arrangement." The old practice of maintaining distance has almost entirely disappeared.

EXTERNAL SOCIABILITY

One might imagine that *miai* couples replace solitary dating with familistic occasions. This is only partially true. As Table 2–17 shows, *miai* courtships are just too short to allow much sociability with anyone, inside or outside the relationship.

Table 2–17—Pre-engagement Contacts with Families and Friends by Type of Introduction

| | INTRODUCTION | | | |
	None	Friendly	Informal	Formal
Mean number of contacts				
With man's family	13.1	11.2	10.8	4.1
With woman's family	15.7	13.0	11.3	4.9
With man's friends	26.2	15.3	10.1	1.4
With woman's friends	14.3	7.2	3.6	0.9
Mean monthly rate				
With man's family	0.7	0.6	1.0	0.8
With woman's family	0.8	0.7	1.1	0.9
With man's friends	1.4	0.8	1.0	0.3
With woman's friends	0.8	0.4	0.3	0.2
N	212	70	35	127

In contrast to the original system, in which the bride's appraisal by the groom's family was crucial, contacts with the wife's family predominate. This resembles the Western pattern in which the boy meets the girl's parents at her home when picking her up to go out on a date. However, we should not assume that dating customs are necessarily the same. According to one informant, "Parents wouldn't know what to say to a child's dates, creating an embarrassing situation. As a result, the boy doesn't pick the girl up at her house but meets her at the station, theater, etc. She goes home alone after the date, too."

The amount of contact with peers differs more sharply than the amount of contact with parents. *Miai* couples have almost no contact at all with each other's friends, but self-introduced couples often have common friends, especially when they are employed in the same place or meet in some other structured setting. *Miai* couples, by definition, have no friends in common; otherwise they would know each other and would not need an introduction. Moreover, they have relatively little time and therefore concentrate on getting acquainted with each other. So strong is this concentration that three quarters of the men and two thirds of the women never meet any of the partner's friends before getting engaged.[7]

When dating is extensive, it broadens out into double-dating and parties which acquaint friends with each other. Male initiative in dating patterns gives this contact a strong masculine bias. For the total sample, contacts with the man's friends are twice as frequent as with the woman's.

Comparing contact with families and with friends in Table 2–17, we see the direction of sociable contact in arranged and nonarranged marriages reversed. In arranged marriages the vertical dimension predominates. Contact with families (presumably concentrated on parents and other older relatives) is more frequent than that with friends. In love matches, on the other hand, the horizontal dimension eclipses the vertical (even though *both* dimensions are stronger in the absolute sense).

When attention shifts from the absolute number of contacts to the rate of contact, this contrast between the two systems is intensified. Love-match couples excel in contact with both partners' friends, but formally introduced couples edge them out in their rate of contact with their families. The difference is not great, but throws into relief the contrasting patterns of the two systems of mate-selection.

This contrast is consistent with the two forms of introduction. Those who meet on their own select their marriage partners from among their peer contacts. The *miai* system, on the other hand, relies on the older generation to bring the partners together. After the first encounter, these contrasting starting points continue to structure behavior during courtship.

INTERNAL DISCUSSION

We have suggested that *miai* couples eschew external sociability with peers in order to get acquainted with each other. Does this involve an interrogation so intensive as to outrank the more casual and spontaneous interaction of love-match couples? Or do the latter's more frequent dates allow them to get better acquainted despite less concentration on each other?

Table 2–18 shows that the latter hypothesis is correct. On all seven topics, love-match couples talk more frequently than *miai* couples.

The items are arranged in the table in order of size of difference between the extreme types of introduction. Note that personal topics top the list, and more theoretical ones come last. Presumably it is safer for *miai* couples to talk about politics and marital theory than about inner feelings. It takes a degree of

7. One *miai* couple advised me that in arranged marriages the man and woman usually meet each other's friends for the first time at the wedding ceremony. Engagement parties involving peers are "very rare."

acquaintance and mutual trust which few *miai* couples achieve prior to engagement to be ready to "let one's hair down" before a prospective marriage partner.

Table 2–18—Frequency of Pre-engagement Discussion by Type of Introduction

INTRODUCTION

Discussion Topic	None	Friendly	Informal	Formal	Net Difference*
Her emotional problems	2.27	2.04	1.66	1.35	+0.92
His emotional problems	1.72	1.43	0.74	0.91	+0.81
Her happenings since last date	2.38	2.28	1.89	1.70	+0.68
His happenings since last date	2.15	2.16	1.37	1.66	+0.49
Partners' vocational plans	2.31	2.11	2.09	1.79	+0.52
National or international politics	1.34	1.28	1.17	0.82	+0.52
Traditional *vs.* modern husband-wife relationships	1.77	1.62	1.40	1.36	+0.41
N	212	70	35	127	

* Net difference between mean frequency for nonintroduced minus formally introduced. Means are computed according to the following weights: 3, often; 2, sometimes; 1, seldom; 0, never.

On the other hand, there may be a positive reason why *miai* couples discuss old and new styles of husband-wife relationships so much. Perhaps love-match couples can more nearly take for granted that their marriage will be modern. Perhaps, having begun in the old-fashioned way, *miai* couples need to devote a greater proportion of their more limited time to achieving an understanding of just how traditional they intend to be for the remainder of their life together.

From this perspective, the axis of Table 2–18 is not merely from personal to impersonal but from personal to structural. *Miai* couples apparently find marriage customs a salient problem by virtue of the nature of their introduction, whereas love-match couples can afford to spend their time meeting each other's personal needs for companionship and emotional therapy without worrying so much about their future marriage style. Indeed, their extra year of courtship enables them to *create* their marriage style rather than to *speculate* about it. Their relationships are farther advanced by the time they get engaged than many *miai* couples' are by the time they get married. Love-match couples are already engaged in "the art of loving" when *miai* couples are only deciding whether marriage might blossom into love.

In the few dates they have, however, *miai* couples manage to explore a remarkable range of topics. Vogel's (1963) discussion of dating applies especially well to formally introduced strangers:

> Because opportunities for dating are limited, each date takes on great significance. . . . On dates, most young people try earnestly to set forth their entire philosophy of life, their ambitions and goals, their interests in reading and music.

Love Match and Arranged Marriage

Throughout this chapter it has been apparent that the two systems of mate-selection are not entirely separate. In various ways they shade into one another, overlap, and interpenetrate. Japanese matchmaking has incorporated features of the Western system, while the latter has not entered Japan without "contamination" by traditional Japanese elements.

Nevertheless, there are still two systems, not one. They differ in numerous ways (even though the differences may diminish in the future). By way of summary, we may sketch the distinguishing features of each system as it operates in contemporary Tokyo among the couples we interviewed.

We will begin with the modern version of marriage arrangement and conclude with the Japanese version of free selection.

MARRIAGE "ARRANGEMENT"

The key defining element in an arranged marriage is ceremonial introduction of the young man and woman as potential marriage partners. The *miai* is presided over by a matchmaker and attended by mothers of both parties (this trio having been instrumental in bringing the prospects together). However, the young people have already previewed each other by way of the matchmaker's personal and family credentials and photographs of each other. They, the parents, and the matchmaker have preselected each other as promising prospects, rejecting less favorable candidates. Both partners have typically met and rejected two previous prospects and both have dated several members of the opposite sex. Hence marriage arrangement is not conducted blind, not exclusively a parental prerogative, and not a foregone conclusion.

If first-hand impressions in the *miai* are favorable, follow-up opportunities take the form of limited dating, limited contact with families, and rare contact with each other's friends. In less than six months from the introduction the couple seal their relationship with the traditional engagement ceremony and exchange betrothal gifts. By this time they have discussed traditional and modern marriage patterns relatively often (that is, seldom rather than never) and explored such practical matters as each other's vocational plans. They have seldom shared their emotional problems, nor have they had time enough to develop much feeling for each other. Usually both partners feel rather cool this early in their relationship. However, if either partner is warm, it is the man, perhaps because he and his family have taken the initiative in developing the relationship, perhaps because Japanese women today have a good deal of ambivalence about entering old-fashioned marriages. Arranged marriages today are largely a last resort for young people who fail to contract a successful love match. Only the more old-fashioned segments of the younger generation (less educated, less emancipated girls) are apt to rely on this system.

SELF-SELECTION

Love matches differ at least in degree on every point. By definition, the man and woman fall in love before getting engaged. Love is made possible by courtship three times as long and four times as extensive (in terms of number of dates). Contacts with each other's friends are particularly numerous but even the partners' families are better known than in *miai* couples' limited pre-engagement experience.

Though parents are better known, they less actively promote the marriage. Indeed their feelings are often mixed when their children take responsibility into their own hands for an unsponsored marriage. Fathers are especially skeptical of the young men their daughters intend to marry. The girls themselves, however, are conspicuously more enthusiastic than their passive *miai*-marriage counterparts.

Love-match couples have previously dated hardly any more individuals than those who marry the old-fashioned way. The difference is that one of their dating relationships blossoms over a longer period of time into marriageable love. The social structure which makes that evolution possible is most often the company where both partners work. Hence women who enter such marriages are often those qualified for employment by college degrees and a masculine sex-role preference. Partly because of these situational factors, love matches are more equalitarian than arranged marriages (by age and education). Nevertheless, compared to American couples, even the love matches in Japan happen later in life and involve greater discrepancies between husband and wife. On the whole, however, Japanese self-selection is closer to the Western system than to the traditional Japanese system. Perhaps the same can be said for the contemporary "arranged" marriage system in actual operation. Both represent major departures from Japanese tradition.

How do these two systems work out after marriage? That is the subject of the next chapter.

LOVE MATCH

AND ARRANGED MARRIAGE—

AFTER MARRIAGE

"Love matches start out hot and grow cold. Arranged marriages start out cold and grow hot."

We have seen that love matches indeed start out hotter, particularly for the wife. We have seen differences in the roles couples play in the two systems and in the intensity of courtship prior to engagement. We come now to the acid test. Do love matches really freeze up after marriage? American experience suggests they easily could. (For a summary of the evidence for progressive disenchantment and disengagement in American marriages, see Blood, 1962: 200–207.)

A second hypothesis might be that a few years of marriage give *miai* couples a chance to catch up in their courtship. Married prematurely, before their relationship has fully developed, they may progressively close the gap between themselves and love couples. As more years of marriage are added, the missing year at the beginning of courtship may dwindle in significance. Eventually perhaps the influence of introduction systems on marriage is superseded by more immediate environmental factors.

A third possibility is that the traditional saying is wrong. The initial coolness of arranged marriages may be more than a temporary effect of truncated courtship. It may reflect different styles of interaction in the two systems. If arranged marriages, even in modernized form, emphasize the wrong criteria, couples may be poorly matched at least regarding the determinants of love.

Having speculated that our epigram may be quite right, half right, or dead wrong, it is time to examine the facts. How do our contrastingly introduced couples differ after marriage in their feelings and behavior toward one another?

We must remember that our sample extends only a few years beyond the wedding day. We cannot say what happens later on. However, given the presumed gradual eclipse of premarital events (specified in the second hypothesis), it is well to focus on the immediately post-nuptial years.

Moving progressively from the concrete to the intangible, we will examine first the structure of marriage, second the interpersonal dynamics, and finally the participants' subjective evaluations.

The Structure of Marriage

When we examined the value systems of those who marry with and without a formal introduction, we saw that *miai* couples were more traditional in their values as well as in their method of introduction. If this pattern continues after marriage, we should expect *miai* couples to have a more traditional power structure, division of labor, and deference pattern.

POWER STRUCTURE

To measure the power structure of Japanese marriages, we asked "Who

Table 3–1—Power Structure in Love Matches and Arranged Marriages

	MATE-SELECTION SYSTEM*		
	Love Match	Arranged Marriage	Love Margin
Husband's aggregate power	5.19	5.33	−0.14
Number of shared decisions	3.85	3.68	+0.17
Number of unilateral decisions	1.91	1.96	−0.05
Husband's specific power			
Sexual intercourse	2.81	3.09	−0.28
Holiday outing	2.14	2.29	−0.15
Gifts	2.07	2.11	−0.04
Wife's clothes	1.49	1.51	−0.02
Children's spending money			
Actual (N 47)	1.08	1.09	−0.01
[Predicted† (N 286)	1.34	1.34	0.00]
Radio, TV programs	2.26	2.23	+0.03
Life insurance	2.74	2.70	+0.04
Children's school			
Actual (N 53)	2.16	2.00	+0.16
[Predicted (N 282)	2.21	2.26	−0.05]
Children's special lessons			
Actual (N 51)	1.64	1.35	+0.29
[Predicted (N 281)	1.75	1.76	−0.01]
N	212	127	

* A love match is operationally defined as one in which the couple were not introduced to each other. An arranged marriage is initiated by a formal introduction (*miai*).

† Childless couples or parents who had not yet made such a decision were asked to predict how they would decide.

usually makes the final decision?" in nine topical areas. Summing the total battery yields male power scores ranging from 10 to 0 (reduced from 36–0). Individual items were scored 4 if the husband decides unilaterally, 2 for equality, and 0 for wife-always responses (see Appendix for details).

Table 3–1 shows that *miai* husbands are slightly more powerful than love-match husbands, sharing fewer power decisions with their wives and making a few more unilaterally. We infer, however, from the small size of the latter difference that the chief difference lies not in "husband-always" decisions made by the *miai* group but rather in "husband usually" decisions. This reflects the fact that in Japan (as in the United States) shared decision-making is the norm, and departures rarely extend all the way to unilateralism.

In these three ways, therefore, *miai* marriages are more patriarchal than love marriages. The net result is that when marriages are classified by their general decision-making pattern, there are a few more husband-dominant power structures (24 as opposed to 20 per cent) and fewer wife-dominant structures (10 as opposed to 15 per cent) among *miai* couples than among love couples. However, the detailed breakdown of decisions at the bottom of Table 3–1 shows how tenuous this distinction is.

The greater power of *miai* husbands is wielded chiefly in two areas—sexual intercourse and holiday outings (40 per cent of the *miai* husbands but only 23 per cent of love-match husbands decided unilaterally when to have intercourse).

These are significant topics, as they involve distinctively personal power over the wife.[1] Nevertheless, *miai* husbands are clearly not more powerful in all areas of marriage. On many questions there is hardly any difference, and on two

---

1. Deciding when to have intercourse, according to Wagatsuma, not only exerts power over the wife but expresses the *miai* husband's "egocentricity" and his "lack of genuine relatedness" to his wife.

> In the traditional culture of Japan, the wife was not important as a sexual partner for the husband. Many textbooks which taught Confucian ethics to feudal Japanese women emphasized the importance of wives hiding their orgasm and suppressing their sexual interest. Feudal Japanese husbands, even as late as the 1930's and 40's, simply did not care whether their wives had sexual orgasm. Reciprocity and mutuality in sexual intercourse were relegated to the world of the gay quarter (even though the prostitutes' pretense of having orgasm was completely professional and the existence of mutuality in sexual intercourse in a gay quarter was very often an illusion). But there tended to be a rather nice division of labor among Japanese women—the wife being housewife and desexualized servant on the one hand, and the women in the gay quarter (that is, *geisha* and bar girls, etc.) playing the role of sexual partner for the Japanese husband. I would imagine that many of the *miai* husbands who were tradition-oriented might not consider it very important that their wives enjoy and participate in sexual intercourse. They simply discharge their sexual tension and for that simple, almost biological purpose make use of their wives. For such husbands, intercourse is physical and mechanical rather than psychological. Egocentric husbands who lack real relatedness to their wives may decide by themselves when to have intercourse. *Miai* wives may also be more repressive of their sexuality than love-marriage wives and may simply accept (not without frustration) such egocentric behavior and the lack of reciprocity in their sexual life.

The personal authoritativeness of *miai* husbands may be converted into cruelty when the marriage goes awry. The Ministry of Justice reports cruelty as a more frequent source of trouble in *miai* marriages coming before the Family Court than in love marriages (1957).

children's items the love-match husbands are more powerful. Indeed, the only reason *miai* husbands appear more powerful in the aggregate is that so few couples have yet made the last two decisions. By and large, children in this sample are so young that these questions do not apply to them. Hence the sex and holiday questions are primarily responsible for the net difference in power between the two types of marriages.

If *miai* marriages are more traditional in two areas of husband-wife interaction, what shall we say about the area of the children's formal and informal schooling, in which love-match husbands are more powerful and *miai* couples do more sharing or leave it up to the wife? We shall see shortly that child-care activities are the responsibility of the wife in *miai* marriages. Perhaps the greater involvement of love-match fathers in decisions about the children's schooling represents not a traditional role but a new interest in a formerly feminine sphere. Without historical data, this is a tenuous assertion. But the overall pattern is suggestive: love-match wives move into the traditionally masculine sphere of sexual decision-making while their husbands reciprocate with greater interest in the children. This decreases the traditional sex-role differentiation, creating shared concern with various aspects of married living.[2]

In summary, however, the differences in power structure between arranged marriages and love matches are marginal at best, suggesting only residual traditionalism within *miai* marriages and limited modernization in love marriages.

THE DIVISION OF LABOR

Even in the United States, where the decision-making norm is thoroughly equalitarian, the main responsibility for housework remains with the wife (Blood and Wolfe, 1960). For a postfeudal country like Japan, the division of labor should be even more skewed in the wife's direction.[3] In searching for tasks in which the Japanese husband ever participates, we had to emphasize personal services to the husband himself.

In such services we might expect *miai* wives to excel. They have more submissive personalities and fewer ideological objections to the traditional servant role of Japanese wives. Love-match wives, on the other hand, are more emancipated from the bonds of servitude in both attitude and practice. More nearly their husband's equals in education, age, exposure to Western influence, and preference for the masculine role, they should not enjoy waiting on their husbands unilaterally. Moreover, they often work prior to marriage and more often continue working after marriage (38 as compared with 24 per cent of *miai* wives at the time of interview). Hence they are not only philosophically

2. Wagatsuma reports that "the feminization of husbands is one of the common topics of conversation among the Japanese. Husbands seem to be paying more attention than before to such feminine matters as child-rearing, even participating in diapering and bathing the babies."

3. "The wife who served the other members of the family well in the patriarchal family did not hesitate to torture herself by working very hard. She withstood pain, she remained patient, and she rarely went to bed even when she was suffering from sickness" (Koyama, 1961).

but structurally emancipated from their traditional role in the division of labor.

From studies in the United States we know that employment outside the home impedes the wife in performing her usual household tasks (Blood, 1963). Particularly reduced is any help she might otherwise give in tasks that husbands are capable of handling by themselves. For our Japanese respondents, therefore, we have many reasons to expect *miai* wives to do more housework than love-match wives.

Table 3-2—The Division of Labor in Love Matches and Arranged Marriages

	MATE SELECTION SYSTEM		
	Love Match	Arranged Marriage	Love Margin
Wife's aggregate task performance	4.27	4.75	—0.48
Number of shared tasks	1.60	1.44	+0.16
Number of unilateral tasks	3.38	3.67	—0.29
Wife's specific task performance			
Putting away the husband's clothes	2.27	2.68	—0.41
Putting away the *futon**	2.40	2.73	—0.33
Disciplining the children			
Actual (N 168)	2.74	3.00	—0.26
[Predicted (N 167)	2.60	2.47	+0.13]
Shopping for the husband's favorite foods	2.85	3.10	—0.25
Making repairs	1.45	1.65	—0.20
Helping the children with homework			
Actual (N 59)	2.77	2.86	—0.09
[Predicted (N 280)	2.42	2.32	+0.10]
Taking the children out Sundays			
Actual (N 179)	1.90	1.97	—0.07
[Predicted (N 156)	2.04	1.85	+0.19]
Buying husband's ordinary clothes	3.24	3.23	+0.01
Carrying heavy objects	0.76	0.64	+0.12
N	212	127	

* The quilt-like blankets Japanese families use for sleeping on the floor, which are put away on closet shelves every morning.

Table 3-2 shows that the division of labor in arranged marriages is more traditional. (Further analysis shows that this difference does not "wash out" even if controlled by the wife's employment status.)

Miai wives do more of the total housework. This involves both more tasks done entirely by themselves and fewer tasks shared with their husbands. This resembles the patterning of power structure, except that the differences here are larger and more consistent.

When tasks are considered individually, the largest difference is in the most personal area of service: laying away and hanging up the husband's clothes after he undresses on return home from work and on going to bed at night.[4] (Traditionally the Japanese housewife is last to bed and first to rise in order to

4. Many Japanese men abandon Western dress in favor of loose-fitting traditional garments for relaxation at home.

perform such domestic duties.[5]) No task in this list is less enthusiastically performed by American wives—who believe that grown-up men should care for their own clothes. Our love-match wives still carry more responsibility than their husbands in this area, but fall conspicuously short of providing complete maid service.

The only task at which *miai* husbands excel is carrying heavy objects such as suitcases or children when the couple are out together. The traditional Japanese wife was a beast of burden. If tradition alone operated here, we would expect more *miai* wives to carry these burdens. However, this question focuses on public situations where both partners are present, introducing a new factor— public etiquette. Chivalry is a novel concept, alien to Japanese culture, imported from the West. In both West and East, etiquette is more important during courtship than after marriage. The fact that our young *miai* husbands are still courting their wives may account for their eagerness to carry these burdens.

For tasks involving children, there is a sharp distinction between actual performance (*miai* wives do more of the work) and the hypothesized pattern for couples whose children have not yet been disciplined, tutored, or taken on holidays: inexperienced *miai* wives expect their husbands to help more than they actually do—so their predictions involve wishful thinking. Apparently *miai* husbands delegate both the control and the servicing of children to their wives, preferring not to be bothered. Their failure to help must rudely disappoint their otherwise courted wives.

DEFERENCE PATTERNS

In equalitarian marriage systems, deference is seldom noticed because it is bilateral. Husband and wife may defer to each other, Alphonse-Gaston fashion, but the net result is zero, leaving the marital relationship unskewed. Wherever the pattern of marriage is symmetrical and reciprocal, deference is inconspicuous.

Not in traditional Japan. In patriarchal family systems, the husband not only wields power and receives services but acquires symbols of authority as well. His superior status is ceremonially acknowledged by his subordinate wife (and children). Privileges are granted the head of the house which carry more emotional than practical significance.

In old Japan, the husband bathed first in the family tub, enjoying the day's arduously heated water when it was cleanest (though preliminary washing outside the tub left it cleaner for his successors than Western bathing habits). At meals he ate first or was served first and given the choice portions of food. He walked down the street three paces ahead of his wife. In general, his superior status within the family was expressed in a pattern of precedence.

There were other forms of deference, too. Women bowed lower to men

---

5. "The wife was expected to get up first and not after her husband so that she might make herself neat and presentable to him. The saying was that she must 'get up early so that he might not catch sight of her dishevelled appearance' " (Koyama, 1961). No one seems to have been concerned about *his* dishevelled appearance.

than vice versa. Women addressed men respectfully, whereas they talked down to women the way adults do to children. Families assembled in the front hall to greet the man on his return from work—but not the women or children.

In short, the interaction of the sexes proclaimed the man as lord and master, the woman subject and servant.

Modernization has undermined these patterns, especially in cities. Today it is rare to see women even one pace behind.[6] Indeed, precedence has often been reversed. Most Tokyo wives enter the door first, followed by the husband. The caste privileges of Japanese men have not only disappeared, they have been replaced by the Western code of "ladies first."

Theoretically modernization should proceed farthest in love matches. However, our formally introduced couples may adhere more closely to the new norm of chivalry in precedence and deference, as we have already seen in regard to carrying burdens.

Terms of address—The traditional term of address for husbands is *anata* (a polite way of saying "you"). Forty-five per cent of our *miai* wives employ this formality, but only 36 per cent of our love-match wives. By contrast, 13 per cent of the latter use pet names for their husbands; only 4 per cent of the *miai* wives are so daring. Thus, *miai* wives are more respectful and polite, love-match women more affectionate and informal.

When Japanese husbands address their wives, they normally use first names, just as Western husbands do (or else call them "Mother" after the children arrive). The two types of marriage do not differ significantly in practicing these customs.[7] There is some difference, however, with less common terms. Paralleling their wives, love-match husbands more often use pet names (11 as opposed to 4 per cent) or call their wives very informally "darling" (*omae*).

6. One exception: wives of Buddhist priests are still bound by traditional customs:

> Chief priests of 20 Tokyo temples have launched a campaign to fight the still-strong prejudice which prevents priests from walking in public with their wives. "We are going to begin walking the streets with our spouses just like any other citizen and even hand-in-hand just to emphasize our contempt for this tradition," said Ryuzen Hosoda, chief priest of Seishin Temple in Koto Ward. He said that the people still regard Buddhist priests as a symbol of feudalism and that to combat this, "we have decided to relinquish tradition by holding an all-out party with our wives" (*Asahi Evening News*, December 10, 1958).

7. Although 56 per cent of our respondents are parents, less than half of them are so addressed (19 per cent as "Mother," 25 per cent as "Father"). Presumably, as their children become older and more verbal, more parents will address each other as such. Wagatsuma believes that

> this prevalent way of address still reflects the Japanese marriage being oriented heavily toward parenthood, after they become parents. This is very common among middle-class and lower-class families. This is practiced even among the very young generation of married couples. In many cases the Japanese husband and wife become for themselves more important as parents of the children rather than as a marital spouse. Addressing the spouse as mother and father may also reflect an unconscious identification of the spouse with the parent of the opposite sex. That is to say, a husband addressing his wife as "Mother" may get vicarious satisfaction of his dependent need.

Perhaps, however, our respondents should be described as surprisingly seldom using "Father" and "Mother" at the stage in life when they were interviewed.

Conversely, some *miai* husbands are extraordinarily formal, addressing their wives, with the respect ordinarily reserved for men, as *anata* (2 per cent, as opposed to one out of 212) or using the "Mrs." title and first name, as *Yasuko-san* (10 as opposed to 7 per cent). Such practices can only be described as super-formal.

Curiously, more *miai* husbands (as opposed to 4 per cent) call their wives *oi*—the equivalent of "hey!" Hardly a term of respect, it contrasts with the love-match preference for terms of endearment.

In general, love-match partners of both sexes favor affectionate terms, whereas *miai* couples use more formal terms of address. A few exceptional *miai* husbands, however, go to the opposite extreme and use terms of disrespect reminiscent of the haughty male tradition:

> Japanese men hate to be thought henpecked and so they pretend not to be nice in public. When my husband refers to me in public, he speaks of me as "my foolish wife" (*gusai*). Our younger friends thought that was funny and teased him about it. He just naturally used the term—at first I was surprised but I got used to it. It expressed his way of liking to be master (a middle-aged informant).

When the terms used by husband-wife pairs are combined as comparative terms of address, love-match couples are more equalitarian (39 as opposed to 30 per cent). *Miai* couples use terms more respectful of the wife than of the husband relatively often (14 as opposed to 9 per cent) but also present the opposite pattern of greater deference for the husband (55 as opposed to 51 per cent). This reflects the fact that both *miai* husbands and their wives tend to use courtly terminology, producing a formal reciprocity instead of the informal reciprocity of love-match couples.

Our interviewers noticed how respectfully *miai* wives talked about their absent husbands. As one interviewer put it, "They seem to be afraid to say anything bad about their husbands," whereas love-match wives talk matter-of-factly about their husbands' bad points as well as good points. Apparently the stiffness and propriety of the *miai* do not wear off with the wedding ceremony.

Deference to the husband's friends—In an unpublished manuscript on "Changing Patterns of Friendship in Contemporary Japan," Hiroshi Wagatsuma describes how deference to the husband is extended to his friends as well:

> In the old pattern, a man's friends are his and not his wife's. When they visit in each other's homes, wives serve the meal but do not join them. A wife who joined in the conversation of her husband and his friends would tend to be regarded as immodest. In the new pattern, a wife may eat with her husband and his friends and may join, or at least listen to, their conversation.

In our sample the old pattern has gone out of style. However, the change has progressed farther with the love-match wives, 83 per cent of whom usually or always join in the conversation with the husband's visiting friends, compared to only 67 per cent of the *miai* wives. In short, love-match wives are less modest and less submissive. Just as love-match couples abandon formality in addressing each other, so they address each other's friends more freely:

> There are two types of good wives in Japan: (1) quiet, well-disciplined doll vs. (2) sharing, marching-along-together partner. Men who prefer the second type often get the first, resulting in unhappiness. E.g., when I entered into conversation with my husband's colleagues, the visitor expressed surprise and said he wished his wife would stay around instead of leaving the room after serving tea. The usual wife would say she was too stupid to learn, he shouldn't have married her. "I'm no good, you are clever. I'm sorry" (young career woman who had studied in the United States).

Precedence—Who goes first, ladies or men? For the sample as a whole, the answer is clearly the ladies. Almost half the wives routinely get in taxis before their husbands, and two-thirds always sit down on trains and buses while the husband stands. In the latter situation, *miai* husbands are more consistently chivalrous (73 as opposed to 61 per cent). Love-match husbands are not traditionally patriarchal but take turns with their wives or at least occasionally sit down (perhaps when they are more tired than their wives). In short, the love-match pattern is more flexible, whereas the *miai* pattern conforms more closely to code.

Detailed analysis shows, however, that *miai* chivalry evaporates as the years go by (declining from 84 to 60 per cent "always" from the first two years to the second decade of marriage). Chivalry is therefore part of the "delayed courtship" of arranged marriages. Love-match pragmatism, by contrast, results in growing chivalry during the same period of time—not because values change, but because children arrive and make bus seats for wives more useful. By the ninth year of marriage these contrasting trends reverse the precedence patterns of our two types of marriages, *miai* husbands reverting to greater patriarchalism and love-match husbands responding more thoughtfully to the changed circumstances of child-burdened wives.

For taxis the pattern is more complicated. Love-match couples emphasize the middle categories ("wife usually" gets in first and "50/50"—43 as opposed to 31 per cent). On the other hand, *miai* couples split into extremes, either chivalrous (51 as opposed to 43 per cent) or old-fashioned (18 as opposed to 13 per cent).[8] At either extreme they are less flexible and more sex-oriented in their behavior, but the winning sex may be either the old king or the new queen. This is not to say that they are equally apt to go in either direction. Not only does the queen usually win in both mate-selection groups, but *miai* husbands more often turn in the new direction than in the old. Hence the old-fashioned subgroup within the *miai* category is doubly deviant.

Appreciation—Traditionally Japanese wives expressed appreciation for small favors but husbands were not expected to. After all, wives were supposed

---

8. Nadler and Morrow (1959) find that (a) chivalrous and (b) openly subordinating attitudes toward women are not antithetical but positively correlated with each other and with other authoritarian attitudes in a sample of American college males. Perhaps, then, both groups of *miai* husbands have something in common.

to be servants and servants do not expect to be thanked for doing their duty.

Here again, however, things are changing in Japan: husbands are beginning to emulate their wives in expressing appreciation for the partner's labors.

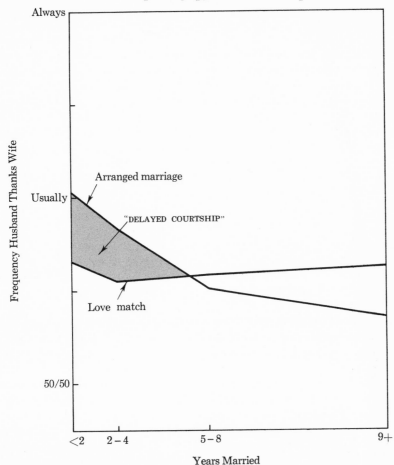

Figure 3–A. Husband's Expressed Appreciation for Small Favors in Love Match and Arranged Marriage by Length of Marriage

Between *miai* wives and love-match wives there is hardly any difference—both are modally appreciative (46 and 44 per cent respectively). However, the total group of *miai* husbands again outstrips love-match husbands in their politeness (36 as opposed to 25 per cent "always" thanking their wives for small favors). However, "This, too, shall pass." By the second decade of marriage, fewer *miai* husbands are still chivalrous. Moreover, their modal category shifts from "usually" thanking her to expressing appreciation less than half the time. The latter category rises progressively from a mere 13 per cent at the beginning of marriage to nearly half (45 per cent) in the later years. As with bus seats, this reverses the two types of marriages, leaving love matches more appreciative than arranged marriages once the delayed courtship is completed. The point here is not that love matches become more appreciative than they were at the beginning of marriage, but that their thoughtfulness resists the corrosion of time, whereas the brittle chivalry of *miai* husbands crumbles rapidly.

Reviewing these precedence patterns as a whole, *miai* husbands seem much like an American boy on a first date with a new girl (Blood, 1962). Both hope to impress new partners whose loyalty is not entirely certain. Both hesitate to alienate their girls by unconventional behavior. No wonder, then, that the deference patterns observable in new *miai* marriages give way later just as American marriages sink into taken-for-grantedness once the social relationship is secure.

Structurally speaking, then, love marriages tend to be consistently more equalitarian—in shared decision-making, shared housekeeping, and mutual informality. *Miai* marriages, on the other hand, are less symmetrical. In power structure and division of labor, they are patriarchal, especially in activities traditionally associated with sex role such as sexual initiative and household chores.

However, it takes two to make a power structure and a division of labor, and my hunch is that these represent less masculine arrogance than feminine desire to please the new master, especially when we see how assiduously the "master" courts her favor in return. *Miai* wives, in other words, try to be good wives in the traditional sense of the term, and *miai* husbands try equally hard to be good husbands in the new sense of that term. The net result is an old-fashioned division of labor (and, to a lesser extent, power structure) combined with a strikingly modern deference pattern—at first.

The Dynamics of Marriage

During the feudal era in any country the emphasis in marriage is on duties and responsibilities of the sort involved in the structure of marriage. Relations between husband and wife are de-emphasized, especially in three-generation households representing the feudal ideal.

With the disintegration of the extended-family system and the loss of associated customs such as concubinage and courtesanship, men turn to their wives for the stimulation and solace they once found elsewhere.

New dynamic aspects of marriage include companionship, emotional therapy, love and affection, and, perhaps, sex (though that was traditionally a wifely duty of sorts).

We already know that (with the possible exception of sex) these are distinguishing characteristics of love matches before marriage. Do "lovers" continue to excel in interpersonal areas after marriage or do *miai* couples catch up with them in the interval we have under scrutiny? Given the substantial head start of love-match couples, it seems unlikely that *miai* couples would reverse their premarital handicap so soon after marriage.

COMPANIONSHIP

Husband-wife companionship is not considered important in Japan—though part of the problem is semantic (Blood and Takeshita, 1963). The Japanese language has no word for marital companionship—which may be one reason why our couples list it last among the potential values of marriage.

Nevertheless, its traditional absence in Japan and its pre-eminent importance in the United States (Blood and Wolfe, 1960) make companionship an index of the modernization of the family.

Companionship is the ground from which love matches spring. Partners typically meet as fellow workers or colleagues in some other enterprise. They get acquainted, become friends, and begin dating. If they prove to be good companions, they fall in love and decide to marry.

Miai courtships provide less opportunity for companionship. There is too little time, too little contact. After a meager beginning, friendship grows during engagement. But, even so, companionship is only half-developed by the wedding day.

What about after marriage? The asymmetrical structure of *miai* marriages suggests that they are not likely to catch up with equalitarian love matches. It's hard to feel chummy with a man to whom one feels subservient or with a woman whom one keeps on a chivalrous pedestal.

Table 3–3—Companionship in Love Matches and Arranged Marriages

	MATE-SELECTION SYSTEM		
ANNUAL FREQUENCY BY TYPE OF COMPANIONSHIP	Love Match	Arranged Marriage	Love Margin
Get together with friends	8.8	6.6	+33%
Get together with relatives	14.5	12.9	+12%
Go out for a good time (date)	22.6	21.5	+ 5%
Wife tells husband what happened during the day	236	225	+ 5%
Discuss the news	174	169	+ 3%
Husband tells wife what happened during the day	179	177	+ 1%
N	212	127	

From this viewpoint, it is understandable that love matches excel, however slightly, in every one of the six forms of companionship presented in Table 3–3.

These may be divided into activities outside and inside the home. External companionship is the rarer of the two, requiring more effort, more time, the only expenditure of money, and (in the case of friends and relatives) a co-operative commitment from other parties. The more costly the activity, the greater the ratio by which love matches excel.

The differences between the two groups of marriages are less for internal companionship. Noteworthy, however, is the asymmetry of the two directions of informative companionship. *Miai* husbands almost catch up with love-match husbands in reporting the day's events, reflecting their efforts to be good husbands. However, the difference for wives is greater, with *miai* wives relatively shy as usual and love-match wives more verbal.

Controlled analysis by length of marriage shows that *miai* wives overcome their shyness as they get more used to their husbands, increasing their reporting from the first to the middle years of marriage. In some years, *miai* wives and husbands even outstrip love-match couples in informative and intellectual companionship. We can properly call this a "delayed honeymoon" (following their delayed courtship) only when there is an actual upsurge in interaction.

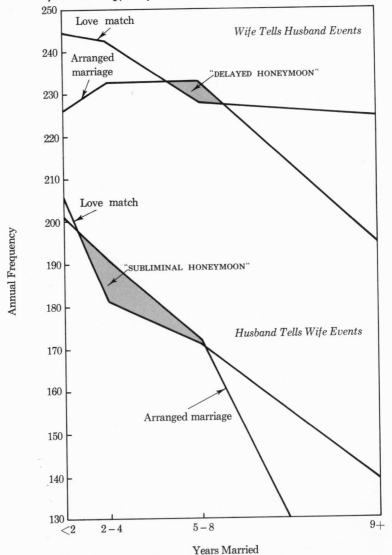

Figure 3–B. Informative Companionship in Love Match and Arranged Marriage by Length of Marriage

More often there is a "subliminal honeymoon" which retards the normal rate of attrition in companionable phenomena. However, by the second decade even this quasi-honeymoon ends and *miai* couples sink to conspicuously low levels of communication, far lower than the normally depressing effect of time produces in love matches (see Chapter 7).

The love margin in external sociability is so great that control by length of marriage never puts *miai* couples ahead of love couples, even though it reveals a delayed-honeymoon upsurge in kinship companionship. Dating, on the other hand, exhibits the delayed courtship pattern: husbands still courting their wives date them slightly more often in the first four years of marriage, then slack off sharply below the love-match level, the same way they express appreciation less after the courtship ends.

EMOTIONAL THERAPY

In their longer courtship, love-match couples rely on each other emotionally more than *miai* couples. They often tell each other their troubles, whereas *miai* couples are more reserved.

Table 3–4—Emotional Therapy in Love Matches and Arranged Marriages

	MATE-SELECTION SYSTEM		
Therapeutic Utilization of Partner	Love Match	Arranged Marriage	Love Margin
Husband tells his troubles	2.48	2.21	+0.27
Wife tells her troubles	3.12	2.88	+0.24
Partner's Therapeutic Response			
Husband's response			
Advice	40%	32%	+8
Helps wife get away	8	6	+2
Passive	7	7	0
Dismissal as unimportant	23	24	—1
Criticism	*	2	—2
Sympathy	3	6	—3
Helps wife solve the problem	19	23	—4
Total	100%	100%	
Wife's response			
Helps husband get away	20%	14%	+6
Passive	12	10	+2
Advice	10	10	0
Criticism	2	2	0
Helps husband solve the problem	14	15	—1
Dismissal as unimportant	13	15	—2
Sympathy	29	35	—6
Total	100%	101%	
Partner's Therapeutic Effectiveness			
Wife feels better†	2.41	2.37	+0.04
Husband feels better	1.84	1.81	+0.03
N	212	127	

* Less than 0.5%.
† Code: Much better, 3; a little better, 2; about the same, 1; worse or never tells, 0.

Table 3–4 shows that the greater mutual reliance of love-match couples continues after marriage, though the gap narrows. The two groups differ primarily in the larger proportion of love-match husbands who "always" tell their troubles (28 as opposed to 17 per cent) and of wives who do the same (47 as opposed to 37 per cent). In this sense, love-match couples turn to one another more indiscriminately when they are in trouble. Their relationship is more open. They hold less back.

Although *miai* couples are no more apt *never* to tell their troubles (a rare state among newly married couples), they are fairly reserved, telling "seldom" or about half the time (49 per cent of *miai* husbands as opposed to 38 per cent of love-match husbands; for wives, 30 and 19 per cent respectively). They more discreetly unload their burdens on the partner's shoulders. Presumably they turn to the partner only when their own ability to cope is inadequate and when the partner is most available. With less equality and sharing in the structure of *miai* marriages, the partner seems less accessible. Structural separation is compounded by the more circumspect attitude of *miai* partners to one another. The net result is that *miai* marriages are less interdependent, less useful in meeting personal needs, and therefore weaker dynamically (however they may be conceived structurally). Detailed analysis shows delayed honeymoons in thera-peutic utilization by both partners in arranged marriages. The increase by *miai* husbands fails to catch up with love-match husbands. However, *miai* wives overcome their initial reserve by the fifth to eighth year of marriage and out-strip their love-match counterparts, only to withdraw again into extraordinary reticence (a majority seldom or never telling their troubles). Since the modal frequency for all love-match wives and for middle-years *miai* wives is "always" telling, these longer-married *miai* wives prove again how extraordinarily cold an arranged marriage can become once the delayed courtship and honeymoon fade into the past.[9]

Therapeutic responses—The responses made by husbands and wives after hearing the other's troubles are similar in the rank order of differences between the two mate-selection systems. Love-match couples more often help each other forget their troubles by getting away from them. This technique is reminiscent of the way some couples in love escape from their families by eloping. Leaving one's troubles behind may mean a night out on the town in characteristic love-match dating fashion.

Miai couples provide sympathy and active help in solving each other's problems. These seem at first glance to involve sharing emotion and work. Ordinarily there is less emotional intimacy and less shared work in *miai* marriages. Note, however, that it is primarily wives who provide the sympathy (illustrating their submissive-maternal attitude), whereas husbands give the most help, discharging their patriarchal responsibility. Perhaps, similarly, the

9. *Miai* husbands and wives have twice as many illness-caused cases coming before the family court as do love-match couples (Ministry of Justice, 1957). This may be due to greater emphasis on physical health in the traditional mate-selection process and greater disappointment when illness develops. However, it may also be that the reticence of *miai* couples means they turn their troubles in upon themselves, producing psychogenic illnesses.

tendency of love-match husbands to confine themselves to advice (which I take to be less supportive than either sympathy or help) reflects greater confidence in the wife's ability to solve her own problems, once she has suggestions to go on. In other words, if love-match wives are more independent, they may be able to cope with their problems with a little advice (or perhaps even no response at all, as the "passive" category suggests). Or the couple can leave home in mutually enjoyed escape from it all. *Miai* marriages, on the other hand, being less symmetrical, react in more nurturant and protective ways, parent-child fashion.

These interpretations are hazardous at best and definitely *ex post facto*.

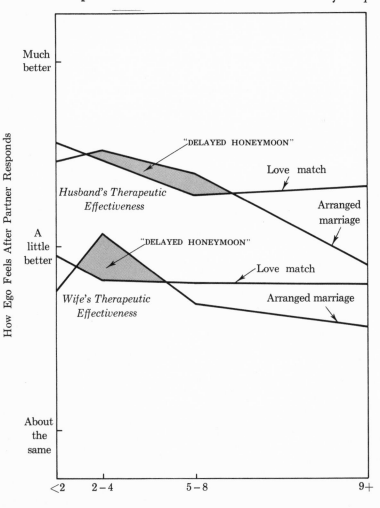

Figure 3–C. Partner's Therapeutic Effectiveness in Love Match and Arranged Marriage by Length of Marriage

Nevertheless, they may illuminate the marginal differences between the two kinds of marriage.

Therapeutic effectiveness—When our subjects were asked how much better they felt after they had told their troubles and the partner had responded, overall differences between the marriage types almost disappeared.

However, analysis by length of marriage shows that both men and women in *miai* marriages experience delayed-honeymoon reactions reminiscent of Figure 3–B. Love-match couples as usual report a slow decline in the partner's therapeutic effectiveness as the partner becomes more passive and unresponsive. However, for *miai* husbands married two to four years, the wife's effectiveness rises to surpass even the initial love-match starting point. In this dimension, arranged marriages start out colder (and end up much colder) than love matches, but glow more warmly in the temporary flare-up of the delayed honeymoon.

Although both systems work well when they are utilized, we should not forget that love-match couples invoke the partner's aid more often. Hence their aggregate gain is quantitatively greater.

AFFECTIONAL EXPRESSION

Expression of sentiment for the girl in Japan is traditionally quite indirect. For example, the man talks about the beautiful moon instead of telling the girl he loves her (elderly female informant).

In public, not only was affection prohibited, but "a number of husbands went so far as to imagine that they could gain personal credit by speaking ill of their wives to others, even though in their own private life they were tender to their wives" (Koyama, 1961).

The classic three-generation household structurally inhibited expression of affection between husband and wife:

The house is small and crowded. [It] offers almost no privacy for intimacies, nor is there much possibility of wandering unobserved on the hill or in the fields. The expected pattern of daily behavior, during the first year especially, tends to curb any show of affection, caresses (kissing is regarded as a paraphrase of the sex act), or sense of humor in the husband and virtually bans all sexual allurement on the part of the girl. The outstanding thrill, some say, comes from concealment (Beardsley, Hall, and Ward, 1959).

The traditional reserve between husbands and wives chaperoned within the home by their elders and outside by their neighbors has been relieved by the privacy afforded to young couples behind the concrete walls of their apartments. Hence our urban sample should behave quite differently from the rural situation described above.

But which half of our sample should be more affectionate? Since love matches are explicitly based on love, we might expect love-match husbands to tell their wives more often that they love them (or show it by gesture or facial expression). On the other hand, there is the familiar danger that premarital love may give way to taken-for-grantedness. Perhaps the continued courting behavior of *miai* husbands expressed in more chivalrous etiquette includes courting in the language of love.

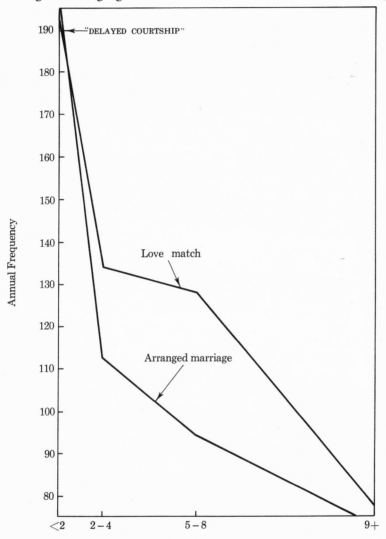

Years Married
Figure 3–D. Husband's Expression of Affection in Love Match and Arranged Marriage by Length of Marriage

Figure 3–D shows that by the time they were interviewed, *miai* husbands had initially caught up with love-match husbands and then slacked off sooner.

If we had looked only at the total frequencies (138 versus 127), we might have mistakenly assumed that *miai* husbands had not yet caught up with love-match men. However, the breakdown by length of marriage shows that *miai* courtliness demonstrates at least as much affection by the second year of marriage as love-match spontaneity. However, that courtship is not long sustained. Though both sets of husbands become less affectionate in subsequent years, the *miai* men quit faster. Perhaps the effort required is too strenuous to sustain long. Once the delayed courtship is over, *miai* marriages revert sooner to the traditional emphasis on practical matters: money, children, and keeping house. In any case, arranged marriages start off cool and grow hot, but that heat is a "flash in the pan" rather than a sustained glow.

The 9 per cent difference in total frequency is greater than for all save the most strenuous kinds of companionship. Hence, relatively speaking, this is a significant difference. Translated into medians, the typical love-match husband expresses affection "almost every day," whereas the typical *miai* husband does so only "once or twice a week." Percentage-wise, *miai* husbands are particularly over-represented in the category "two or three times a month" (14 as opposed to 7 per cent). The expression of love, therefore, characterizes love matches not only before marriage but in most years after marriage. Here is yet another area in which *miai*-marriages are more reserved, less communicative, less interactive.[10]

SEXUAL BEHAVIOR

Sex is an ambiguous aspect of marriage. In traditional marriages it is the wife's duty to submit to her husband's advances:

> [In Niiike] the sex act itself usually is a brief, businesslike affair with a minimum of foreplay. The husband, after waiting in the quilts at night for the rest of the household to settle into slumber, grasps his wife and satisfies himself as quietly and inconspicuously as possible, releasing his tensions and settling his duty to posterity at the same time (Beardsley, Hall, and Ward, 1959).

In a modern marriage the wife is more emancipated sexually. She is expected to achieve personal satisfaction "in bed." This makes the husband responsible for arousing her potential responsiveness. It may change the quality more than the frequency of intercourse.

We have already seen that sexual decisions are conspicuously more husband-dominated in *miai* marriages than in love matches. Since power is relative, we

---

10. One corollary of the continuing love-match emphasis on love and affection is greater touchiness if the spouse gets involved extramaritally. Among Kenji Tamura's marriage-counseling cases, over half the love-match wives complained that their husbands were "playing around," compared to less than one fourth of the *miai* wives. In the larger Ministry of Justice study (1957), the difference was smaller but in the same direction. Cox comments that love-match wives are "much less tolerant of husbands playing around, although *miai* husbands probably play around just as much." According to the concept of relative deprivation, love-match wives lose more, feel more explicitly rejected, when their husbands fall in love with another woman. To be hurt more deeply is one of the risks in marrying for love.

do not know how much this is due to the dominance of *miai* husbands or the submissiveness of *miai* wives. However, from the standpoint of social change, we suspect it was the emancipation of love-match wives that altered the sexual power structure more than "demasculinization" of love-match husbands. In any case, sexual initiative is more bilateral in love matches than in *miai* marriages.

Table 3–5—Sexual Behavior in Love Matches and Arranged Marriages

	MATE-SELECTION SYSTEM		
	Love Match	Arranged Marriage	Love Margin
Mean annual frequency of intercourse	55	56	—2%
Mean length of foreplay (in minutes)	9.6	9.6	0
N	212	127	

Neither measure of sexual behavior reported in Table 3–5 is very reliable. Wives were asked to choose from our standard list of frequencies and overwhelmingly chose "once or twice a week" when questioned about frequency of intercourse. Since the major variations are likely to be *within* this range (once a week *or* twice a week) our list did not offer fine enough distinctions.

Analysis by length of marriage shows that the slight overall difference between the two types of marriage results from intensified intercourse by *miai* couples married nine or more years. Perhaps this should be called a "second honeymoon" after so many years. Perhaps it results from the emancipation of those conscientious mothers from the burdens of child-rearing as their children grow older (see Chapter 7). In any case, it coincides with increased feminine sexual satisfaction. Prior to that point, the love-match couples are both more active and more satisfied sexually.

The husbands were asked to estimate the number of minutes involved in foreplay. Their problem was not awkward response categories but the difficulty of judging something so variable and untimed. (Probably this is the chief reason why 96 of our 444 husbands failed to answer this question. On the other hand the greater failure of *miai* than love-match husbands—26 as opposed to 21 per cent—suggests a greater sense of propriety.) Presumably if we asked the same husbands again, they would vary a good deal in their responses. Nevertheless, group averages may be more reliable than individual responses.

Table 3–5 shows that the two groups engage in identically long foreplay, on the average. When this is broken down by length of marriage, familiar differences appear. *Miai* husbands court their wives with longer foreplay during the first four years of marriage. After that, the length of foreplay subsides below that of love-match husbands.

That foreplay is a masculine burden is suggested by corresponding changes in the husband's sexual satisfaction. During the courting years, *miai* husbands are less satisfied than love-match husbands; but once their courtship ends, they remain sexually satisfied, whereas love-match satisfaction continues to ebb.

If foreplay is a masculine burden, it is also a feminine benefit, for the sexual satisfaction of *miai* wives sags when courtship ends, reviving only subliminally when the burden of motherhood lightens.

On the whole, the sexual area is one of the least differentiated facets of marriage we have found in our search for contrasts between love matches and arranged marriages. Measured in terms of overt behavior, the two groups can hardly be distinguished at all with our crude measuring instruments.

The Evaluation of Marriage

Having surveyed how marriages differ in actual behavior, we come to the crucial question of their success from the standpoint of the participants. We began this study with contradictory opinions, both of which cannot be right. Love matches cannot be both more and less successful than arranged marriages, as different segments of Japanese society believe.

Success could be measured in various ways, most of them intercorrelated. We chose to ask the participants' satisfaction with various facets of marriage. These evaluations were weighted by the individual's own sense of the relative importance of those facets so as to compute a general satisfaction index (see Appendix). We also asked the partners how much they love each other, testing more directly the "hot-cold" controversy. We expected these approaches to yield similar results as alternative ways of reporting the subjective reactions of participants in marriage.

MARITAL SATISFACTION

"Satisfaction" is a tricky concept. It tells how much people get of what they expect. Some people are "highly satisfied" with an objectively low level of achievement which fulfills modest expectations. In other cases the same satisfaction results from higher expectations superbly fulfilled. Despite this ambiguity, satisfaction is real enough for the people involved and correlates roughly with objective phenomena insofar as members of the same society share cultural norms about marriage.

The fascinating feature of Table 3–6 is that love matches lose out on all the structural facets of marriage and win on all the dynamic ones. The weakest links in the two marriage systems appear to be the financial recklessness of love-match wives and the lack of companionship in *miai* marriages. Could love-match wives be so emancipated that they spend money independently without getting their husband's approval?

Miai husbands find themselves thoroughly respected by their conformist wives. They have good reason to be satisfied with their wives' devoted housework and the marginally patriarchal power structure of their marriages. Since their wives carry more decision and task responsibility for the children, the husbands find them good mothers also.

Table 3–6—Husband's Marital Satisfaction in Love Matches and Arranged Marriages

MATE-SELECTION SYSTEM

Husband's satisfaction with	Love Match	Arranged Marriage	Love Margin
Wife's financial management	3.99	4.36	—0.37
Wife's courtesy and respect	4.32	4.62	—0.30
Wife's housework	4.04	4.31	—0.27
Wife's interest in decision-making	4.44	4.55	—0.11
Own share in decision-making	4.49	4.60	—0.11
Wife as mother	4.56	4.66	—0.10
Wife's love and affection	4.85	4.83	+0.02
Wife's understanding of his problems and feelings	4.26	4.23	+0.03
Companionship in doing things together	4.14	4.06	+0.08
Sex	4.45	4.31	+0.14
N	212	127	

In the dynamic areas of marriage, however, *miai* husbands are relatively dissatisfied. Differences in love and understanding are marginal, but the asymmetrical structure of *miai* marriages interferes particularly with companionship between the partners. It isn't possible to "have one's cake and eat it, too." One can't have a loyal servant and an equal partner in the same wife—these are intrinsically contradictory roles.

Finally, in the sexual area the freer, more spontaneous, less inhibited, and more aggressive love-match wives are qualitatively more satisfactory sex partners than more submissive *miai* wives. If sex is partly what is meant in the saying that arranged marriages grow "hot" after marriage, then the saying must be wrong.

When husband's responses are analyzed by length of marriage, satisfaction with the dynamic aspects of marriage generally declines for both groups. However, *miai* husbands' satisfaction declines more slowly, perhaps because they expect less in this area. Love-match husbands, on the other hand, become so disillusioned with the affectional, therapeutic, companionable, and sexual aspects of marriage that by the later years of marriage the love margin is replaced by a sizable *miai* margin. Only the extraordinary satisfaction of love-match husbands during the early years of marriage (before children arrive!) creates the love margins in the first place.

From the man's viewpoint, then, love matches have their own prolonged courtship. Not that love-match wives *need* to be courted—their affection has long since been won. But the "dyadic withdrawal" of love-match couples which began with premarital courtship continues after marriage until disrupted by the intrusion of children (Slater, 1961). Children may or may not be resented (see Chapter 7), but their arrival destroys the bliss of love marriages, and its passing is mourned by increasingly unhappy men. Arranged marriages, on the other hand, are more businesslike in orientation and can absorb the responsibilities of child-rearing with less alteration of basic features and less awareness of dynamic losses.[11]

Table 3–7—Wife's Marital Satisfaction in Love Matches and Arranged Marriages

	MATE-SELECTION SYSTEM		
Wife's satisfaction with	Love Match	Arranged Marriage	Love Margin
Husband's interest in decision-making	3.84	4.02	—0.18
Own share in decision-making	4.31	4.45	—0.14
Husband's ability as a breadwinner	3.92	3.96	—0.04
Husband's helpfulness with household tasks	3.69	3.72	—0.03
Husband's understanding of her problems and feelings	4.36	4.35	+0.01
Husband's love and affection	4.77	4.74	+0.03
Sex	4.09	4.00	+0.09
Companionship	3.86	3.76	+0.10
Husband as father	4.58	4.48	+0.10
Husband's courtesy and respect	4.50	4.30	+0.20
N	212	127	

In general, wives feel the same amount of satisfaction as their husbands. Table 3–7 shows again structural superiority in *miai* marriages and dynamic superiority in love matches. Understanding, love, sex, and companionship are all reciprocally appreciated in love marriages.

However, two facets of marriage look quite different from the wife's perspective. The more active child care by love-match men is just as appreciated by their wives as is the converse situation by husbands in *miai* marriages. Love-match wives know how to recognize a good father when they see one and give their husbands full credit for helping with the children.

Miai wives, on the other hand, have a remarkable ability to perceive their structural inferiority even though their husbands court them with extra courtesy. A little chivalry cannot mask the disrespect implicit in the role of servant. Hence, *miai* wives fail to share the sense of mutual respect that love-match wives find in informal, equalitarian marriages.

We might have expected satisfaction with the division of labor also to be

11. Wagatsuma points out that one feature of the traditional orientation of marriage is toward parenthood:

> For those who are married according to arrangement, the marriage does not become complete until they produce children. The arrival of the first child is the consummation of the marriage, the fulfillment of the expected function of the marriage. In other words, they get married not so much for the purpose of becoming husband and wife as for becoming father and mother. Furthermore, many husbands and wives in arranged marriages (who lack, at least in the beginning, genuine interaction and reciprocity in their married life) may find emotional satisfaction from interaction with the newly arrived child. This seems to be especially the case with wives. Dissatisfied with their life with their husbands, they look forward to becoming mothers. They receive not only emotional satisfaction but even substitutive social satisfaction from their babies and children.

reversed from husband to wife. Though it is not, the *miai* margin is sharply reduced, suggesting that whereas husbands are enthusiastic about servant wives, the latter merely tolerate their master husbands.

With respect to power structure, the trend is in the opposite direction. Since their marginal satisfaction with their decision-making pattern is greater, *miai* wives obviously are not unhappy with their more submissive role. Apparently they enjoy having someone to lean on and would not want it otherwise.

Many of the marginal differences in Table 3–7 prove unstable when analyzed by length of marriage. Delayed courtships make *miai* wives temporarily more satisfied at the beginning of marriage with the husband's helpfulness, understanding, affectionateness, and expected functioning as a father (in the years before the children arrive!). However, the end of courtship consolidates the long-run dynamic advantages of love marriages for women. Indeed, by the time marriage has lasted nine or more years, love-match wives are even more satisfied structurally than *miai* wives, at least as far as decision-making roles are concerned.

One general comment needs to be made about the pattern of responses to the satisfaction questions. In the *miai* marriages responses tend to cluster in the middle range, whereas in love marriages they are more dispersed, particularly for wives. Love matches either succeed more gloriously or fail more miserably than arranged marriages, perhaps because couples enter the latter with modest expectations—less hope, less bravery, more compliance. Since these premarital contrasts are sharper for wives than for husbands, we can understand why wives are more differentiated in their evaluations. For a Japanese girl to "go out on a limb" and enter a love match unsponsored by her elders is still a daring act. If her boldness pays off, all is well. But if she is disappointed, no *miai* wife could feel so let down.

Aggregate satisfaction—When all ten facets of marriage are combined, the positive and negative features of each sytem largely cancel out. Moreover, the contrast between the two systems is minimized by the fact that we gave greatest weight to whatever facets the individual valued most. Since *miai* couples place a premium on structural aspects and love-match couples stress dynamic aspects, each system's strong points were accentuated. Hence couples in the two systems should be equally satisfied with their situation as a whole.

If we combine the men's and women's mean satisfaction scores shown in Table 3–8, the overall satisfaction of love-match *couples* is 5.47 and that of arranged-marriage *couples* 5.56. The difference between these combined scores is so small as to be hardly worth discussing. From the standpoint of pair satisfaction, the two systems work almost identically well.

However, the two systems work less identically from the standpoint of the two sexes. Wives are marginally happier in love matches, but husbands are considerably more positive about arranged marriages. Since wives generally tend to be less satisfied than husbands, the net result is that love marriages are nearly symmetrical, whereas *miai* marriages are strikingly asymmetrical. Indeed, the bottom half of the table shows that when standard cutting points are used

Table 3–8—Aggregate and Comparative Satisfaction in Love Matches and Arranged Marriages

| | MATE-SELECTION SYSTEM | | |
	Love Match	Arranged Marriage	Love Margin
Aggregate satisfaction			
Husband's	5.54	5.92	—0.38
Wife's	5.40	5.21	+0.19
Comparative satisfaction			
Husband only satisfied	14.0%	21.2%	—7.2
Both satisfied	36.8	41.3	—4.5
Both dissatisfied	32.2	29.8	+2.4
Wife only satisfied	17.0	7.7	+9.3
	100.0%	100.0%	
N	212	127	

on the satisfaction scales, three times as many *miai* marriages are asymmetrical in the husband's favor as in the wife's, whereas love marriages equally often favor either partner.

To American ears the contrasting reactions of men and women carry a familiar ring. Perhaps at one time Japanese men and women were equally satisfied with the patriarchal system. Women, after all, knew no alternative and had been trained from childhood to become servant wives. Today, however, the submissive complacency of Japanese women has been disrupted. They have discovered an alternative way of life—a way of freedom and spontaneity, equality and comradeship—which their Western sisters enjoy. This is one reason so many Japanese women dated American soldiers after the war.

From the male standpoint, however, such women seem spoiled. Infected with álien ideas, they are too demanding, too selfish, too bold. Some men long for the "good old days" when women were properly deferential. These men resent the loss of status caused by feminine emancipation from feudalism.

For Americans, the closest parallel is the relationship between Negroes and whites. In the past most Negroes accepted their inferior status without question. Now, however, their slave mentality has been replaced by a desire for freedom and equality. Now they challenge old customs that held them down, demanding equal rights. These demands are resented by reactionary whites, but the clock cannot be turned back. The democratization of American society is just as inevitable as the democratization of Japanese marriages.

During transitional eras, however, some people get hurt. Dissatisfied love-match husbands envy the privileges, services, and prestige that went with being "king of the castle." Sometimes both partners are dissatisfied with the new system. Pioneers in an uncharted style of life, both sexes have little to guide them. They have been poorly schooled in the arts of communication and accommodation required by the new system. Presumably in the long run the new system will work better for both sexes. In the meantime, its novelty creates risks for both, but especially for husbands. To lose not only the wife's services but her respect and then to be drafted as an active parent and cohousekeeper comes hard to husbands in love marriages; they are apt to become nostalgic about the old system. Only when that system has finally passed into oblivion can we expect Japanese men to be as satisfied as their wives with the new equality.

Analysis by length of marriage shows that both systems please both sexes at first. Discrepancies emerge in the later years, when love match husbands become dissatisfied with their wives' structural ineptness and *miai* wives become restive in their structural subordination. Their partner's satisfaction declines also, but less precipitously.

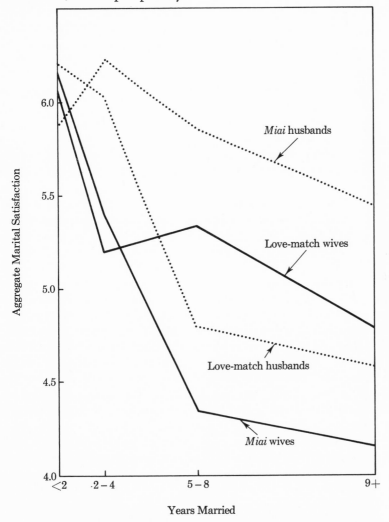

Figure 3–E. Husbands' and Wives' Aggregate Satisfaction in Love Match and Arranged Marriage by Length of Marriage

These comparisons show that love matches indeed start out hot and grow cold. In this sense they confirm the misgivings of the older generation. However, this does not mean that arranged marriages grow hot. Aggregate satisfaction for *miai* wives declines progressively as time passes. Their initial satisfaction is higher but their ultimate dissatisfaction greater than that of love-match wives. Hence, as far as wives are concerned, the hot-cold sequence applies even more forcibly to arranged marriages. Only for *miai* husbands is there any evidence of a warming trend, and that proves to be short lived. Hence the slogan must be revised; from the man's standpoint, arranged marriages start out cool and end up cool, but enjoy a hot spell in the middle years. The trouble with the old prediction is that it fails to recognize that time generally chills marital satisfaction. Japanese arranged marriages are no more exempt from falling temperatures than any other kind of marriage. Hence the prediction about arranged marriages had to be wrong ultimately. Only in the short run—in the early years of marriage—could it be right. Even then, it is right only for the chief beneficiary of the old system, the man.

LOVE

Marital satisfaction reflects both the structural and the dynamic aspects of marriage. Hence the ambiguous trends we have seen.

Love, however, is a dynamic feature, in which love matches should excel. At engagement, love is much more intense for couples who meet on their own. We have also seen that both men and women are more satisfied with the partner's expression of love and affection in love matches than in arranged marriages. It follows logically that love-match couples should be more in love throughout the marriage.

I have added premarital love to Figure 3–F for comparative purposes. Otherwise the general trends of love resemble those of satisfaction. Love decreases after the first years of marriage for everybody, except *miai* husbands with their usual delayed honeymoon. The rank order of intensity is the same: love-match couples are in the middle and *miai* couples sharply divided. The chief difference is that love in arranged marriages never attains the highest peaks of love in love matches. To be sure, in the later years of marriage, *miai* wives at one point and their husbands at several points exceed their love-match counterparts. But those are the cooler years of marriage. Only in a relative sense and chiefly for husbands can it be said that *miai* marriages start out cold and grow hot. Only after love matches have cooled considerably are arranged marriages relatively warm. And for wives in arranged marriages, the ultimate fate of love is conspicuously chilly.

Another relative sense in which arranged marriages grow hot is in the sequence from engagement to marriage. Prematurely engaged after truncated courtships, *miai* couples have little chance to fall in love. In their prolonged courtships extending into marriage, they almost catch up with their love-match counterparts—but not quite. Even their peak intensity after marriage never reaches the honeymoon intensity of love marriages. Not in comparison with love matches, then, but only relative to their own original coldness do arranged marriages thaw out. So cold are they at engagement that even after nine years of marital cooling, they are not *that* cold again. By contrast, love is so hot when love marriages begin that they cannot help cooling down. From this perspective we can say that love matches cool off and arranged marriages warm up, but the average temperature is lower throughout the cycle in arranged marriages—especially for wives.

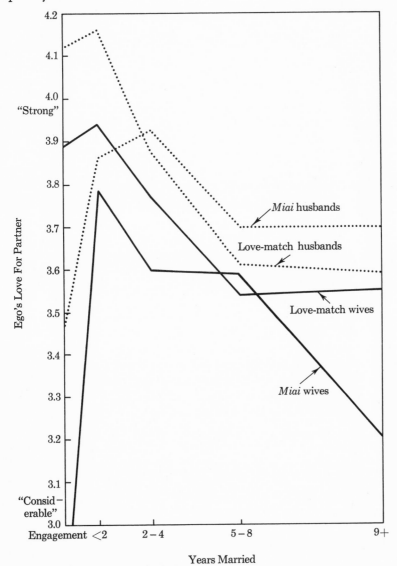

Figure 3–F. The Course of Love in Love Match and Arranged Marriage

This difference in averages between systems masks a wider range of variability within love marriages. Love-match wives still feel "intense and powerful" love twice as often as *miai* wives (12 as opposed to 6 per cent) but are the only ones to report hardly any love left. As with satisfaction, the riskiness of love offers both greater rewards and greater penalties to those who by-pass the conventional system. By contrast, women marrying conventionally more often wind up with merely "considerable" love (36 as opposed to 24 per cent). For husbands, however, the patterns are almost identical in the two groups.

"THE BEST OF BOTH WORLDS"

So far we have treated love matches and arranged marriages as opposites. But our respondents' comments in Chapter 1 warned us that the two systems overlap. Perhaps we should pursue a Hegelian dialectic beyond the usual thesis (the traditional system) and antithesis (the modern system) to a synthesis embracing both. Especially if contemporary Japan is in transition, the most fruitful system may be neither the old nor the new but a hybrid containing elements of both.

The strength of the old system is parental involvement in choosing the partner. This insures against wild and irresponsible love. Parents and children combined are wiser than either generation by itself. Moreover, parental support

Table 3–9—Marital Satisfaction by Betrothal Love and Mate-Selection System

	MATE-SELECTION SYSTEM		
Husband's marital satisfaction	Love Match	Arranged Marriage	Love Margin
Love at betrothal			
Intense	6.46	7.83	—1.37
Strong	5.30	5.77	—0.47
Considerable	4.64	5.08	—0.44
Little	(3.38)*	4.73	—1.35
Hardly any	—	(6.00)	
None	—	(3.00)	
Total	5.54	5.92	
Wife's marital satisfaction			
Love at betrothal			
Intense	6.64	(8.00)	—1.36
Strong	5.54	6.03	—0.49
Considerable	4.13	5.18	—1.05
Little	3.25	4.28	—1.03
Hardly any	(6.00)	(5.11)	
None	—	(1.00)	
Total	5.40	5.21	
N	212	127	

* Categories with less than ten cases are printed in parentheses. The love margin is not shown unless at least one mate-selection group has more than ten cases.

provides extra resources (emotional, social, and financial) for establishing the new home more securely.

The strength of the new system is the involvement of young people in choosing their own partners. Couples may need parental guidance in a country weak in heterosexual experience, but today's parents are less competent than previous generations to arrange marriages singlehandedly in view of the changing attitudes of the younger generation. Young people must take the basic steps of dating, courting, and falling in love before they get engaged. For them, love is a sign that the choice is wise.

Some *miai* couples proposed that their marriage should be labelled "*miai-plus-love*" because they began with a formal introduction but fell in love before getting married. Table 3–9 tests their claim that this combination is auspicious.

The table shows that they are right. We have discovered already that *miai* husbands are generally more satisfied than love-match husbands. But this difference is magnified when we equate the husbands' intensity of love at engagement.[12]

More importantly, the same difference holds true for wives. Although love-match wives generally are more satisfied than *miai* wives, this difference is sharply reversed when they are equated on their premarital love. This reflects the fact that most *miai* wives are pressured into marriage (and therefore concentrated in the lower brackets of love).

For both partners, given a particular amount of love, those with a *miai* consistently have an extra measure of marital satisfaction. The most satisfied couples are those who combine a *miai* with love. Thereby older and younger generations join forces to produce the most satisfactory marriages.

Table 3–10—Marital Satisfaction by Self-Classification of Marriage

| | Self-Classification of Marriage | | | |
| | LOVE MATCH | | ARRANGED MARRIAGE | |
Marital Satisfaction	Pure	Modified	Modified	Pure
Husband's	5.81	4.85	6.03	5.46
Wife's	5.36	5.62	4.85	4.91
N	218	68	40	89

Similarly, when couples are asked to classify their marriages subjectively, the most satisfied husbands are not those in pure *miai* marriages but those who rate their marriages as "modified *miai*" in type (see Table 3–10). As a matter of fact, pure *miai* marriages are even less satisfactory for husbands than pure love matches. The *miai* system, then, comes out on top only when it is modernized in form by adding enough courtship to allow love to develop before marriage.

For wives, Table 3–10 fails to disclose a similar superiority in modified

12. Wagatsuma warns that retrospective distortion may affect reported love at engagement, spuriously heightening the correlation between prior love and present satisfaction. However, if such distortion is a *general* process, it fails to explain why *miai* couples reporting intense premarital love are more satisfied than comparable love couples.

arranged marriages. It does, however, present an analogous finding in the top satisfaction of modified love matches.

For neither partner, therefore, is the most satisfactory marriage a pure love match or a pure arranged marriage. The greatest satisfaction always involves a combination.

Another way of comparing purely arranged marriages with quasi-arrangements is to examine who was "chief promoter" of the marriage. Originally the chief promoters (indeed, the only promoters) were the parents. Today, however, the most purely arranged marriages in that sense are the least satisfactory, especially for wives. Although *miai* wives generally are less satisfied than love match wives, there is an even sharper distinction between wives who are the chief promoters of their own marriages (regardless of introduction) and those who allow themselves to be pushed into marriage by someone else (usually their own parents). This differential satisfaction (5.45 as opposed to 4.82) suggests the obsolescence of the old system in the modern world. Parents are no longer equipped to choose partners singlehandedly for their children.

However, the child's failure to assume the role of chief promoter means not that he has not been consulted, but that he has reservations—and people who marry when in doubt tend to have poor marriages. All of which suggests that one predictor of the success of a marriage is the individual's subjective reaction to the prospect.

For husbands the differences are not nearly so great, but are in the same direction (5.66 for chief promoters, 5.58 for secondary promoters, and 5.50 for those who play neither role). Though small, these differences point in an important direction: even the sex that usually likes the old system finds it more satisfactory in the modified form in which parents do the introducing but the man does the deciding. For both sexes, then, parents may play useful roles in mate-selection, but they can no longer override the child's judgment without negative consequences for the marriage. Even for the dominant sex, the old system is no longer satisfactory unless it is drastically modernized.

Table 3–11—Marital Satisfaction by Number of Dates Prior to Engagement by Mate-Selection System

	NUMBER OF DATES	
	0–9	10 *or more*
Husband's aggregate satisfaction		
Love match (*N* = 21, 159)	6.43	5.38
Arranged marriage (*N* = 68, 37)	5.38	6.62
Wife's aggregate satisfaction		
Love match (*N* = 18, 180)	4.72	5.45
Arranged marriage (*N* = 77, 46)	4.97	5.62

How much courtship is necessary in an arranged marriage to allow love to develop? Table 3–11 suggests the value of at least ten dates prior to engagement for formally introduced husbands. Aggregate satisfaction is markedly less for husbands who rushed into engagement with fewer than ten dates following the *miai*. Curiously, the reverse is true among nonintroduced husbands. For them, long periods of dating often reflect obstacles to marriage, whereas quick engagements signify love at first sight.

For wives, no such contradiction appears. In both mate-selection systems, marriage benefits from lengthier courtship. And for wives as well as for husbands, the best marriages of all are those that combine a formal *miai* with adequate dating.

Does this mean, that the old marriage system should be reinstituted universally in Japan? Are couples who happen to meet on their own fore-doomed to unsatisfactory marriages because they by-passed the traditional form of parental sponsorship? Or is there a modified love match which is the equivalent of "*miai*-plus-love"? Is it possible for parents to become sponsors and give their blessing to a marriage even though they didn't happen to arrange the initial contact? Is there, in short, a "love-plus-parental-approval" form of marriage that works equally well?

Table 3–12—Marital Satisfaction by Parental Approval and Mate-Selection System

| | MATE-SELECTION SYSTEM | | |
	Love Match	Arranged Marriage	Love Margin
Husband's marital satisfaction			
Mother's attitude			
Eager, enthusiastic	8.30	6.52	+1.78
Happy	5.88	6.04	—0.16
Indecisive	5.14	(5.12)	+0.02
Indifferent	4.50	(4.43)	+0.07
Reluctant, hesitant	5.91	(1.00)	+4.91
Opposed	4.70	—	
Total	5.54	5.92	
Wife's marital satisfaction			
Father's attitude			
Eager, enthusiastic	7.40	5.10	+2.30
Happy	5.88	5.67	+0.21
Indecisive	5.04	4.43	+0.61
Indifferent	4.40	4.83	—0.43
Reluctant, hesitant	5.64	(6.25)	—1.41
Opposed	5.22	(1.67)	+3.55
Total	5.40	5.21	
N	212	127	

Table 3–12 suggests that there is. Especially when the opposite-sexed parent's attitude is considered (but also to a lesser extent with the parent of the same sex), the best marriages combine parental enthusiasm with the approval implied in personal selection. Although the general pattern at lesser levels of parental enthusiasm is not so clear as in the "*miai*-plus-love" combination, self-introduction appears to be generally an added benefit when the control variable is parental approval.

Within each mate-selection system, parental enthusiasm is generally correlated with marital satisfaction. However, there are two exceptional situations. Some love matches succeed remarkably well in spite of reluctant and hesitant parents. These cases demonstrate that marriage in spite of parental skepticism is not necessarily disastrous in contemporary Japan, even though outright opposition is more ominous. The most difficult situation of all, however, is the odd one of arranged marriages with parental opposition. Originally there must have been parental cooperation in the *miai*. Presumably the parents developed doubt or opposition later. Even though few in number, these marriages are so extraordinarily unsatisfactory to both husband and wife that they deserve attention. They can claim neither parental approval nor personal selection. Perhaps, indeed, the only person favorably disposed was a powerful matchmaker whose influence neither parents nor children could resist.

The bias toward patriarchal initiative (that is, from the husband and his family) in arranged marriages introduces two distinctions between the husband's and wife's satisfaction profiles: (1) Not one mother opposed her son's marriage outright, but even hesitation is disastrous. Negative evaluations by the father of the bride are more extensive and less disastrous—he shares some of his daughter's initial ambivalence about marrying this comparative stranger. (2) At the opposite extreme, enthusiasm by the wife's parents can be excessive. The lesser satisfaction of women whose fathers were "eager and enthusiastic" suggests that they allowed their fathers to push them into incompatible matches.

In a love match, whether in the U.S.A. or in Japan, there is little danger of excessive parental enthusiasm because initiative and judgment are in the young people's hands. Even for young men in contemporary arranged marriages, parental enthusiasm rarely overwhelms the son's judgment. But in postfeudal Japan there are still girls meek enough to allow themselves to be manipulated into mediocre marriages by overeager parents. Only with further emancipation will Japanese girls be immune to such manipulation.

Our basic comparisons demonstrate that the best marriages come from neither extreme—neither pure *miai* marriages in which parents are the primary promoters and children the passive pawns, nor pure love matches in which love triumphs over outright opposition. Rather, marriage thrives when both generations join in mutual enthusiasm for the proposed match. Under these circumstances it matters little whether couples are formally introduced or never introduced at all. To be sure, those who follow the conventional path tend to establish more old-fashioned marriages. But they also prefer that kind of marriage. Under either system, as long as both generations approve, marriage can be satisfactory. Styles of mate-selection and of marital interaction may change—and in this transitional era old and new styles exist side by side in the same community—but each style offers satisfaction in its own way to those who choose it. Provided, that is, it is not pushed to extremes but carried out with due regard for the interests of all those concerned in both generations. Six heads are better than two young ones or four old ones!

The hot-cold epigram implies that only parents are able to contract satisfactory marriages for their offspring. The younger generation is equally convinced that only they can do the job. Both generations are partly right and partly wrong. Both have something to offer. Neither is right alone. The best marriages require collaboration between the two. In contemporary, conflict-ridden Japan such collaboration is rare—it is almost unthinkable. But happy is the family that achieves it.

Love Match and Arranged Marriage—After Marriage

Even though our general conclusion is that the best marriages in contemporary Japan are hybrids, we can see the total picture better if we draw together the distinctive features of each type of marriage. This is not so much summary as caricature, highlighting the marginal differences, ignoring the overlap.

ARRANGED MARRIAGES

Marriages initiated by a formal introduction come closest to the traditional Japanese marriage. They tend to be patriarchal in power structure, the husband dominating particularly decisions about his precious leisure time. The children, on the other hand, are relegated to his wife's care, for he is too busy to be bothered with feminine affairs.

The man's world and the woman's world are more sharply divided in household tasks. *Miai* wives are servants, waiting on their husbands like valets, raising children for him like governesses. Only tasks which chivalry requires the man to shoulder does he take over—and then only as long as he is still courting the stranger who has become his wife.

Chivalry extends beyond practical tasks to symbolic gestures between husbands and wives. *Miai* husbands address their wives more formally and treat them more courteously, save for a few unreconstructed tyrants.

The structural split between *miai* husbands and wives reduces dynamic interaction. Specialized roles do not lend themselves to companionable activity either inside or outside the home. The more costly the form of companionship, the less apt are *miai* couples to practice it. The same is true for emotional therapy. Couples who seldom join in other activities seldom share their troubles.

The strengths and weaknesses of arranged marriages are reflected in subjective evaluations. Arranged marriages excel in their structural features, especially from the standpoint of the male beneficiary of that structure. However, for wives, structural benefits are outweighed by the dynamic defects of old-fashioned marriages. The net result is that arranged marriages are skewed both objectively and subjectively in the husband's direction. Wives feel left in the lurch, especially after the husband's delayed courtship peters out.

LOVE MARRIAGES

Love matches are the Japanese equivalent of Western marriages.

Structurally they are not only equalitarian in power but syncratic. Husbands and wives share decisions, share housekeeping and child-rearing responsibilities and—for better or for worse—disdain the formalities of chivalrous etiquette. Between husband and wife there is an easygoing intimacy symbolized by terms of endearment.

Intimacy is also expressed in the dynamic aspects of marriage. Love-match couples spend more leisure time together, do more things together, and communicate more frequently to each other a variety of messages: informative, affectionate, therapeutic.

For wives, this new style of marriage is eminently satisfactory. Even for husbands, the loss of servant wife is partially offset by gaining an emancipated woman, a more satisfactory sex partner and companion in other recreational activities. Though the average love-match husband is relatively less satisfied than a *miai* husband, he is not absolutely dissatisfied. Both sexes find the new pattern of marriage reasonably satisfactory, in contrast with the split reaction of the two sexes to arranged marriages.

To return to the quotation with which we began the chapter, love matches indeed start out hot for both partners and grow cold (or at least cool). And arranged marriages do start out cold; but they grow hot only from a short-range, male viewpoint. The long-range trend of arranged marriage temperature is as clearly downward as that of love matches. The difference is that *miai* heat waves roll in later because premarital warming opportunities are inadequate. Moreover, these delayed heat waves never equal the passionate love of appropriately named "love" matches.

For *miai* wives, the ultimate despair is colder than for either partner in love matches.

Hence, the second half of the original quotation must be revised to read: Arranged marriages start out cold, grow temporarily warm, and then freeze up for wives.

However, the dichotomy posed by the whole quotation is basically false. The best marriages in Japan are neither love matches nor arranged marriages, but combinations of the best elements of both. When both generations join forces in mate-selection, marriages are most likely to start out hot and retain their warmth.

COURTSHIP— 4

FOUNDATION FOR MARRIAGE

THE last three chapters have compared two systems of mate-selection in ideology, in the processes of courtship, and in the ensuing years of marriage. In each case our purpose has been to contrast what happens in the two systems.

But we have found that the two overlap. Although unsponsored couples usually date often and long, some rush into marriage knowing as little about one another as the traditional sponsored couple. Does it make any difference? Does it matter whether couples take time to date, to visit their families, to get acquainted before getting engaged? Is marriage more successful for couples who build their relationship solidly in advance?

In the Japanese tradition, the answer was "no." Premarital involvement did not strengthen marriage, but ruined it. When my Hiroshima professor-interpreter heard that one of his nephews had fallen in love, he feared the worst. Nevertheless, he agreed to serve as matchmaker and began his investigation:

I was pleasantly surprised to find that this was a pure love based only on occasional glances at each other on the streetcar which both rode every day. There were no conversations, no dates, no intimacy. I felt that such a couple *should* marry because this was not a sordid love affair involving pleasure and self-indulgence in which people have already reaped rewards. Rather this was a restrained, self-disciplined, spiritual love.

The Western viewpoint is just the opposite—to look askance at decisions so flimsily based, to encourage more acquaintance so that realism can replace rose-colored glasses.

The purpose of this chapter is to test these contradictory philosophies. Ignoring the distinction between systems of introduction, we shift our focus to the marital consequences of premarital interaction patterns.

The activities to be explored include dating, contact with the partner's social networks, discussing varied topics, and spending enough time to build a strong relationship. We focus on the interval prior to engagement, because that is when the relationship first takes shape.

Dating

In order to build a relationship the partners must interact. Except for those thrown together institutionally (who interact even when they are not dating), intentional association provides the means by which more specific forms of interaction may take place. Dating involves either exclusive companionship for the couple alone or broader sociability with family or friends. In asking our respondents how much dating they had done, we referred only to "pure" dates—that is, those on which they had been alone together.

Table 4–1—Dating as the Basis for Love

Love at Engagement	Number of Dates								
	0	1–2	3–4	5–9	10–19	20–49	50+	Fre-quent	Inde-pendent*
Man's	2.93	3.11	3.47	3.91	4.15	3.82	3.92	4.18	4.12
Woman's	2.21	2.60	3.25	3.18	3.33	3.52	3.75	4.00	4.04
N	14	34	37	45	39	56	89	51	75

* Contact independent of intentional dating (e.g. colleagues at work).

Dating makes love possible. Love seldom occurs by spontaneous combustion. It depends on continued rewarding interaction. Table 4–1 shows that for both sexes, the more they date the more they love each other. For women, love is especially inhibited by lack of dating. This is less true for men, who are more likely to fall in love at first sight. As the initiators in arranged marriages, they would not have scheduled the *miai* in the first place if they had not already been attracted by the girl's photograph. Men also achieve high intensity faster (by 10–19 dates) whereas women's love rises continuously within the limits of our categories. From the woman's standpoint, the more dates the better if love is to be firmly established before the fateful step of engagement. For the man, five or ten dates are enough.

Whereas premarital love can hardly exist without the opportunity provided by dating, marital interaction patterns are less predetermined by the number of dates before engagement. Only where dating is almost completely by-passed before engagement is there fair warning that a couple may not date after marriage either. To be more specific, couples in our sample who rush into engagement after only one date or none at all date only half as often after marriage as the rest of the sample (11–12 times per year as opposed to 22). At least two dates (three in longer courtships) are necessary to indicate that dating will be a continuing activity after marriage.

Men who date more often before engagement also are somewhat more emotionally expressive after marriage. For this purpose the prerequisite minimum is three dates. Men who date three or more times before getting engaged convey their affection to their wives an average of 137 times per year, whereas those who fail to date that much express affection only 102–108 times a year on the average. A little dating is necessary to guarantee that men will ever get around to courting their wives at all. Men who are willing to get engaged without bothering to date the girl several times are apt to neglect her after marriage, too.

Roughly the same amount of dating is necessary for the wife to be satisfied with various facets of marriage. For example, to be satisfied with the husband's companionship, four dates are needed; with his love and affection, three dates. The larger the minimum, the better the premarital activity previews that aspect of marriage. (That is, the higher the correlation between number of dates and marital interaction.)

For men, however, there is no connection between premarital dating and the satisfactoriness of marriage. Dating is something the man does for the woman. He takes her dating; he pays for it. His willingness to invest time and money in giving her a good time means he will be a lovable husband. If he neglects this activity, she may manage to be a good wife, but he is not likely to measure up to her image of a good husband.

Because dating is an intrinsic part of the love-match system, it can be taken for granted for couples who meet on their own. When couples are formally introduced, however, the woman's fears of being trapped in an unsatisfactory marriage can be allayed by dating. We have already seen that the best *miai* marriages combine the *miai* with love. Since dating provides the basis for love, it creates a modified *miai* marriage likely to be more satisfactory than a purely "arranged" one. More detailed analysis shows that the wife's love for her husband is hardly correlated with dating in love marriages but rises steeply with dating after a *miai*. This illustrates how dating mitigates the potential dangers of the *miai* system and guarantees the combined benefits of both personal and parental approval.

By taking his girl to the movies and to coffeeshops to listen to classical music, the man proves his interest in her as a person and as a companion. But if he presses her into a quick engagement, the chances are he is interested only in getting a cook, a maidservant, a sexual outlet, and a mother for his children. In postfeudal Japan, a traditionally introduced man's willingness to engage in nontraditional dating demonstrates his willingness to develop the nontraditional marriage pattern most women prefer.

Time

Closely related to the man's willingness to date before engagement is his willingness to spend time before pressing the girl to become his wife. For our total sample, the median interval from first date to engagement is nine months, only half the typical American interval (Hollingshead, 1952). Japanese custom telescopes courtships, especially in *miai* marriages.

What is the optimum interval? Not the longest possible one—a lifetime of previewing would be absurd. Sooner or later one must move on to engagement and marriage. Theoretically one should spend enough time to develop confidence in the future, but should launch oneself into that future before losing momentum. Beyond the point of diminishing returns, external obstacles and internal doubts create frustration and presage marital difficulties. Therefore the most satisfactory marriages should lie somewhere in the middle range.

Table 4–2—Comparative Marital Satisfaction by Length of Courtship Before Engagement

	LENGTH OF COURTSHIP			
COMPARATIVE SATISFACTION	<4 months	4–6 months	7–35 months	3 years or more
Both satisfied	37.8%	38.1%	39.6%	30.5%
Husband only	23.0	17.5	15.7	18.6
Wife only	9.5	11.3	17.2	13.6
Neither satisfied	29.7	33.0	27.6	37.3
Total	100.0%	99.9%	100.1%	100.0%
N	74	97	134	59

The relationship between time and marital satisfaction is so weak that successive intervals fluctuate erratically. Table 4–2 portrays broad time intervals which correlate slightly with satisfaction.

Our curvilinear hypothesis (that moderately long courtships promote marital satisfaction) is just barely supported. The most satisfactory single time interval in more detailed analysis is 7–11 months (50 per cent of the couples are satisfied). Whether this is a causal relationship is debatable. Perhaps these are lucky couples for whom everything goes swimmingly in courtship, who marry in due time and "live happily ever after."

At the opposite extreme are dissatisfied couples who marry only after years of going together. Why do they take so long to get married? Several interviews describe delays due to parental opposition, ill health, and other "external" obstacles. In others, inner doubts prolong the agony of decision. Either objective or subjective problems bode ill for the future. Perhaps long courtships symbolize rather than cause difficulties.

Table 4–2 suggests contradictory trends in asymmetrically satisfactory marriages. "Quickie" marriages often satisfy the husband but not the wife.

We have noted before how quickly some Japanese men fall in love. Theirs is the initiative in marriage and theirs the pleasure when the invitation is promptly accepted. Many such marriages are patriarchal, rewarding the man but costing the wife. In short, a speedy courtship yields maximum dividends to the man from minimal investment of effort.

To a woman, on the other hand, a man's willingness to court her proves his love. If she is the bargaining type, she may postpone saying "yes" until she exacts enough promises and receives enough gifts to feel ready to capitulate. Within limits, satisfaction rises for the woman at the expense of the man. If this game is prolonged for more than two years, it is less apt to be carried off successfully, even from the standpoint of the woman. It is a dangerous game, souring first the man and eventually the woman too.

However, these are speculative interpretations. Varying lengths of courtship are variously motivated by special circumstances. If we could control those circumstances by conducting a grand experiment, randomly assigning couples varying amounts of time, we might learn the effect of time itself.

As it is, we learn only that courtship requires a man to persuade a woman to marry him and that their bargaining process determines the length of courtship and coincidentally the nature of their relationship more than time itself determines the success of either the selection process or the subsequent marriage.

Contact with the Partner's Social Networks

Pre-engagement sociability sets the pattern for later social life. After marriage, leisure-time dating involves more parties, entertaining, and other external social contacts. Early social contacts may be expected to resemble sociability after marriage.

CONTACT WITH THE PARTNER'S FAMILY

Our respondents' contacts with each other's families before engagement are skewed in the girl's direction. The median number is five contacts with her family but only three with the man's. Presumably this bias occurs in any country whenever the girl lives at home and the man calls to take her out. Sixty-seven couples met only the girl's family (more than double the reverse situation).

Table 4–3 shows that marital satisfaction is not affected by prior contact with the girl's family. However, contact with the man's makes a difference (especially if we ignore the zero category, in which geographical barriers probably intervene). Optimum contact covers a very broad range from 4–49 times. Less contact either yields inadequate knowledge of the man's family or reflects too much knowledge of their skepticism about the match. Whichever the reason, rare visits are a bad omen.

Table 4–3—Marital Consequences of Pre-engagement Contact with the Partner's Family

Annual number of marital contacts with families	NUMBER OF PRE-ENGAGEMENT FAMILY CONTACTS					
	0	1–3	4–49	50+	Fre-quent	Inde-pendent
With man's family	11.6	13.2	13.5	13.3	16.5	18.5
With girl's family	12.9	12.6	12.6	15.4	18.1	20.6
Comparative marital satisfaction						
By contact with man's family						
Both satisfied	39.1%	32.2%	46.2%	38.5%	31.6%	35.0%
One satisfied	34.4	30.3	33.0	23.1	31.6	30.0
Neither satisfied	26.6	37.4	20.9	38.5	36.8	35.0
Total	100.1%	99.9%	100.1%	100.1%	100.0%	100.0%
By contact with girl's family						
Both satisfied	38.2%	37.3%	37.1%	36.8%	47.4%	30.8%
One satisfied	26.5	32.5	33.1	26.3	21.0	38.5
Neither satisfied	35.3	30.2	29.7	36.8	31.6	30.8
Total	100.0%	100.0%	99.9%	99.9%	100.0%	100.1%
Minimum Number of Cases						
Contact with man's family	64	155	91	13	19	20
Contact with girl's family	34	126	148	19	19	13

At the opposite extreme, excessive contact appears. Presumably the problem is not so much that pre-engagement contact mars the relationship as that it foreshadows a continuing eclipse of the dyadic relationship by the man's ties to his parents. Remembering that the traditional Japanese family system was patrilocal (that is, the couple lived with the husband's parents), we see in excessively close patrilineal contact a dangerous remnant of that system. Though we have excluded actually patri*local* cases from our sample, excessive visiting can inhibit young marriages almost as much as excessive proximity.

Evidence of the intervening mechanism appears in the top segment of Table 4–3. Couples who meet the man's family most before engagement do the most visiting with relatives after marriage. Apparently, the girl's family is less dangerous: intensive contact can continue after marriage without impairing marital satisfaction. Though the two families differ in their potential impact on the marriage itself, pre-engagement relationships with either family tend to continue after marriage. Individuals whose contact with the partner's family occurs independently of dating (for example, a man who marries the boss's daughter) are structurally guaranteed the highest frequency of kin contact after marriage.

CONTACT WITH THE PARTNER'S FRIENDS

Whereas the girl's parents are seen most often, the man's friends are best known. Men arranging dates presumably recruit their friends for double dates and group parties. Contacts with either set, however, are rare by American standards: only three with his friends and two with hers.

Table 4-4—Marital Consequences of Pre-engagement Contact with the Partner's Friends

| | NUMBER OF PRE-ENGAGEMENT CONTACTS | | | | | |
	0	1–4	5–49	50+	Fre-quent	Mutual Friends
Annual Number of Marital Contacts with Friends						
By contact with girl's friends	6.4	7.1	8.0	(15.9)	15.7	12.4
By contact with man's friends	6.6	6.6	6.4	6.9	13.9	10.7
Relative Frequency Wife Talks with Husband's Visiting Friends						
By contact with girl's friends	2.94	3.17	3.26	(3.38)	3.24	3.07
By contact with men's friends	2.98	3.08	3.30	3.00	3.18	3 14
Comparative Marital Satisfaction						
By contact with girl's friends						
Both satisfied	37.8%	36.6%	39.2%	(60.0%)	50.0%	34.8%
One satisfied	31.5	37.5	27.6	(40.0)	21.4	30.4
Neither satisfied	30.7	25.9	33.4	(0.0)	28.6	34.8
Total	100.0%	100.0%	100.2%	(100.0%)	100.0%	100.0%
By contact with man's friends						
Both satisfied	36.4%	41.1%	40.4%	30.0%	29.6%	35.5%
One satisfied	31.8	28.4	31.6	30.0	33.3	35.5
Neither satisfied	31.8	30.6	28.1	40.0	37.0	29.0
Total	100.0%	100.1%	100.1%	100.0%	99.9%	100.0%
Minimum Number of Cases						
By contact with girl's friends	127	112	69	5	14	23
By contact with man's friends	110	95	57	10	27	62

Table 4-4 shows that marital sociability can be predicted better from contact with the girl's friends than from that with the man's. Perhaps the very fact that men less easily become acquainted with the girl's friends than vice versa makes his willingness to do so significant. After marriage, executive husbands enjoy expense-account entertainment in public restaurants, bars, and night clubs where professional hostesses replace missing wives. For wives, however, there is no substitute for a sociable husband, which is why they especially value a man's early demonstration of his leisure time thoughtfulness and interest in their social circles.

The wife's ability to talk to the husband's visiting friends also correlates more closely with his premarital sociability than with hers. Here continuity of behavior is manifested less than selectivity. Men willing to meet the girl's friends before marriage give her verbal access to their own friends after marriage. Both are "modern" acts.

Generally speaking, frequent contact with the girl's friends before engagement is associated with satisfactory marriages. However, the concept of excessive contact arises for the man's friends just as it did for his family. Beyond forty-nine contacts, the proportion of dissatisfied couples suddenly jumps. Hence we can hardly conclude that contact with the man's friends is beneficial, save perhaps the first few times. Whether male friends are equally "dangerous" in less patriarchal societies remains to be seen from further research.

For both sexes, mutual friends yield poorer predictions of marital behavior than frequently contacted separate friends. When both have the same friends, no effort is required to meet them. So the situation of such couples yields fewer clues about their commitment to a companionable way of life.

In most other respects, contacts with families and friends are parallel phenomena. Contacting the girl's family and friends is especially beneficial, whereas the man's associates may be excessively close. However, the lesser contact with mutual friends after marriage has no parallel among mutually linked families. Proverbially, "blood is thicker than water." If one must choose, ties with families take precedence over ties with friends. So friendships may wane after marriage while kinship remains solid.

Discussion

Besides social activities, a second means of preparing for marriage is discussion. Sharing thoughts furthers the development of a sharing, equalitarian relationship.

The greater the frequency of discussion before marriage, the more satisfactory the marriage should be, especially for the wife.

We investigated five discussion topics. Each will be reviewed in relation to corresponding facets of marriage. Then the five will be compared as bases for general marital satisfaction.

DISCUSSING MARRIAGE PATTERNS

Because old-fashioned and modern marriages exist side by side in Japan, potential marriage partners need to inquire which type the prospective spouse prefers. We asked, "How often did the two of you discuss traditional and modern husband-wife relationships?"

In an unchanging society, such discussion is unnecessary; traditional patterns can be taken for granted. In a changing society the fracturing of tradition makes both conservatives and radicals wary. Conservatives may take the tradition somewhat for granted and be less interested in debating the issue from a philosophical point of view. Particularly in the early stages of a social revolution, it is the revolutionaries who endlessly argue the advantages of the new over the old. In the Japanese family revolution, it is the modern-minded *woman* who is most likely to broach this question. She has the most to lose if she marries an old-fashioned man. He would try to crush her efforts at self-realization. By contrast, a "modern" man with an old-fashioned wife faces less difficulty—disappointment, perhaps, but not a power struggle.

Lacking direct evidence, we can only guess that structural discussions are mostly wife-initiated. We can test, however, whether they are linked with modern marriages.

Table 4–5—Marriage Structure by Pre-engagement Discussion of Marriage Patterns

	DISCUSSION OF TRADITIONAL AND MODERN RELATIONSHIPS			
	Never	Seldom	Sometimes	Often
Power Structure				
Husband's power	4.98	5.35	5.29	5.09
Number of shared decisions	3.63	3.62	3.95	4.03
Division of Labor				
Wife's task performance	4.86	4.86	4.16	4.17
Number of shared tasks	1.43	1.45	1.68	1.64
Wife is employed	22%	29%	40%	38%
Deference Patterns				
Wife enters taxi first	3.02	3.14	3.14	3.06
Wife sits down in bus	3.47	3.57	3.59	3.60
Husband expresses appreciation	2.55	2.60	2.62	2.71
Wife expresses appreciation	3.07	3.13	3.17	3.25
Wife talks to husband's friends	3.01	3.00	3.15	3.18
Minimum Number of Cases	91	109	126	115

Table 4–5 shows that couples who discuss marriage styles most have relatively modern marriages, whereas those who seldom or never do have more traditional marriages. For example, girls who often discuss this topic do less work in the home and more out of it. They also make more decisions. The change, however, is not from husband-dominant marriage to wife-dominant ones. Rather, in both decision-making and housekeeping, there is increased teamwork between husband and wife.

In one sense, these discussions are a form of sharing in themselves—verbal sharing. For this reason they foreshadow other forms of verbal communication, as the last three deference patterns suggest. To talk to the husband's friends is both modern and communicative, but to thank the husband for his favors is hardly modern and simply reflects the way all forms of discussion reveal the partners' verbal fluency.

Non-verbal patterns of precedence in taxi and bus are less closely related to discussions about marriage. Nevertheless, those who never discuss the topic behave most traditionally in both situations.

In general, then, those marriages most thoroughly discussed in advance are most modern in structure. Husbands are particularly cooperative, equalitarian, and chivalrous. Wives do not take these unusual services for granted but are extra-appreciative. Both partners are rewarded for their pre-engagement exploration of ideal designs for marriage.

Given this improved version of marriage, we should expect both partners (but especially wives) to be satisfied with their marriages. Table 4–6 shows that intensively discussed marriages do result in skewed evaluations of the structural aspects of marriage.

Wives find their new power very satisfactory, but husbands react ambivalently. Men feel both deprived of their old pre-eminence and gratified by the new sharing. In the division of labor, the sense of loss, while small, is mutual.

Even though wives get more help from their husbands and less often feel like servants, they are still less satisfied in the most "discussed" marriages. Perhaps increased employment outside the home increases their need for help faster than husbands supply it.

Table 4–6—Marital Satisfaction by Pre-engagement Discussion of Marriage Patterns

	DISCUSSION OF TRADITIONAL AND MODERN RELATIONSHIPS				
Power Structure	Never	Seldom	Sometimes	Often	Net Difference
Satisfaction with own decision-making role					
Wife's	4.22	4.29	4.40	4.73	+0.51
Husband's	4.51	4.40	4.66	4.49	—0.02
Division of Labor					
Wife never feels like a servant	3.45	3.50	3.63	3.64	+0.19
Wife's satisfaction with husband's helpfulness	3.75	3.55	3.71	3.67	—0.08
Husband's satisfaction with wife's home management	4.12	4.04	4.31	4.11	—0.01
Deference Patterns					
Satisfaction with courtesy and respect					
Wife's	4.26	4.27	4.56	4.56	+0.30
Husband's	4.41	4.31	4.45	4.62	+0.21
Comparative Marital Satisfaction					
Both satisfied	36.6%	32.6%	38.5%	41.5%	+4.9
Wife only	7.0	15.2	15.4	13.8	
Husband only	18.3	17.4	18.3	19.1	
Neither satisfied	38.0	34.8	27.9	25.5	
Total	99.9%	100.0%	100.1%	99.9%	
Minimum Number of Cases	71	92	104	94	

Only in the area of deference does pre-engagement discussion benefit both partners. Increased masculine chivalry is matched by increased appreciation from the wife, enabling satisfaction with courtesy to rise mutually. Moreover, willingness to explore the partner's views before getting engaged is a form of deference in itself, providing a foundation for deference after marriage.

The direct impact of structural discussion on structural satisfaction is ambiguous. Why then does aggregate satisfaction increase? The answer is that structural discussion not only previews the form of marriage but is a dynamic activity in itself. In this sense, couples who talk about *anything* are likely to find marriage dynamically satisfying no matter how they feel about it structurally.

To talk about structure is to pave the way to structural alteration, to produce a more dynamically satisfying marriage, but to leave husbands wondering whether they have gained or lost in the structural area itself.

DISCUSSING VOCATIONAL PLANS

Next we asked how often couples discussed the man's vocational plans and whether wives should work. This is a double-barreled question, the latter half overlapping considerably with our marriage-patterns question. When wives answer "often", we have no way of knowing whether their discussions focused on the man's plans, on her own, or on both. In view of these ambiguities, it deserves less investigation than the previous topic.

Table 4–7—Marital Consequences of Pre-engagement Discussion of Vocational Plans

	DISCUSSION OF BOTH PARTNERS' VOCATIONAL PLANS			
	Never	Seldom	Sometimes	Often
Wife is now working	13%	29%	33%	39%
Wife's satisfaction with husband's income	3.78	3.87	3.94	3.90
Comparative Marital Satisfaction				
Both satisfied	28.6%	26.6%	37.9%	42.4%
Wife only	8.6	18.8	12.6	13.0
Husband only	14.3	18.8	17.2	19.2
Neither satisfied	48.6	35.9	32.2	25.4
Total	100.1%	100.1%	99.9%	100.0%
Minimum Number of Cases	35	64	87	177

Table 4–7 shows that this topic is closely connected with the wife's current employment. For a middle-class married woman to work outside the home is still sufficiently unorthodox in Japan to be worth discussing in advance. (By contrast, women's services have long been utilized in domestic enterprises such as the family "farm" or cottage industry.) Not only is there a general correlation between advance discussion and being employed at all, but those who discuss it most are more often employed full time than less than 40 hours a week.

Discussing job plans at least "sometimes" is highly conducive to mutual satisfaction after marriage, while never discussing either the husband's or the wife's plans is especially ominous.

DISCUSSING POLITICS

Rarest of all our topics is national and international political issues. Studies in many countries show that they are primarily masculine affairs (Duverger, 1955). Even in the United States, most wives vote the way their husbands tell them to (Lane, 1959). In Japan, women have had the right to vote only since World War II, and even though Japanese students are more involved in politics than American ones, the sex segregation of Japanese universities means that student political action is concentrated on male campuses. Presumably many of our men were interested in political events during the turbulent postwar era when they were dating, yet only 9 per cent of our couples talked politics "often," and three times as many never did. To discuss politics with a girl, then, indicates an unusually companionable style of dating.

Table 4–8—Marital Consequences of Pre-engagement Political Discussion

DISCUSSION OF NATIONAL OR INTERNATIONAL POLITICS

	Never	Seldom	Sometimes	Often	Net Difference
Wife Prefers Masculine Role or Is Uncertain	25%	36%	33%	55%	
Continuity After Marriage					
Annual frequency of discussing the news after marriage	143	169	202	204	+43%
Satisfaction with Companionship					
Wife's	3.53	3.83	3.99	3.92	+0.39
Husband's	3.88	4.18	4.26	4.00	+0.12
Comparative Marital Satisfaction					
Both satisfied	28.3%	40.6%	42.7%	35.5%	+7.2
Wife only	9.1	16.1	10.1	25.8	
Husband only	23.2	14.7	21.3	9.7	
Neither satisfied	39.4	28.7	25.8	29.0	
Total	100.0%	100.1%	99.9%	100.0%	
Minimum Number of Cases	99	143	89	31	

Table 4–8 demonstrates anew the masculinity of politics. A majority of those rare women who talk politics often before engagement either prefer the masculine role in life or cannot decide which sex they would rather be if they could live their lives over again. Women whose rejection of the feminine role is manifested in intense concern for political issues do not make very good wives: their husbands are notably dissatisfied with them as mothers and as purveyors of courtesy and respect. The best marriages from the standpoint of both sexes follow "some" discussion of politics rather than frequent discussion. To be politically oriented means to value external affairs more than domestic chores. If the husband's values are similar, mutual satisfaction is possible. But unilateral feminine satisfaction is highly correlated with political discussion, suggesting a feminist revolt against domesticity that many husbands deplore. Conversely, men alone are often satisfied with marriages preceded by no political talk whatsoever.

Companionship between the partners may suffer, then, when the wife is too externally involved. Nevertheless, pre-engagement intellectual activity strikingly forecasts this aspect of marriage. For the sample as a whole, discussions of "the news" are almost half again as frequent among those who talked politics often as among those who never did. Some Japanese courtships are so short that couples hardly have a chance to get around to politics. Among those that endure a year or more, the pre-engagement precedent is even more clearly established (with a 75 per cent differential after marriage between the two pre-engagement extremes).

Politics, then, rarely intrudes in Japanese love-making, but for those for whom it does very often, it signifies so much emancipation from traditional sex roles that their marriage is not simply modernized but disintegrated. The forecast may be accurate, but it calls for stormy weather.

INFORMATIVE COMPANIONSHIP

Some may doubt the legitimacy of politics as a discussion topic for young daters, but few will question the value of telling each other what happened since they last met. Husbands claim their girls reported to them a bit more frequently than the wives claim in reverse—but since husbands tend to think more positively than wives, we can discount the difference and emphasize how much informative communication occurs in both directions before engagement.

We assume that hearing personal news provides the individual with both knowledge about the partner and pleasure in having the partner share his private life. There may also be, however, a third gain to the individual, namely pleasure in acquiring an audience. Therefore, even one-way communication may simultaneously benefit both partners.

Table 4–9—Marital Consequences of Pre-engagement Informative Companionship

	FREQUENCY OF TELLING/HEARING PERSONAL EVENTS				
	Never	Seldom	Sometimes	Often	Net Difference
Continuity After Marriage					
Husband tells annually	135	140	165	208	+54%
Wife tells annually	213	171	229	253	+19%
Benefits of Man's Telling Events					
Satisfaction with companionship					
Wife's	3.44	3.41	3.83	4.08	+0.64
Husband's	3.69	3.74	4.39	4.22	+0.53
Comparative Marital Satisfaction					
Both satisfied	24.4%	26.8%	39.2%	45.3%	+20.9
Wife only	8.9	14.1	10.3	16.9	
Husband only	15.6	21.1	19.6	16.2	
Neither satisfied	51.1	38.0	30.9	21.6	
Total	100.0%	100.0%	100.0%	100.0%	
Minimum Number of Cases	45	71	97	148	
Benefits of Woman's Telling Events					
Satisfaction with companionship					
Wife's	3.41	3.56	3.62	4.05	+0.64
Husband's	3.86	3.59	3.96	4.40	+0.54
Comparative Marital Satisfaction					
Both satisfied	28.2%	26.2%	34.9%	43.6%	+15.4
Wife only	5.1	9.5	15.1	15.1	
Husband only	25.6	16.7	12.3	20.3	
Neither satisfied	41.0	47.6	37.7	20.9	
Total	99.9%	100.0%	100.0%	99.9%	
Minimum Number of Cases	39	42	106	172	

Table 4–9 shows straightforward continuity between the man's pre-engagement and marital behavior. The less he tells of his personal life before engagement, the less he does after marriage. This is largely true for women also, except that some who are silent before engagement open up later. Controlled analysis by length of courtship shows that most of these women had short ones. The shorter the interval between first encounter and getting engaged, the skimpier the preview of later behavior. Only when a woman has a chance to talk before engagement and fails to do so is she likely to be silent after marriage.

The bottom section of Table 4–9 suggests that women who blossom out only after engagement make reasonably satisfactory wives from the man's point of view. However, the most satisfied men are those whose courtships get off to a less ambiguous start with wholehearted sharing of personal news whenever the couple meet.

For wives of initially silent men there is a slight reversal in the satisfactoriness of marriage between the "seldom" and "never" categories. However, this relationship straightens out when long courtships are distinguished from unpredictable short ones. For wives more than husbands, then, a reticent dating partner is a bad sign, partly because Japanese women prize an open relationship more than men, partly because men are less apt to change this behavior pattern than women.

In general, then, the man's postmarital information flow can be prejudged from his pre-engagement expressiveness or reticence. For a Japanese girl, loquaciousness is similarly indicative. However, girlish silence may be only circumstantial. In a whirlwind courtship, pushed by the man and both families, she may be too timid to reveal her personal life. Once the relationship is sealed, communication channels may open. Yet the removal of impediments does not guarantee a high-pressure flow of information. Only pre-engagement demonstration of conversational skill and energy can guarantee that. Hence for women as well as men, informative companionship before marriage leads most certainly to informative companionship after marriage.

SHARING EMOTIONAL PROBLEMS

To tell one's troubles is a special form of informative companionship—the less cheerful part. It involves more than just conveying information, for the teller hopes to get a helpful response. For most people this is the "deepest" form of sharing. To tell troubles means to take the other into one's confidence, to "open up" to an unusual degree, to make oneself vulnerable to hurt and shame. It may even risk ending the relationship. Revealing inner problems takes courage and requires trust. The partner may be offended by what is revealed and critical of the difficulties encountered. He may resent being burdened with unpleasantness and rebuff the overture. Such reactions will discourage further attempts. On the other hand, helpful responses encourage individuals to share subsequent troubles and build a dynamic relationship of emotional therapy between partners.

Unlike informative companionship, telling troubles is asymmetrical in Japanese dating. Of the men, 41 per cent often "discussed the girl's emotional problems" before engagement. Barely half as many of the women (23 per cent) said the man often "told her about his emotional problems." (The questions are not quite identical, but the difference in percentages is probably meaningful.)

Why do Japanese girls tell their troubles more often than their partners? For one thing, men in most countries are less sensitive emotionally and probably feel less need to tell in the first place (Tyler, 1956). Also, Japanese men (presumably more than men in equalitarian countries) hesitate to share problems even when they have them. Men, after all, are the superior sex, supposed to solve their own problems and not lean on others for solace. (A similar difference appears after marriage when 43 per cent of the wives but only 22 per cent of the husbands "always" tell their troubles.) If Japanese men feel they have fewer problems to start with and are less apt to confess them, the search for emotional relief becomes characteristically feminine.

If telling troubles is standard practice for Japanese women but rare for Japanese men, we would expect the differences between men who tell and those who don't to be sharper than for women. Presumably variations in the premarital frequency for women depend on such situational factors as length of courtship or difficulty of problems. On the other hand, men who tell their troubles before they even get engaged are deviant individuals breaking cultural norms. They seem likely to become unusually communicative husbands.

Table 4–10 confirms our reasoning that premarital differences in male behavior are more predictive of marriage patterns than those in female behavior. Continuity after marriage is similar to that for informative companionship—straightforward for men but slightly reversed for short-courtship women who never get a chance to tell their troubles.

Premarital habits of crying on the partner's shoulder are not only related to continued emotional reliance after marriage but to the kind and effectiveness of therapeutic responses given by the partner and made by the self. Men not embarrassed to admit problems to their wives make particularly effective therapists. After marriage they often give helpful advice[1] rather than brushing off problems as unworthy of attention.[2] As a result, the one who tells his troubles feels appreciably better and is more satisfied with the partner's understanding of his problems and feelings. Finally, these effective therapies are part of generally satisfactory marriage patterns.

Such beneficent outcomes, however, occur less regularly in response to the woman's premarital problem-sharing than to the man's—for the peculiarly Japanese reasons we have suggested before. Presumably as Japanese courtship is extended in the future, feminine emotional reliance on the fiancé will more consistently portend an interactive marriage.

In the meantime, old-fashioned Japanese men prefer wives who keep their troubles to themselves. They prefer to hide their own troubles, too. Although

1. 50 per cent "often" *vs.* 33 per cent "never" tellers.
2. 19 per cent *vs.* 30 per cent respectively.

Table 4–10—Marital Consequences of Pre-engagement Emotional Reliance

FREQUENCY OF TELLING EMOTIONAL PROBLEMS

	Never	Seldom	Sometimes	Often	Net Difference
Continuity after Marriage					
Husband tells troubles now	1.96	2.06	2.47	2.87	+0.91
Wife tells troubles now	2.75	2.67	3.03	3.39	+0.64
Benefits of Man's Telling Troubles					
Wife's Therapeutic Effectiveness	2.27	2.40	2.42	2.54	+0.27
Satisfaction with Understanding					
Husband's	4.22	3.97	4.31	4.37	+0.15
Wife's	4.28	4.17	4.20	4.62	+0.34
Comparative Marital Satisfaction					
Both satisfied	36.5%	33.0%	29.6%	50.0%	+13.5
Wife only	10.4	13.8	19.7	12.2	
Husband only	18.3	17.0	29.6	9.8	
Neither	34.8	36.2	21.1	28.0	
Total	100.0%	100.0%	100.0%	100.0%	
Minimum Number of Cases	115	94	71	82	
Benefits of Woman's Telling Troubles					
Husband's therapeutic effectiveness	2.35	2.24	2.39	2.49	+0.14
Satisfaction with Understanding					
Husband's	4.44	3.71	3.98	4.47	+0.03
Wife's	4.30	4.10	4.10	4.54	+0.24
Comparative Marital Satisfaction					
Both satisfied	37.1%	32.1%	28.1%	45.3%	+8.2
Wife only	6.5	10.7	13.5	17.3	
Husband only	27.4	7.1	17.7	18.7	
Neither satisfied	29.0	50.0	40.6	18.7	
Total	100.0%	99.9%	99.9%	100.0%	
Minimum Number of Cases	62	56	96	150	

mutually satisfied and wife-satisfied marriages are common among frequent tellers, husband-satisfied marriages are more common among never-tellers.

Pre-engagement emotional dependence, then, is a feminine characteristic. However, the rare Japanese men who imitate this feminine pattern before marriage make extraordinarily satisfactory husbands. To be a good husband ordinarily means to acquire a good wife; marital satisfaction therefore reaches its peak for couples where the man dares tell his troubles even before getting engaged.

COMPARATIVE EFFECTIVENESS

So far our five discussion topics have been treated separately. It is apparent, however, that many possess similar patterns. Because all utilize the same responses, we can compare them statistically to see what most effectively previews satisfactory marriages for our Japanese men and women.

Table 4–11—Comparative Effect of Five Discussion Topics on the
Marital Satisfaction of Men and Women

Discussion Topic	NET DIFFERENCE IN MARITAL SATISFACTION*		
	Mutual	Wife's	Husband's
Personal events since last date	+15.4	+1.22	+0.66
Both partners' vocational plans	+13.8	+1.16	+0.56
Individual emotional problems	+8.2	+0.83	—0.02
National and international politics	+7.2	+1.02	—0.05
Traditional and modern husband-wife relationships	+4.9	+0.64	+0.12

* Aggregate satisfaction of those "often" discussing *minus* those "never" discussing the topic. Difference between percentages mutually satisfied; difference between mean satisfaction for all wives and for all husbands.

Inferences from Table 4–11 are that the most effective means of promoting marital satisfaction for both sexes include informative companionship and discussing vocational plans. Also highlighted is the consistent difference between the sexes in the usefulness of discussion for predicting marital satisfaction. The more women discuss these topics before getting engaged, the happier their marriages turn out to be, but for men, two topics predict negatively. Moreover, no topic makes as much difference to men as it does to women.

Perhaps this, too, reflects a society in a state of transition. Japanese men are still old-fashioned enough to prefer wives who don't talk about politics and don't burden them with emotional problems. Marital asymmetry results from the contrasting needs and preferences of a rising group of women *vs.* a challenged group of men. The feudal legacy of subordination and discrimination has been felt so keenly by Japanese women that they respond warmly to men who demonstrate respect for their opinions by entering into premarital and marital discussions. Men, however, feel more ambivalent about surrendering old prerogatives and learning to cope with the intellectual and emotional welfare of their wives. There are advantages, after all, in having a servant wife. And if one wants to keep a servant in her place, one shouldn't talk politics with her.

Although some topics ambiguously disappoint the men while they please the wives, the proportion of mutually-satisfied couples rises with discussion of every topic. This is not so for the involvement of couples with outside parties. Although limited involvement with families and friends is mutually beneficial, couples can become so involved externally that their relationship to each other suffers. Perhaps this explains the difference between discussion and sociability. The former is a purely internal activity and therefore builds a more dynamic relationship. By contrast, external activity weakens the relationship when one partner becomes more involved with outsiders than with the spouse, or when the couple are jointly dominated by outsiders. In postfeudal Japan, both threats are especially strong from the husband's quarter.

Just as families and friends may become "too much of a good thing," so may time. Moderately long courtships enable love and understanding to grow. But prolonged courtships may also result from external obstacles or inner doubts signifying trouble ahead. Otherwise, why not get married? The fact that

Japanese courtships begin so late means that delay is seldom necessary because lovers are too young to get married. By contrast, in the United States, long courtships seldom have the ominous meaning they often do in Japan (Burgess and Wallin, 1953).

Dating, on the other hand, is an interpersonal activity with generally beneficial results, especially counteracting the danger of excessive parental influence in *miai* marriages.

Since some pre-engagement activities ambiguously affect the satisfactoriness of marriage, we cannot assume that the more a couple do together before engagement the happier they will be. Far less ambiguity applies, however, to continuity of behavior. Every type of pre-engagement activity produces more marital activity. In this sense, courtship sets the pattern for marriage. The only exceptions occur in courtships too short to allow relationships to unfold enough to glimpse their full potential. In such cases, inactivity may mean "no opportunity" rather than "no potential." With this exception, the courtship is father to the marriage. A familiar American saying is that one can look at her mother and see what a girl will look like twenty-five years hence. Similarly one can look at a dating pair and see what their marriage will be like. Even while going to the movies, they are laying the foundations of their marriage structure. And life subsequently will be constrained by the foundations they have laid.

Part II

Husband-Wife Relationships in Japan and the U.S.A.–An International Comparison

IF JAPAN is being Westernized, how far does it have to go to "catch up"? My original reason for going to Japan was to study a family system strikingly different from what I had known in America. What I found was not as different as I expected. However, comparison of the two will detail the similarities and differences between them (Chapter 5).

For scientific purposes, the crucial question is not simply how people behave in Japan and America but *why* and *so what*? What forces outside the family influence its shape (Chapter 6), and how do the inside forces of time and children alter that shape? (Chapter 7). Finally, what is the impact on the two partners of the ways they treat each other? How do they react subjectively to various action patterns and how do those patterns interact on each other? (Chapter 8).

The final three chapters offer an opportunity to test principles discovered in our earlier American investigation and see whether they hold up in a new setting. If they do, our confidence in their validity as principles of human behavior will increase. The very fact that Japan is so different makes this test more crucial than would a comparative study of European families.

When things seem to work differently in the two countries, we will be in a dilemma. Do environmental differences between the countries account for the difference? Were the measuring instruments different or were the samples different? In other words, are the differences characteristic of the two societies as a whole or are they more apparent than real?

The problems involved in making international comparisons are innumerable. (They are discussed in greater detail in Blood and Takeshita, 1963, and in Blood, Hill, Michel, and Safilios-Rothschild, 1965.)

My American couples are a cross-section sample of the Detroit metropolitan area. Wives alone were interviewed (in the Spring of 1955) so there is no data directly from husbands. The original report was published by the Free Press in 1960 under the title *Husbands and Wives: the Dynamics of Married Living* (by Blood and Wolfe).

Since the Tokyo sample was restricted to postwar marriages, it is concentrated in the early stages of the family life cycle. To make the Detroit sample more comparable, I decided to discard couples who had been married long enough to have children age 13 or older. However, the proportion of childless young couples is much higher in the Tokyo sample and the average length of marriage correspondingly less. Hence it is only in the life-cycle tables in Chapter 7 that the two groups are really matched on length of marriage and presence of children. Even there, the American couples have *more* children—which seems a pity, scientifically, but is one of the differences between ambitious Japan and affluent America.

The other major problem relates to social status variables such as occupation, income, and education. The Japanese sample is almost exclusively middleclass. Does that mean we should throw out our working-class Detroiters? Or does the fact that the latter own their own homes and one or two cars and have five times the income (but not necessarily the purchasing power) of the Japanese sample mean that they are not so different after all? After struggling with this question, I decided not to attempt to match on status. So we must remember that the comparison is between a cross-section sample of 405 young Detroit couples and a vanguard group of 444 young Tokyo couples. However, for certain purposes, breakdowns by education, occupation, and other socio-economic variables in Chapter 6 will enable us to explore some of these complexities.

THE SHAPE OF MARRIAGE 5

IN JAPAN AND THE U.S.A.

BEFORE making a detailed analysis of the way marriages function in our two samples, we need to see how their profiles compare. What are the similarities and the differences in their everyday style of operating?

Our primary resource is American and Japanese wives answering similar interview questions. In some cases phraseology was deliberately (or accidentally!) modified. Moreover, we must keep in mind that the Tokyo questions were in Japanese. Hence, what appear to be equivalent English wordings may involve connotational differences introduced in translation despite elaborate attempts to avoid them. When languages differ as sharply as English and Japanese it is often impossible to translate concepts "exactly" (see Blood and Takeshita, 1963, for examples).

Sometimes we have information for Japan alone from husbands, but we unfortunately have no equivalent American data at all. This lack is frustrating, but the addition of the former is often illuminating. Hence, this chapter involves a double set of comparisons: Americans *vs.* Japanese on the one hand, and husbands *vs.* wives on the other. This tests both the similarity of marriages in the two samples and also the degree of symmetry within Japanese marriages.

Power Structure

For reasons discussed by Blood and Takeshita (1963) and by Blood, Hill, Michel, and Safilios-Rothschild, it is always difficult to compare power structures

Figure 5-A. Decision Making in Tokyo and Detroit Marriages

Who Decides	Husband's Mean Power	Tokyo Decision	% Equal*	Detroit Decision	% Equal*
Husband always	4.0				
	3.5			Husband's job choice	3
Husband more than wife	3.0	When to have sexual intercourse	33	Choice of automobile	25
	2.5	Whether to buy life insurance	31	Whether to buy life insurance	42
		Choice of radio, TV program	45	Choice of vacation place	70
		Choice of holiday outing place	53	Choice of house, apartment	59
Equal	2.0	Cost of obituary, congratulatory gift	58	Whether wife should work	18
		Choice of children's school	72		
	1.5	Whether wife can buy new clothes	31	Choice of family doctor	46
		What special lessons for children	51	Weekly food budget	33
Wife more than husband	1.0	Amount of children's spending money	16		
	0.5				
Wife always	0.0				

*Percentage of couples reporting equal decision-making.

cross culturally. Since cutting points between husband-dominant, equalitarian, and wife-dominant structures are arbitrary, differences within a culture are relative. Hence, it is impossible with present methods to compare the percentage of husband-dominant power structures in different countries.

When dealing with particular decisions, comparison is more reliable. However, even this is complicated by the fact that many decisions studied in Detroit were irrelevant to Tokyo (for example, the fact that in 1959 practically nobody in Japan owned a car). For various reasons (which hindsight suggests weren't always good ones!) most of the Detroit power questions were discarded and replaced by new ones. Our comparisons must therefore be cautious and impressionistic.

The only identical item in the two studies is: "Who usually makes the final decision about whether or not to buy some life insurance?" Despite possible differences in the role of life insurance in the two societies, decisions are remarkably similar in the two samples. The fact that the Tokyo group is slightly more husband oriented does not prove a general patriarchal tendency, since middle-class husbands within the Detroit sample also make this decision more often.

When the overall patterns are compared, the two countries are remarkably similar. Masculine influence is greater in areas of special masculine interest: his occupation, financial security, sex, and the family car. Conversely, the wife influences decisions in her specialties: housekeeping and child-rearing.

In between is an area where decision-making tends to be not only equally balanced in frequency but conducted jointly. (A breakdown of "equal" decisions in Tokyo shows that they are made "always together" about ten times as often as "50/50 separately." Hence, we can treat equal decision-making as generally shared.) This area of joint concern includes choices about how to spend leisure time—and decisions of overwhelming mutual importance to the family such as what house or apartment to take in Detroit or what school to send the child to in Tokyo. The latter matters more in Tokyo than in the United States because access to subsequent schools and employers is heavily influenced by personal and institutional ties in Japan's particularistic, nonmobile social structure.

Generally speaking, the rank order of means corresponds to the percentage of joint decisions in both samples. However, there are two major exceptions. Whether the wife buys new clothes in Tokyo or whether she goes to work in Detroit is seldom decided jointly. For both questions there is an extraordinary diversity. In Tokyo clothing decisions, powerful wives are partially balanced by powerful husbands (27 per cent to 10 per cent), while in Detroit, the split over the wife's employment is deadlocked 33 per cent to 33 per cent at the unilateral extremes. Perhaps these decisions are controversial because they allocate resources between husband and wife. If the wife buys new clothes (for her exclusive use, unlike a house or a joint gift), less money will be available to the husband. If the wife goes to work, the family's financial resources will increase but the wife's time resources will decrease (forcing the husband to become a substitute housekeeper). Such issues pit one partner against the other (each one's gain is the other's loss). So they are difficult to settle by accommodative methods. Ultimately many couples decide unilaterally when no consensus emerges.

Except for these controversial decisions focused on the wife's activities, the emphasis in both societies is equalitarian. Equality of the sexes is a compound of joint decision-making in areas of mutual concern and unilateral deciding in areas that concern only one partner. Given the limitations of our measuring instruments, the least we can say is that no difference in power structure appears between the two groups. This doesn't mean that there may not be differences in untapped facets of decision-making. Even less does it mean there may not be other groups within the two countries whose power structures are less equalitarian. Especially in Japan, where we so often refer to our sample as a "vanguard" segment, it seems likely that other groups are more patriarchal—the older generation, provincial groups from rural Tohoku or traditionalistic Kyushu, and so forth. In the next chapter we will see which segments within our Tokyo and Detroit samples are less equalitarian in order to gain a fuller sense of possible international variations. For the moment, however, the general pattern of power is remarkably similar.

The Division of Labor

Having mentioned the "servant wife" concept in discussing traditional Japanese marriages, we should expect Tokyo wives to do more housework than Detroit wives. Indeed we took it so much for granted that Japanese housewives do practically all the dishwashing, cooking, grocery shopping, and cleaning up at home that we were afraid we would be laughed at if we repeated those American questions in Tokyo. Hence, we either discarded them or gave them a husband-oriented twist in the hope that a few Tokyo husbands might occasionally share in them.[1]

Take for example the question of foodshopping. Most Detroit wives shop once or twice a week at a supermarket many blocks from home. Buying in large quantities, they can hardly carry the heavy bags home. In some cases, a wheeled basket solves the problem. More often, the wheeled vehicle is the family car. Since the husband usually drives to work and few families have more than one car, the shopping must be done when the husband is home. This increases the possibility of doing it jointly, because men do most of the driving.

1. "The urban husband's and wife's activities remain clearly segregated, and the husband has virtually no household duties. In a very recent survey of a modern middle-class Tokyo apartment area, for example, fewer than 1 per cent of the husbands participated in cleaning, shopping, cooking or washing. The only work that was done by as many as 8 per cent of the fathers was putting up of the bedding and caring for the children" (Vogel, 1961a, citing Koyama, 1960). In my sample, the percentage of participant husbands is higher but marriages are still basically segregated.

In Japan, by contrast, the first supermarket in the entire country opened in Yokohama in 1959. Even though Tokyo department stores have large food departments, few housewives depend on them for ordinary supplies. Instead, neighborhood food shops (butcher shop, fish market, fruit store, and so forth) within easy walking distance of home are the main source for everyday shopping. The term *everyday* is literally correct because tiny Japanese kitchens lack storage facilities for keeping food fresh from day to day. Most housewives shop at least once a day for small quantities of food.

Department stores are more frequently used for special occasions. Hence, we thought husbands might stop on their way home from work to buy some special delicacy to suit their own taste. Figure 5–B shows, however, that Japanese husbands do less specialty shopping than American husbands do of general food shopping.

The husband's clothes are another case in point. Although we unfortunately have no parallel question from Detroit, it seems doubtful that American wives so consistently buy his ordinary clothes (such as underwear and handkerchiefs). In Tokyo, 55 per cent of the wives carry this responsibility exclusively, contrasted with only 2 per cent of the husbands. Even more strange to Americans is the task of picking up after the husband undresses. The American norm is clearly self-reliance and any man who leaves his clothes strewn around is sure to be labelled "messy." But the traditional Japanese norm is for the wife to be valet. Even in our vanguard sample, wives typically do all the picking up (41 per cent of the wives—twice the proportion of self-reliant men). To be sure, the lack of closets in most Japanese homes would cause many an American husband to call for help in folding up his clothes so they could be laid away successfully in a dresser drawer. Nevertheless, the dominant note in the Japanese pattern seems to be not technical competence so much as personal service: "The servant wife at your service, sir!"[2]

Home repairs are carried out in different settings which make comparison difficult. Most Detroit families live in their own homes where repairs are often structural in nature. Since all of our Tokyo families live in apartment houses, it is the government's responsibility to do most of the repairing. Perhaps if we asked who repairs precisely the same objects, masculine mechanical skill would be as important in Tokyo as in Detroit.

Only where sheer biological factors are involved do the two groups behave the same. Carrying heavy objects in Tokyo and mowing Detroit lawns are done primarily by the sex with the sturdier physique and the larger muscles.

2. The traditional norm of personal service is revealed in the comments of a middle-aged housewife on the radical ways of the younger generation:

> Young wives no longer take abuse without complaining the way my mother did. Some of the youngest wives are very demanding. I know a couple of university grads where the wife expects the husband to do as much as she does around the house, like shining his own shoes. She is a very dominant woman—she makes him shine his own shoes!

This woman complained that in a sudden rainstorm her husband would never notice clothes getting wet outside, much less help her retrieve them. Nor would he ever answer the phone, no matter how busy she was.

Figure 5–B. Task Performance in Tokyo and Detroit Households

Who Performs Task	Wife's Task Performance	Tokyo		Detroit	
		Task	% Equal*	Task	% Equal*
Wife always	4.0				
	3.5	Buying husband's ordinary clothes	19	Doing evening dishes	15
Wife more than husband	3.0	Buying husband's favorite foods	26	Straightening living room for company	20
		Helping children's homework	17	Getting husband's breakfast	5
		Disciplining the children	35		
	2.5	Putting away the *futon* bedding	15	Grocery shopping	30
		Putting husband's clothes away (after he undresses)	7		
Equal	2.0	Taking children out Sundays	72	Keeping track of money and bills	34
	1.5	Making repairs at home	14		
Husband more than wife	1.0	Carrying heavy objects	9	Shoveling sidewalk	10
	0.5			Mowing the lawn	9
				Making home repairs	9
Husband always	0.0				

*Percentage of couples reporting equal task-performance.

This efficient arrangement has not always existed in Japan. In the feudal era, patriarchal prestige led servant wives to assume staggering burdens despite biological weakness. Even today, peasant wives labor in rice paddies alongside their husbands, and poverty-stricken urban women labor on road construction. For the middle-class, however, chivalry has arrived and freed women from burdens they used to bear.

With some exceptions, then, the division of labor in Tokyo is skewed in the wife's direction. This is not entirely a matter of ideological differences between the two countries. It is partly a functional adaptation to different stages of economic development. Japan's standard of living may be skyrocketing but it still has a long way to soar to catch up with America's. So Japanese husbands labor longer hours away from home. (The standard work week for Detroit husbands is 40 hours, for Tokyo husbands, 50. Japanese men are thus less available for domestic tasks. In this sense, servant wives are balanced by hardworking husbands in the total division of labor (*outside* as well as *inside* the home).

Feminine drudgery is compounded by inadequate household equipment. Old-fashioned kitchens were tiny, gloomy, and inefficient. In urban apartments they might be just an alcove off the living room or double as an entry way. The stove was hardly more than a hot plate (electric burner or gas jet). The sink usually had only one tap—for cold water. Even new refrigerators hold only one day's food supply, just like the traditional ice box (so small the iceman rides a bicycle). The inconvenience of shopping in decentralized specialty shops has already been mentioned. Add the lack of ready-to-serve foods and it can be seen why Japanese husbands would hesitate to invade the kitchen even if they had the time.

Technological change is whirling through Japan. Electric rice-cookers, portable washing machines, tiny vacuum cleaners, and other adaptations to the Japanese scene are selling like proverbial hotcakes. Economic development will slash the housewife's working hours in Japan as it has in the U.S.A. In the meantime, many a Japanese housewife has stubborn facts to contend with as well as a stubborn husband.[3]

SPECIALIZATION

The Japanese division of labor may be skewed more than the American one, but both are equally specialized. Unlike decisions which are usually shared in both countries, most tasks are performed unilaterally. This can be inferred by noticing the lower percentages of equal task performance in Figure 5–B compared with Figure 5–A. The difference is sharpened when it is realized that even these "equality" percentages are skewed to separate-but-equal performance for several household tasks, whereas they are always skewed to togetherness in decision-making. It can be seen more precisely in the fact that every Japanese

3. The net result of the time-consuming nature of women's work in Japan is that women have less time to spend on self-cultivation or on eating and sleeping than their husbands (Koyama, 1961).

task except child-rearing and every American task except keeping track of the money and bills is more often performed exclusively by the customary-sexed person than by any sharing of responsibilities whether equal or unequal. Money and bills, it seems, are modally shared because they include administrative tasks full of power implications. Taking the children out on Sundays (the only Japanese task which is generally shared) is also not pure work because parents enjoy the chance to be together after a busy week apart. It is more of a recreational activity than a chore. Pure chores, then, with neither power dividends nor recreational dividends, tend to be assigned to one sex or the other for solitary performance. In Japan the wife does more things alone than in the United States, but in both countries the basic pattern is sex-linked specialization.

Companionship

From the sharp, rigid division of labor in Japan we would expect less companionship between husbands and wives in leisure-time activities. Segregation of the sexes in task areas removes a potential foundation for integration of the sexes in nontask areas.

More concretely, the economic underdevelopment that shapes the Japanese division of labor also impedes recreational companionship by reducing available leisure. So much energy must be devoted to achieving a higher standard of living that little is left for anything else. Nor are material resources available. There is too little money for purchasing spectator entertainment, recreational equipment, or transportation to recreation sites.

The net result is that Japanese family life is more task oriented and less leisure oriented than American family life. Paradoxical as it sounds, the world's highest material consumption shifts concern from material things to non-material activities: social, educational, recreational, and spiritual. For example, together American families attend church, take vacation trips, go to concerts, and play their own musical instruments. Classical recorded music, available in Tokyo chiefly in coffeehouses, is part of the background for daily activity in many American homes. This is not to say that spare time is always put to good use in the United States but that the enjoyment of leisure is possible here to an extent hardly dreamed of overseas. Japan is too busy trying to acquire modern gadgets to be able to afford much family frivolity.

This is not to cast aspersions on Japanese character. It *is* to say that the accusation that Americans are "materialistic" while Japanese are "spiritual" or "aesthetic" is ill founded. Americans and Japanese alike are creatures of their environments and Japanese circumstances are harsh compared with American affluence.

We should expect this to affect most heavily those activities that require the most resources. Verbal communication between husband and wife should be impaired least, but activities that require facilities for entertaining, cost money for traveling, or consume many hours should be appreciably reduced in Japan.

EXTERNAL SOCIABILITY

Contact with persons outside the household may occur either in the home or elsewhere, but is *external* in the sense of involving other persons.

In the United States, contact often occurs within the home. So important is entertaining guests that Blood and Wolfe (1960) designate a major role of the middle-class housewife as "hostess-companion." The living room in winter and patio in summer provide space for home-cooked meals, light refreshments, or cocktails for countless guests.

Japanese entertaining is throttled by limited space and equipment. The per capita square footage of indoor and outdoor space is substantially less in crowded Tokyo than in sprawling Detroit. Kitchens that are inefficient for family purposes hardly lend themselves to serving guests. Hence, what little entertaining is done at home is apt to be catered (sent in ready made from neighborhood food shops) at a fancy price. Or if meager accommodations are unworthy of an honorable guest, he will be entertained in a private room in a restaurant, thus incurring costs not only for food but for facilities at a budget-taxing price.

Given inadequate facilities and funds, entertaining is restricted chiefly to social obligations. Because a sense of duty is strong in Japanese culture, care is taken not to impose an obligation on others to reciprocate with entertainment they could not afford. This sensitivity further inhibits handing out invitations broadcast in lighthearted American fashion. To be sure, Emily Post encourages social reciprocity too, but the obligation to return favors is taken less seriously and frequently discharged wholesale in massive cocktail parties or barbecues.

If social invitations are narrowly focused in Japan, we would expect them to be concentrated on relatives to the neglect of friends.

Kinship companionship—Not only should kin contact be relatively important in Japan, but we might expect it to be more common than in America. Disregarding for the moment the problem of resources, how important is the kin network supposed to be in the two countries?

The conventional Japanese norm, for relatives to live together, has never been expected in American culture. To be sure, in Japan this applies primarily to eldest sons—and to younger sons more than to daughters married into other men's families. Nevertheless, the sense of belonging to a family line, membership in a common lineage, obligation to honor one's ancestors, and responsibility for aged parents, are familistic notions unparalleled in the United States. The arranged marriage system itself illustrates the importance of relatives in Japan.

Motivationally, then, we would expect heavy pressure for maintaining contact with kin, particularly with parents. It may be, however, that the social revolution in Japan creates countermotives. A younger generation that labels its elders "feudal" may feel so estranged that they wish to avoid their parents. At the very least, contact must be strained by divergent values, attitudes, and practices. Such strains would counteract the sense of obligation to visit parents—

but not siblings. Since our Tokyo data make no distinction between generations of relatives, we can only hypothesize that rebellious couples see parents more from a sense of duty and siblings purely for pleasure.

Table 5–1—Kinship Companionship in Tokyo and Detroit

FREQUENCY OF GETTING TOGETHER WITH RELATIVES*		Tokyo	Detroit
200†	Every day or almost every day‡	—	32%
50	Once or twice a week	11%	39
20	A few times a month	24	14
10	Once a month	25	4
2	A few times a year	26	8
1	Less often	12	3
0	Never	2	0
	Total	100%	100%
	N	444	405

* Questions were asked as follows:
  Tokyo: "How often do you and your husband visit back and forth with your parents and other relatives?"
  Detroit: "How often do you (wife) see your (relatives)?"
  This question was repeated for each relative of the wife and husband named in a complete listing. Detroit statistics represent an aggregate sum of the frequencies reported for visiting each relative's household.
  † These numbers indicate the weights used in computing mean frequencies in later chapters.
  ‡ Response categories were identical in Tokyo and Detroit, but frequencies greater than once a week were so rare in Tokyo that the first three responses were grouped together into an at least once a week category.

How do these counterbalancing forces come out? International comparison is complicated by the fact that kin contact was a major interviewing topic in Detroit. It therefore covered the kinship networks of husband and wife more thoroughly than our single Japanese question. Nevertheless, contact is so much more frequent in Detroit that the difference could hardly be attributed to Japanese house-wives who failed to remember some of their visiting.

Another problem arises from the focus of the Japanese question on kinship companionship—shared husband-wife contact with relatives. The Detroit question is not limited in this way and covers solitary contacts made by one partner alone. However, a separate question asked: "Who is it that usually sees your (relatives)?" The total Detroit sample answered as follows: whole family, 82 per cent; parents without children, 10 per cent; wife only, 5 per cent; husband only, 2 per cent; wife and children only, 1 per cent, for a total of 100 per cent.

The vast bulk of kin contacts in Detroit are made jointly by husbands and wives. If we reduced the Detroit statistics by 10 per cent to allow for occasional contacts that lack marital companionship, the Detroit couples would still have far more contact than the Tokyo sample. The median frequency in Detroit would still be once a week instead of Tokyo's once a month.

Of course our couples may be unusual for Tokyo, to say nothing of the rest of Japan. Our research design excluded families sharing a household with relatives. But intrahousehold contacts were not included in the Detroit statistics either, as the unit of analysis was contact between separate households. Conceivably, families sheltering relatives are particularly familistic and also have contact with outside relatives. If so, their exclusion may lower the Japanese frequency.

More likely is the possibility that residents of new housing projects include migrants from the hinterlands whose contact with relatives is severed by distance. We have no data on this from Tokyo. However, migration is also frequent in Detroit; only 26 per cent of our sample were born there. Analysis of the Detroit data by Aiken and Goldberg shows that migration is often joint, so that single adult migrants subsequently invite other relatives to Detroit to share the advantages of the big city. Presumably the same thing happens in Tokyo.

We must not assume, just because kinship *companionship* is less frequent in Tokyo, that the same is true of kinship *contact*. Japanese husbands may be too busy to accompany their wives on visits to relatives. Perhaps kin contact in Tokyo is primarily a woman-to-woman affair, as it is in East London (Young and Willmott, 1957). There the primary bond between mother and daughter is hardly disturbed when the daughter marries. In Japan, however, where marriage traditionally severs the wife's relationship to her mother, we would not expect so feminine a bias to kin contact.

Because we lack additional data, these speculations are inconclusive. Our primary concern, however, is not the strength of the kin network but the strength of the marriage bond. On this subject our data are unequivocal. Our Detroit couples have four times as many joint contacts with relatives. Insofar as expeditions and entertaining are mutually enjoyed activities, external sociability with kin contributes more to American marital solidarity than to Japanese marriages.

Friendship companionship—The greater importance of external sociability in American marriages is intensified by contact with nonrelatives.[4]

Fumi Takano contrasted this aspect of family life in Japan and the United States after studying at Radcliffe in 1953–54:

> In America, a man and his wife form one social unit. That is, at nearly all social functions a man is accompanied by his wife, or rather, a woman is accompanied by her husband. But in Japan, on most social occasions, men alone are invited. I heard the other day of the case of a Fulbright professor, and his wife, who invited the faculty, and their wives, of the [Japanese] college they were assigned to, and found to their

4. In the Detroit interviews, nonrelatives were originally subdivided into neighbors, colleagues, and other friends, but for purposes of this comparison they have been reassembled in a composite aggregate. However, because we have not added the data for the three sub-categories but have used each family's maximum frequency in any category (usually the neighbors) the final result underestimates the total frequency of seeing friends in Detroit. On the other hand, though the context refers to *getting together* and to *you folks*, the Detroit respondents may have wondered whether the question meant genuine interaction and joint interaction, respectively. Conceivably, therefore, more carefully equated questions would narrow the difference between the samples. Even so, the difference is so enormous that it can hardly be entirely due to methodological discrepancies.

great surprise that most of the wives had never met each other. That was not at all an exceptional case. Japanese women seldom attend social functions. Men go visiting their friends by themselves, they go to parties by themselves, they go to movies by themselves or with their friends. And most Japanese women would never think of going out with their husbands, leaving their children at home.

Similarly, a twenty-seven-year-old informant reported:

I am never invited to go to a wedding with my husband if it is his friend that is getting married, nor is he invited if it is my friend. We were married at the Heian Shrine in Kyoto. Most of the guests were my husband's parents' male friends. Even though both sexes were invited, the wives failed to come if they didn't know my husband's father.

Vogel (1963) describes the paralyzing impact of uncertainty on how to behave in the strange and unfamiliar role of couple-to-couple sociability that makes the first venture of pioneers less than pure enjoyment:

When talking with us, many [Japanese women] expressed envy of American wives who go out with husbands, and many were curious as to what it would be like. Several went so far as to try it for the first time during our stay, but reported that they were too tense to enjoy themselves. When out with husbands and their friends, they have to be so careful to behave properly that it is difficult to go beyond polite pleasantries. Moreover, they must be so retiring that they generally prefer the more relaxed times with their lady friends. One wife, upon hearing about a husband and wife going on a trip for a few days, responded, "How nice," but after a moment's reflection added, "but what would they talk about for so long?"

Table 5–2—Friendship Companionship in Tokyo and Detroit

FREQUENCY OF GETTING TOGETHER WITH FRIENDS*		Tokyo	Detroit
300†	Every day‡	—	14%
200	Almost every day	—	8
50	Once or twice a week	4%	41
20	A few times a month	11	17
10	Once a month	26	10
2	A few times a year	36	7
1	Less often	12	(1 case)
0	Never	11	3
	Total	100%	100%
	N	444	405

* The following questions were asked:
   Tokyo: How often do you and your husband get together with friends?
   Detroit: Apart from seeing their relatives, people may also get together with their neighbors. About how often do you folks see any of your neighbors? About how often do you folks get together outside of work with any of the people you or your husband work with? And about how often do you get together with other friends?
   Statistics reported here are the maximum frequency of getting together with any one of these three categories of friends (not an aggregate summation of the three questions).
   † Weights used in computing mean frequencies in later chapters.
   ‡ Response categories were identical in Tokyo and Detroit, but frequencies greater than once a week were so rare in Tokyo that the first three responses were grouped together as "at least once a week."

Taken at face value, Table 5-2 shows Detroit social occasions with friends typically once a week compared to only a few times a year in Tokyo. This suggests a difference on the order of twenty to one. Our earlier discussion suggested that the limited resources of Japanese couples were likely to cut more sharply into nonobligatory sociability with peers than into kin contact. This seems indeed to be the case.

This poverty of friendship companionship is striking in a group consisting primarily of love match couples whose marriages sprang from peer relations, who usually had common friends at work, and who double dated friends five times in nine months (the equivalent of seven or eight times a year). This suggests that friendship companionship declines after marriage in Japan, whereas it is generally assumed to increase in the United States.

That assumption may not be true. It is based on the hypothesis that solitary dating predominates when couples are not yet married, but that once married, they turn their attention outward. This shift—if it occurs at all—may not involve an absolute increase in external sociability but a relative increase resulting from decreased pair dating. For the Tokyo sample, however, there is hardly even a relative shift. Before engagement, there are five dating contacts with friends compared to just under fifty exclusive dates (a ratio of less than one in ten). After marriage, there are approximately three dates per year with friends compared to two a month without them (one to eight). This is hardly a trend. Apparently, both before and after marriage, Japanese dating is overwhelmingly restricted to the partner.

The nonuse of the home as a facility for entertaining is clearly implied by the Tokyo statistics. Beyond that, however, even couple-to-couple sociability utilizing commercial facilities is strictly limited. We have mentioned money before as a deterrent to nights out on the town. Yet with close friends there is no reason why going Dutch or reciprocal entertaining should be any more expensive than solitary dates.

Perhaps there is a difference in "national character." Perhaps the large proportion of resources that American married couples devote to activities with friends results from our ease at making friends. Visitors from abroad often remark on the openness of the American character, the friendly smile for strangers, the easy approachability. The Japanese reserve, fear of entangling alliances, and reliance on proper introductions that make the *miai* so valuable a gateway to courtship, must bar the way to friendship between married couples.[5]

5. Bennett and McKnight, 1956, state:

Americans and perceptive Japanese alike have observed . . . that "Japanese are so shy"; that "it takes longer for a Japanese to open up than any other nationality" . . . The most common type of avoidance behavior found in modern Japanese social relations is an adaptation of an old idea in the new setting, namely, the Japanese concept of *enryo*, or "behavioral-emotional reserve." Originally descriptive of the proper behavior of the subordinate to the superordinate individual, *enryo*, in the modern period, describes proper behavior for any situation in which status positions are unclear: when in doubt, retire from the scene and avoid intimate interaction.

Apartment houses with common stairways filled with homogeneous young couples would be a beehive of sociability in most American cities. The setting after all is not so different from Park Forest, Illinois, whose young middle-class couples forged social bonds within weeks after moving into new apartments (Whyte, 1956). Not so in Tokyo. Despite the fact that every family interviewed in Tokyo lived in a public housing project, whereas most Detroiters live in single-family homes, friendship companionship is rare in the propinquitous Japanese setting and common in the isolated American setting.[6] Presumably if we were to interview Japanese families in more diversified housing, sociability would be even less.[7] In apartment houses, propinquity may eventually wear down reserve, but the few years that our Japanese couples had been living together were not sufficient to penetrate the barrier.[8]

External sociability is so rare that it contributes little to husband-wife companionship in Tokyo. This does not mean that there is no companionship of any kind, but that it assumes forms which cost less time, money, and—we should now add—social involvement. External sociability is not the crucial form of companionship in any case. If we define companionship as the couple's

---

6. In summarizing various researches on Japanese middle-class apartment life, Hoshino reports (1964):

> Human relations are fairly widespread in the same apartment house, but their intensity is not very strong; the greater the physical distance is, the more the "friendliness" scores [number of friends] decrease; husbands' relations with other apartment dwellers are weaker than wives', but even wives' relations with other apartment dwellers usually do not go further than chattering on the street; and the acquaintanceship in the same apartment house is nothing more than spontaneous neighboring relations. All of these facts lead to the conclusion that the large majority of *danchi* apartment dwellers belong to the privacy type and that close, friendly relations with neighbors are consciously avoided as much as possible.

7. Wagatsuma is not so sure:

> When we compare those who live in apartment houses with those who live in independent single houses, the apartment people are notorious for their indifference to the neighbors. Many people prefer living in apartment houses for this very reason, that is they don't have to be bothered by interaction with the neighbors. One reason is that there is usually only one entrance into the apartment unit and with a single little key it can be safely locked and left behind when the inhabitants go out. They don't have to worry about burglary or fire. But ordinary Japanese houses cannot be safely locked and left behind. They have very many windows on the first floor and at least two entrances which cannot be locked very well. Also many single houses are not fireproof. So neighbors must depend upon each other for protection from thieves and fire. This leads to more sociability.
>
> Another factor is that in neighborhoods where houses were not destroyed during the war, people were thrown together for the cooperative work of protecting their houses from air raids, of distributing the meagre rice rations, etc. They had not necessarily grown up together but they went through many things together as neighbors, while apartment houses are completely new phenomena and therefore have no history.

Unquestionably, interdependence promotes sociability. However, the crucial question for our purposes is one's readiness to seek out spontaneous sociability. This seems to be an American trait.

8. In this respect, our Tokyo apartment dwellers are like Young and Willmott's East Londoners who still felt isolated several years after moving to a suburban housing estate. Reserve is not an exclusively Japanese characteristic.

enjoyment of each other's presence in joint activity, that presence is most complete when others are excluded.

Exclusive dating—We have no data on exclusive dating in Detroit, so the Japanese statistics need not be discussed in detail.[9] We have already mentioned that our median Tokyo couple go out together just for a good time twice a month after marriage.[10] This dating companionship is the essence of marital companionship. It most directly reproduces premarital dating which is the essence of courtship.

Against the backdrop of Japanese history, this regular married dating stands forth in bold relief. Traditionally, entertainment was designed for men only and supplied by professional women while wives stayed home to defend paper and bamboo houses from theft and fire. The latter could come either from within (should an earthquake occur) or from without (as urban homes were huddled together). Only recently have pioneering builders freed wives from housesitting by using fireproof concrete construction and providing keys for locking doors from the outside:

> The result has been staggering. Getting keys to their own front doors has done more to Westernize many Japanese than any other single factor. The key will emancipate wives. Their husbands will now have no good excuse for leaving them at home and going off alone to the geisha house. (Hisaakira Kano, President of the government's Japan Housing Corporation, in an Associated Press report, 1959.)

When wives no longer have to guard their homes, they are free to go out with their husbands. The fact that they actually do so as often as twice a month suggests considerable motivation in both partners. Dating has captured the imagination of the younger generation. Its near ubiquity before marriage is extended even further after marriage (only 2 per cent of our couples never go out together).

Where they go we did not ask. Tokyo is well supplied with neighborhood movie theaters, night clubs, stage shows, concert halls, sports arenas, and other night life. For the day there are zoos, parks, and arboretums. In the biggest city in the world, there is no end of things to see and do for couples who enjoy each other's company as much as these do.

In this crucial form of companionship, Japanese marriages strikingly resemble American marriages.

9. To enable comparison with the frequency of getting together with relatives and friends (Tables 5–1 and 5–2), the frequency in per cents of going out as a couple for a good time is as follows: at least once a week, 23; a few times a month, 34; once a month, 32; a few times a year, 8; less often, 2; and never, 2 per cent (for a total of 101 per cent).

The vanguard nature of this group is suggested by a 1957 Ministry of Labor report that only 29 per cent of Tokyo women "go out with their husbands to see movies and for recreation. The percentage is only 3 per cent in rural areas, although even here the percentage is higher for the younger age groups and those with a higher education" (Tanino, 1961).

10. A 1962 Gallup poll reports that the typical American wife goes out with her husband three times a month, slightly more than our Japanese wives.

INTERNAL COMMUNICATION

The fact that our Tokyo couples date so often suggests that their relationship is fairly close. On the other hand, their sharper division of labor implies that they may nevertheless fall short of the American level of internal communication.

Table 5–3—Informative Companionship in Tokyo and Detroit

		TOKYO		DETROIT
*FREQUENCY OF TELLING DAY'S EVENTS**		*Wife tells*	*Husband tells*	*Husband tells*
300†	Every day	48%	26%	43%
200	Almost every day	41	41	22
50	Once or twice a week	10	24	16
20	A few times a month	1	9	8
10	Once a month‡	—	—	3
2	A few times a year	—	—	2
1	Less often	—	—	2
0	Never	—	—	4
	Total	100%	100%	100%
	N	444	444	405

* Questions were asked as follows:
  Tokyo: How often does your husband (wife) tell you about things that happened to him during the day?
  Detroit: When your husband comes home from work, how often does he tell you about things that happened there?
† Weights used in computing mean frequencies in later chapters.
‡ Response categories were similar in Tokyo and Detroit, but frequencies less than a few times a month were so rare in Tokyo that the last five responses were grouped together into a "less often" (than once or twice a week) category.

Table 5–3 shows that Tokyo husbands inform their wives of the day's events on returning from work almost as often as Detroit husbands. The norm for Detroit is daily reports whereas the mode in Tokyo is almost daily. The Detroit sample on the other hand, is more dispersed toward nonreporting, with 19 as contrasted with Tokyo's 9 per cent providing information less than once a week. This dispersion results from greater heterogeneity in education, since less educated, working-class husbands are more reticent than the middle class (as we shall see in the next chapter).

The table also shows that Japanese wives are more loquacious than their husbands—more than even the American husbands. This is probably a sex difference, since numerous psychological studies in the United States reveal a verbal facility in women that men do not match (Tyler, 1956). Given this innate loquacity, American wives may be even more informative than Japanese wives. On the other hand, sex differences are often reduced by the greater symmetry of American marriages.

We know for sure that American husbands are normally more informative than Japanese men. This difference may even be underestimated because a slight difference in question wording tends to restrict the American reference to work-related events.

What are the possible reasons for less informative companionship in Japan? We have already mentioned the interference created by a sharper division of labor and less leisure. These factors are intensified by voluntary segregation of what little leisure time there is. In a fashion reminiscent of working-class Americans, Tokyo salary-men linger after work with their company friends and give them some of the informative messages that might otherwise go to wives:

> Various polls have shown that it takes the husband an average of two to three hours to get home. While commuting may take a long time, it could not possibly take that long. It is rather that this is the time for recreation. After work, the men stop off someplace to sit and chat, have a drink and perhaps a bite to eat. . . . It is here that they talk and laugh freely about sports, national and world events or the daily happenings in the company, complain about bosses and wives, and receive the consolation of their friends and of the sympathetic girls behind the counter (Vogel, 1963).

A Japanese weekly magazine blames the wife's traditional seclusion for the husband's failure to find her a stimulating audience:

> In Japan the wife is nailed into the home and has few topics in common with her husband. This is the primary reason why her idol and master returns [from work] so slowly (cited from the *Shukan Asahi* of February 23, 1961, in Plath, 1964).

Some Japanese men feel it is unmanly to communicate with their wives. One businessman's reticence was described to me by his wife:

> My husband is a typical Japanese. He's never been abroad and was the eldest son, so his whole family respected him and he feels everyone should do things for him. He is thoughtful of others but doesn't express it very much. He doesn't say much, has to be asked what he is thinking. He's supposed to be home from work at 6:30 but because he has to wine and dine his customers he usually gets home about midnight. He always wants me to have a meal ready for him when he gets home. When we were first married, he never called to say when he would be home because he held that a man shouldn't have to think about his wife, especially in front of other men. But he has been watching other men in the office call their wives to avoid trouble, and now he calls to say he will be late, as a help in preparing his meal.

". . . especially in front of other men"—social pressure even reduces communication of useful messages.

Some Japanese couples feel that they are so intimate that they don't need to communicate overtly. Since the partner knows he is loved, there is no need to say so. However, without sufficient "spaces in their togetherness" (Gibran, 1923), their communication flow is liable to be shortcircuited. There must be two *separate* people if information is to flow from one person to another:

> In the Japanese family . . . "intimate but not personal" relations often exist between husband and wife. The wife may know really very little about her husband, and the

husband know very little about his wife, because they have so structured their relations that good communication between them as separate individuals is not possible (Caudill and Doi, 1963).

Could Japanese men have less to report than Americans? Perhaps their less mobile occupational system (the fact that men rarely change companies and that promotions depend on seniority) produces less exciting news to share. By contrast, Americans change not only jobs but fields in the course of fluid careers. Particularly the young men in our Detroit subsample are still on the make, still mobility oriented, still hoping they'll outstrip their fellows. Men striving for high stakes understandably bubble over with good news or bad news for wives dependent on the outcome. (Blood and Wolfe find that wives don't begin losing hope of further mobility for their husbands until after age 40.)

We should not exaggerate the difference, however. Using our conventional weighting procedure, the means are extraordinarily close: 174 for Tokyo husbands and 183 for Detroit. Obviously these Japanese men have come a long way from the conventional aloofness and mystery of haughty males who did not deign to reveal their "private" lives to servant wives. Westernization and modernization have obviously transformed these men as well as their wives.

In sum, the substantial lag in Japanese external sociability is only faintly echoed in diminished companionship between the partners. A new emphasis on love and understanding in Tokyo marriages has revolutionized the old relationship between the sexes, replacing it with a degree of reciprocity that is within sight of absolute symmetry and even closer to catching up with American informative companionship.

Emotional Therapy

We have commented before that therapy for hurt feelings begins with a cathartic act which resembles informative companionship except for its narrower focus on troublesome problems. We expect the international pattern of therapeutic utilization to resemble the one for informative companionship.

Table 5–4—Therapeutic Utilization of Spouse in Tokyo and Detroit

	TOKYO		DETROIT
FREQUENCY OF TELLING TROUBLES*	Husband tells	Wife tells	Wife tells
(4)† Always	22%	43%	22%
(3) Usually	28	33	26
(2) About half the time	16	10	29
(1) Seldom	27	12	19
(0) Never	7	2	4
Total	100%	100%	100%
N	444	444	405

* "When you have had a bad day, how often do you tell your husband (wife) your troubles?"
† The numbers in parentheses show the basis for computing mean intensities of therapeutic utilization in later tables.

This time we are in for a surprise. The Japanese wives are more verbal than the Americans. As usual, wives are more verbal than husbands. Indeed, a considerable minority (one-third) of Japanese husbands seldom or never tell their wives any troubles. Here the traditional male reserve appears again—maintaining a "front" even within fairly modern marriages. This reserve prevents the wives from nursing their husbands' wounds as much as they otherwise might. When men keep their troubles to themselves, their wives can hardly respond appropriately unless they are clairvoyant (which they apparently are supposed to be!).

The surprise is in the international comparison. We hypothesized that American wives would be more verbal than Japanese wives, but they turn out to be strikingly less so. Only half as many "always" tell their troubles and twice as many "never" do. The biggest difference is in the 50/50 category which is modal for American wives, whereas the Japanese distribution for both sexes is bimodal. We might suspect that bimodality results from combining two types of mate selection, but this is not the case. "About half" is consistently unpopular, no matter how the partners met.

Detroit wives are selective but Tokyo couples seldom are. The wives tell their troubles unusually freely, while a significant minority of the men are stoics. Apparently, conflicting norms in Japanese culture claim adherents.

Wagatsuma points out that:

> According to the Confucian feudal ethics, husbands were considered too much above their wives to tell them their troubles. On the other hand, wives were not supposed to bother their husbands with such trifles as women's and children's affairs. In the postwar democracy, sharing life was emphasized as something good. Phrases such as "sharing both happiness and unhappiness" or "sharing joy and troubles" were repeatedly stated as an important aspect of the new democratic marriage based on the equality of both sexes.

Perhaps the never-tellers adhere to the old norm and the always-tellers to the new, leaving few to practice selectivity.

Such contradictions appear in the village of Niiike where selfcontrol is valued and "restraint put on all expression of emotion", but at the same time even men are allowed "tears of sympathy for others" and people enjoy "*naniwabushi*, which are melodramatic recitals of tales of feudal loyalty, strife, and tragedy. Tears flow, though quietly, in contemplation of these melancholy themes." (Beardsley, Hall, and Ward, 1959.) In the United States, men are forbidden emotional expressiveness. On the other hand, neither do Americans cultivate selfcontrol as a virtue to the Spartan extreme found in Japanese culture. For Americans, therefore, midway selectivity of trouble-telling is more natural than the bimodal dispersion exhibited by our Japanese husbands.

Our main problem, though, is the wives' heavy dependence in time of trouble. One clue is their great emphasis on the importance of understanding in marriage. Whereas Detroit women glorify companionship (which means having "good" times together), Tokyo women bypass that concept to emphasize love and understanding. Even though the Japanese list encompassed twice as many alternatives (10 instead of 5), the Tokyo wives ranked understanding first twice as often as the Detroit wives (19 contrasted with 10 per cent) while their husbands chose it even more often (29 per cent). Both partners therefore want their problems understood—this requires greater dependence in crises.

So far, so good, but we haven't explained very much when we say that Japanese couples tell their troubles because they believe it is important to tell one's troubles! Why do they believe it is important in the first place? One reason may be that Japanese take their troubles more seriously than Americans.[11] This is a sweeping statement, to be sure, but it is one of my indelible impressions of Japan. I will never forget a long evening of tea and conversation in a tiny Hiroshima restaurant with my Hiroshima University professor-interpreter explaining the differences between Japanese culture and American culture as he had encountered them in travelling abroad and studying English literature. The Japanese, he said, have a profound appreciation of nature, and (not unconnected with it) a sense that life is tragic and short. This is symbolized in the cherry blossoms which one day are perfect in their fragile beauty but the next flutter to the ground and die. Japanese by the millions leave their work every spring to view those blossoms and drink rice wine to drown their nostalgic sense that they, too, will soon die.

Death is inevitable in every country. But in Japan it sometimes comes sooner. An extraordinarily high suicide rate among young adults testifies to their frequent sense of the futility of life in the face of an oppressive social structure. Low occupational mobility creates social security within the system but bars the door to those who fail university entrance examinations. In the feudal past, parental authority barred love-match marriages. Even today, emotional romaticism often combines with a Buddhist sense of the evanescence of life to make speeding trains and the proverbial volcanic craters popular ways out of personal disappointment.

Americans, by contrast, are incorrigible optimists. Nurtured on activistic Protestant Christianity, they call suicide "chicken." Born in a new country whose frontier just closed and whose labor force is remarkably mobile, they see life and opportunity unrolling endlessly. Characteristically, they make best sellers of books titled *The Power of Positive Thinking* or *Life Begins at 40*.

Perhaps, then, American wives (and surely husbands, too) can manage half their troubles alone because they take them lightly. Better to ignore troubles, forget them, cover them over with activity, than to brood about them cross-legged on the *tatami*.

This is not to say that American culture is better than Japanese culture. Perhaps we have something to offer each other. I came home from Japan feeling enriched by the sensitive perspective on life that I found in novels, movies, and lives.

From the standpoint of marriage itself, the American approach may be

11. Caudill endorses this observation.

worse. Personal needs could be met if the partner knew about them. But instead of turning to her husband, the American wife turns to the TV set or goes to bed. For the sake of her mental health, those are hardly the most therapeutic measures available (although she usually does seek help with more difficult problems).

From several perspectives, Japanese wives win first prize for emotional openness. After all our comments about emotional reserve this sounds inconsistent. Then we referred to reserve with strangers. Now the openness is with a legitimate audience—the marriage partner. In fact, public reserve probably increases the need for private openness.

But husbands and wives are not equally open. Communicating troubles is another aspect of feminine expressiveness—of words and of emotions. Not only verbal facility but emotional lability are feminine predispositions. (Tyler, *op. cit.*) Whatever the reasons, this is an era in which Japanese men and women do not behave the same. Our guess is that American men, too, are less emotionally expressive than their wives. (How husbands in the two countries compare remains to be discovered.)

With twice as many wives as husbands always telling their troubles, Japanese marriages are conspicuously asymmetrical. Another way of saying this is that Japanese wives are more emotionally dependent on their husbands than vice versa. Feminine dependence may reflect residual patriarchalism. When men are older, better educated and more worldly wise, we should expect them to offer shoulders to cry on. Perhaps the selectivity practiced by American wives requires more emancipation and more structural equality than Japanese wives have yet achieved. If so, feminine emotional dependence may decline in Japan as Westernization continues.

It may also be that Japanese wives do not so much desire individual autonomy as a new style of marital interdependence. More dedicated to marital modernization than their husbands, they are more emotionally expressive. Perhaps as Japanese men become more modernized, they too will become more expressive, making their marriages intensely interdependent.

On the other hand, without historical data, we cannot tell whether our wives' emotional dependence is a new achievement or simply an expression of the classic Japanese preference for being cared for by others. Caudill, 1962a, sees "tenderness . . . handled well and adaptively in Japan" as a result of the extension of mother-child nurturance into other relationships. Perhaps Japanese women have always relied on their husbands to take care of them more than autonomous American women. In any case, the difference between wives in our two samples is sharp and important.

THERAPEUTIC METHODS

Culture affects quantitative matters like therapeutic utilization. It even more sharply affects the kind of response the spouse makes.

American and Japanese responses differ strikingly in practically every category of Table 5-5.

Table 5–5—Therapeutic Responses in Tokyo and Detroit

	TOKYO		DETROIT
SPOUSE'S ACTIVITY OR VERBAL RESPONSE	*Wife's*	*Husband's*	*Husband's*
AFTER INDIVIDUAL TELLS TROUBLES	*Response*	*Response*	*Response*
Advice and suggestions	11%	37%	23%
Sympathy and affection	33	5	30
Help in solving the problem	13	20	9
Help in getting away from the problem	18	7	3
Dismissal as unimportant	14	25	7
Passive listening	11	7	21
Criticism and rejection	1	1	7
Total	101%	102%	100%
N*	399	434	381

* Omitting those who never tell their troubles and those whose response is not ascertained.

Japanese husbands rely particularly on authoritative, "strong man" responses appropriate to patriarchs. Either they tell their wives how to deal with problems, brush them off as unworthy of consideration, or assist in dealing with the problem. Although these methods differ among themselves, all place the man in an Olympian position, dispensing superior knowledge, descending to do battle with the forces of evil, or aloof and imperturbable.[12]

Their wives—to confirm the asymmetry of the picture—present a converse pattern. They are strongest where the men are weakest (sympathy and distraction), weaker where the men excel. Their favorite responses are characteristically feminine. Either they respond emotionally with sympathy and love, or they help their husbands forget their troubles (presumably by nurturant activities such as a hot bath, good food, or a back rub).[13]

American husbands give almost as much sympathy as Japanese wives (recalling the fact that they resemble each other in informative companionship). We might hazard a tentative generalization and say that American men have

12. The greater emphasis on giving and receiving advice in Japan is part of a broader pattern of dependence. Caudill, 1961b, states:

> In adulthood . . . the Japanese person tends to stay with the same company, university or hospital for the major part of his productive career. Moreover, in his relations with his supervisors he asks for and receives their advice on many matters which would be considered personal in the United States—problems in the family, marriage partners, financial difficulties and so forth.

The supervisor-employee relationship serves as a model for the husband-wife relationship.

13. Massages may have less of an explicitly sexual connotation in Japan than they would in the United States. Caudill, 1962b, finds a negative correlation between sexual and non-sexual physical gratification responses to TAT pictures:

> In brief, many everyday-life events in Japan, whether for children or adults, offer greater opportunities than is true in the West for the gratification of simple physical pleasures in situations of close contact with other persons—as in bathing, sleeping arrangements, nursing care, child-rearing, and so on . . . If sexual feelings were allowed to intrude into these events, then this would complicate matters, and the simple pleasures to be derived from these situations would be reduced.

Presumably, then, nurturant activities should be distinguished from sexual acts in the usual Japanese behavior pattern.

become feminized (since we assume that in former generations their reactions would have followed the Tokyo masculine pattern). Feminization sounds unfortunate, and is considered dangerous by Freudian psychologists. However, it is essential to the development of skill and sensitivity in human relations as American marriages evolve from husband dominance to equalitarian companionship. Feminization is the male counterpart of the emancipation (or masculinization) of women that is now occurring in Japan and that long since occurred in the United States.

Both labels indicate the direction of change—away from stereotyped sex roles. They do *not* mean that the sexes have changed places—that men have become women or women men. Rather, the gap between the sexes has narrowed so that a "real" man and a "real" woman are no longer polar opposites.

Convergence of the sexes requires the development of latent talents that were once taboo. Margaret Mead points out in *Sex and Temperament in Three Primitive Societies* that human sex temperament is capable of being molded in almost any direction by culture. In both East and West men traditionally were forbidden to be emotionally expressive while women were forbidden to think for themselves. Today's patterns of marriage encourage the development in each sex of the other's talents. As a result, husbands and wives can collaborate in decision-making and intellectual discussion and men can come down the mountain to feel and express sympathy for their wives' troubles. Presumably in the future Japanese men will also become more capable of sympathy.

But American men are not like Japanese wives in every respect—only in in sympathy and affectionateness. They are more like Tokyo men in their secondary readiness to give advice and suggestions and in their unreadiness to help wives get away from their troubles. The latter response may not be as nurturant when given by men as we assume it is for women. Perhaps husbands distract their wives by taking them out to dinner more often than by brewing them a cup of tea.

The remaining Detroit husbands are unlike either sex in Japan. Passive and critical responses are rare in Tokyo but common in the working-class segment of the Detroit sample (see Chapter 6). To feel unable to do anything except provide a sympathetic ear is one consequence of the inferiority feelings that some Americans develop in a wife-dominated household. In this respect, low-status American husbands *are* like Japanese women, only more so. Presumably these men have lost the power to be authoritative (like Japanese husbands) and have not yet developed the capacity to be sympathetic (like Japanese wives). They feel stymied and do nothing at all.

To criticize one's wife for having gotten into trouble in the first place or rebuff her attempts to tell her troubles is not to be therapeutic. Such attacks—which frequently make the wife wish she had never opened her mouth—tend to estrange her and may eventually drive her to divorce. They indicate callousness and insensitivity which contrasts with the modal sympathetic husbands. Perhaps this is one of the dangers involved in shifting from romantic to companionable conceptions of marriage. American marriages have an air of casualness, a rough-and-ready equality, that allow husbands and wives to attack each other unmercifully when they feel like it. Steeped in pseudo-Freudian psychology the attacker may rationalize his aggressiveness as healthy catharsis (though hardly as good for the victim). Casualness produces smugness about marital success, regardless of how one behaves. Such smugness is illusory when critical and rejecting responses lead to the divorce court. Nevertheless, these individuals claim they have a "right" to do whatever they feel like, to act spontaneously regardless of the impact on the partner. Behaving naturally might be labeled "postromantic" both in the historic sense that it is a later stage of social evolution and in the personal sense that it supersedes romantic courtship.

Tokyo, on the other hand, is in the midst of a romantic era. Both husbands and wives—regardless of marriage type—rank love ahead of everything else as the chief value in marriage. Love-match couples feel challenged by their parents and by hostile traditions to prove they can make a go of unconventional marriages. Arranged-marriage couples are challenged by the new romantic ideal to see if they can measure up to their more emancipated contemporaries. Their postmarital courtship insures against taking each other for granted and inhibits both partners from criticizing each other—the husband for fear of losing his wife, the wife for fear of her husband. In either case, restraint minimizes derogatory responses and encourages positive therapy in crises.

A peculiarly Japanese response is to dismiss the problem as not worth worrying about. As we shall see in Chapter 8, this is not only much more common in Japan but is evaluated positively there, whereas Americans consider it worse than no response at all. Apparently dismissal has a legitimacy in Japan that it lacks here.

Could it be the Buddhist strain in Japanese culture? Does the Buddhist belief that the way to peace of mind is to rise above suffering and become oblivious to the cares of the world make dismissal seem a good thing? Or is it the stoic element in Japanese character—a "grin and bear it" philosophy? Does the strong sense of duty, of the importance of carrying on, of "the mail must go through" and "the show must go on" (to cite American slogans), lead some Japanese to dismiss the partner's troubles as trifles not worth the dignity of taking seriously? The warrior *samurai* tradition has not lost all its influence. The "stiff upper lip" that disregards soft human feelings still has some admirers.

We should remember, however, that dismissal is only relatively popular in Japan, not the dominant motif for either sex. Overshadowed by masculine advice and by feminine sympathy and nurturance, it is a minority response that reflects the lingering influence of old traditions in contemporary Japan.

Child-bearing

Our last comparison between the two countries can be made very simply. In the United States the options for family size range from two to four children with less than 20 per cent preferring any other number (mostly more). In Tokyo, the choices are even fewer. Over 90 per cent of our respondents prefer either two or three children. The majority prefer two.

The difference between three children (the Detroit median) and two spells out the difference between the American population explosion and Japan's success in population stabilization. Its cause is partly the crowded *lebensraum* in Japan contrasted with the continuing ability of American suburbs to engulf the countryside. More personally, the limited financial means of even these wealthier-than-average Japanese families force them to limit their procreativity for the sake of their desired standard of living. Contemporary Americans are so affluent that we can afford both things and children. Japanese parents have to choose. So they limit their child-bearing to modest numbers.[14]

Sources of Satisfaction

Because satisfaction is a subjective matter and our respondents expressed it by choosing adjectives whose Japanese and English connotations cannot be precisely equated, we cannot compare the amount of satisfaction in the two countries.[15] However, we can ask which aspects of marriage are most satisfactory.

In Table 5–6 love is conspicuously the most satisfying feature of marriage. In Tokyo, love is both the most highly valued aspect of marriage and the most satisfactory. In Detroit, love is deemed less valuable than either companionship or understanding, but nevertheless ranks first in satisfaction achieved.

The chief differences between the two countries lie in their experience with respect to companionship. Of the four facets of marriage evaluated in both countries, companionship is next to the top in Detroit but last of all for both sexes in Tokyo. From this subjective standpoint as well as objectively, Japanese marriages are less satisfactorily companionable than American marriages.

14. In a cross-section sample of the city of Osaka, Takeshita, 1962, finds a mean "ideal family size" of 2.92 children compared to Freedman, Whelpton, and Campbell's 1959 mean of 3.4 for an American cross-section sample, again showing a lower child-bearing norm for Japan.

15. Our guess would be that American marriages are, like Japanese love matches, symmetrically happy. Japanese marriages in this transitional era seem more apt to be skewed, the husbands unusually happy and the wives unhappy. A suggestive parallel is reported from West Germany by *The Times* of London (May 19, 1959):

. . . While 92 per cent of Germany's married men believe their home lives to be happy, only 19 per cent of married women feel the same.

. . . Especially among younger people, a wife is becoming more of a partner and less of a servant. The man is less authoritative and the woman less helpless.

Probably both German and Japanese women are restless with the past and aspire to greater equality with men.

Table 5–6—Rank Order of Sources of Marital Satisfaction in Tokyo and Detroit*

TOKYO		DETROIT
Husband's Satisfaction	*Wife's Satisfaction*	*Wife's Satisfaction*
1. Love and affection	1. Love and affection	
2. Wife as mother	2. Husband as father	
		1. Love and affection
3. Own share in decisions	3. Courtesy and respect	
4. Wife's interest in decisions	4. Own share in decisions	
		2. Companionship
5. Courtesy and respect	5. Understanding	
6. Sex	6. Sex	
		3. Understanding
7. Understanding	7. Husband's income	
8. Wife's home management	8. Husband's interest in decisions	
		4. Standard of living
9. Wife's financial management	9. Companionship	
10. Companionship	10. Husband's helpfulness	

* Also computed in both cities was satisfaction with expected number of children (see Appendix). Although included in aggregate marital satisfaction scores, this variable cannot meaningfully be listed in this table because the scoring procedures were only roughly equivalent. Husband's income for Japanese wives is equivalent to standard of living for American wives.

Conclusion

What then is the overall shape of marriage in Japan and the United States? At least as far as these samples are concerned, the Japanese shape is narrow and constricted. It rests on a narrow population base—two parents and two children —and has less involvement with the outside world of kin and especially nonkin.

Husband and wife are more sharply separated from each other in their working hours, because external work is more time-consuming and housework is more segregated. But in what little leisure they have, Japanese couples achieve a good deal of intimacy via marital dating, internal communication, and a heavier-than-American emotional reliance in time of crisis. The power structure of their marriages seems just as equalitarian as ours. However, elements of asymmetry in their marriages (and perhaps to a lesser extent in ours) reflect differential sex roles. Wives are more verbally expressive and more emotionally expressive in Japan than in America. In these respects, American husbands are more like Japanese wives than husbands. Hence there is probably more pervasive equalitarianism and reciprocity in America's companionable marriages than in Tokyo's love matches and romantic arranged marriages.

THE IMPRINT   6

OF EXTERNAL FORCES

ON HUSBAND-WIFE RELATIONSHIPS

IN previous chapters we have contrasted American and Japanese standards of living, working hours, and population densities in interpreting differences between marriage patterns in the two countries. Those are external forces which shape the pattern of marriage, and the interpretations were, finally, merely interpretations. Sometimes we proposed alternative ways of explaining differences. In no case could we be sure which factors were more important or indeed whether our supposed explanations had any bearing on the phenomena at all.

Now, however (and in the remaining chapters), we come to a more conclusive task. We have measures of various external variables. Do these measures relate to marriage the same way in both societies? If so, we will have increased confidence in generalizations previously drawn from America alone. If—despite the differences *between* Japan and America—the same relationships hold *within* each country, we will move a step further toward general laws of family behavior.

If they do not, we will be in a more difficult position. Sometimes we will assume that the differences are real in the sense that marriages operate under different laws in the two societies—provided we can invent possible explanations. More often we will have to assume that the differences are not necessarily "real" in the sense of representing consistent differences between the two societies. Rather they may reflect sampling errors—one or both samples being freakishly unrepresentative of the normal state of affairs—or interviewing errors, stemming from the noncomparability introduced in moving from one culture to another (and especially from one language to another). Apparent contradictions in our findings may mask real similarities. In any case, contradictions call for further research in both countries (and third countries, as well) to see which of our findings are generally true.

In other cases, inconsistencies between Detroit and Tokyo findings mean there are no generalizations that hold consistently within either culture—either in the same direction or in the opposite direction. To be sure, even consistencies between our two sets of data may not hold up in later research. Two cases are immensely better than one, but not infinitely better. Hence the international comparisons in the next three chapters will only whet the appetite for further research to strengthen the confirmations we will discover and to check out alternative hypotheses about the discrepancies. This first replication chapter focuses on the relationship between factors outside and inside the family. The remaining two will move inside the family to see whether time and children affect the parents similarly in the two societies and whether marital interaction patterns are equally evaluated in Tokyo and Detroit.

One generalization emerging from the Detroit study was that the balance of external forces impinging on a particular couple shaped their marriage. These forces could frequently be conceptualized as resources brought to marriage by husband and wife. The partner who contributes more financial, intellectual, and other resources especially tends to dominate decisions involving transactions between the family and the external environment. Sometimes these effects can be seen by looking at differences among husbands alone or wives alone, particularly when the role of the opposite sex is fairly standardized. They can be seen best, however, when the comparative resources of marital pairs are examined.

Husband and wife participate in the external world both before and after marriage. Prior to marriage, the partners acquire statuses such as age and education which exert a continuing (though perhaps diminishing) influence on their relationship. After marriage, the partners participate in outside activities to varying extents and with varying degrees of success. These variations influence their attitudes and behavior toward each other.

Premarital Statuses

The external resources to be examined are the comparative age of the partners, the husband's birth order (particularly significant in Japan), both partners' formal education, and the breadth of their travels. Two of these variables (the second and last) are discussed only with reference to Japan, where they acquire special meanings in view of their country's feudal past. Although our main interest is in crosscultural replication of the influence of particular variables, we will make unilateral excursions into both bodies of data because of the riches they add to a broader theoretical context.

AGE

Within the narrow age bracket spanned by our respondents (mostly the twenties and thirties), age in the absolute sense shouldn't affect behavior very much. To be sure, the longer a person is married, the more we expect him to change, but we attribute that to the interval since marriage rather than the interval since birth.

Age is important chiefly as a relative matter. Particularly in childhood, a gap of as little as one year can determine which child will lead and which will follow. As children get older, however, and especially after they graduate from such age-graded institutions as schools, age means less and less. Or, to put it the other way round, the minimum difference in age that "matters" gets bigger and bigger. By middle age, guessing the age of one's contemporaries becomes almost impossible.

Age brings increased experience, to be sure, and with experience come knowledge, wisdom, and self confidence. However, the more years go by, the more an age difference is likely to be eclipsed by qualitative differences in the persons' experiences. For example, knowledge gained by experience may be outstripped by a younger person's formal education.

For such reasons, we do not expect even the comparative age of married couples to influence their interaction very much except where differences are extreme. In those cases we expect the older partner to dominate because of his increased resources—to act as parent surrogate for the spouse who depends on him like a child. Marriage should thus be altered from normal equalitarianism in the direction of a quasi parent-child relationship.

In Detroit this concept is expressed in increased power for husbands married to younger wives. Tokyo couples not only fail to act the same way but reverse the relationship. Whether this is due to differences in the measuring instruments or to a different relationship between the variables we cannot say.

Whereas we expect marital power to vary directly with comparative age, the couple's sense of togetherness should be greatest when their age status is the same. As ages diverge, a sense of distance should appear. The Detroit wives' satisfaction with companionship illustrates this proposition, declining slightly when the husband is seven or more years older and sharply when he is four or more years younger. In Tokyo the relationship is even clearer, with the greatest satisfaction in the same-aged couples (except for two extraordinarily satisfied couples where the wife is substantially older than the husband). Though the statistics are less "pretty" than they might be, they show that companionship is generally produced by similarity in age.

The therapeutic relationship between husband and wife involves more complicated issues. On the one hand, to tell my troubles means to depend on my partner emotionally. Emotional dependence should increase as the partner's age superiority increases. However, there is also the question of my perception of my partner's accessibility—how willing is he (or at least how willing do I perceive he is) to listen to my troubles? The older he is, the less approachable he seems. So a "father-daughter" or "mother-son" relationship may discourage the younger spouse's initiative at the same time that it alters interaction.

Table 6-1 shows that therapeutic reliance on the partner is most frequent among similarly aged couples in both countries and for both sexes in Japan. It is least when the spouse is much younger—one doesn't tell one's troubles to one's "child." The conflicting problems of accessibility and emotional dependence make relationships at the opposite extreme more ambiguous.

Table 6-1—The Marital Imprint of the Comparative Age of Husband and Wife

		Comparative Age						
		HUSBAND YOUNGER		EQUAL		HUSBAND OLDER		
		4 plus	1-3		1-3	4-6	7-10	11 pl
Husband's Power								
Detroit		5.00	4.78	4.97	5.21	5.43	5.80	6.09
Tokyo		(5.50)*	4.85	5.30	5.21	5.23	5.15	(4.60
Satisfaction with Companionship								
Wife's	Detroit	3.16	4.03	3.86	3.86	4.01	3.78	3.87
	Tokyo	(5.00)	3.61	4.02	3.68	3.81	3.65	(3.17
Husband's	Tokyo	(5.50)	4.09	4.35	3.98	4.23	3.94	(4.00
Therapeutic Utilization of Spouse								
Wife's	Detroit	2.00	2.62	2.43	2.52	2.26	2.38	2.40
	Tokyo	(2.50)	3.00	3.18	3.04	3.05	2.81	(3.17
Husband's	Tokyo	(2.50)	2.35	2.61	2.28	2.20	2.26	(2.00
Advice-giving Responses								
Husband's	Detroit	25.0%	21.1%	19.4%	23.3%	16.7%	28.6%	34.8
	Tokyo	— 52.0% —		31.3%	33.9%	37.1%	— 41.4% —	
Wife's	Tokyo	— 13.0% —		10.9%	9.5%	11.6%	— 9.8% —	
Marital Satisfaction								
Wife's	Detroit	4.38	4.89	5.00	4.89	5.10	4.67	4.26
	Tokyo	(6.00)	4.30	5.26	5.16	5.42	5.40	(6.60
Husband's	Tokyo	(6.00)	5.94	5.81	5.38	5.98	5.56	(3.50
Minimum Number of Cases								
Detroit		11	37	36	147	85	42	23
Tokyo		2	22	47	158	125	48	4

* Means in parentheses are based on less than 10 cases. Percentages have not been computed where the base is less than 10.

When the individual does take his troubles to his spouse, the latter's response is affected by the age gap. We have portrayed advice-giving because it is particularly paternal-maternal in tone. Generally speaking, advice is given less to equals. It flows most from elder partners to younger ones (but there is an unexpected countertendency for husbands to advise older wives). We achieve, then, only modest and not entirely consistent support for the notion that advice flows from elder to younger spouse.

Which age combinations make the most satisfactory marriages? In Detroit the ideal marriage is companionable and the satisfaction index focuses on such equality-linked facets as companionship, love, and understanding. So the superiority of more-or-less equal ages is notable.

In Tokyo, however, the norms of marriage are more ambiguous and our index of satisfaction includes decision-making and other structural variables likely to change directly with age. For whatever reasons, the data in Table 6–1 show that equal-aged marriages in Japan satisfy neither sex. For women, the best marriages are to older husbands, and for men the best wives are nurturant mother figures. According to these data, Japanese couples differ from American wives in the age patterns they find most satisfactory. For American women, the ideal husband is an age peer. For our Tokyo men and women, the ideal is an elder.

In general, comparative age has proven to be a complicated variable. As we said in the beginning, age is at best a crude predictor of adult behavior. Our international exploration reinforces this conviction.

BIRTH ORDER

Americans rarely think of birth order in relation to marital behavior (although maybe we should more often because psychological studies suggest that it *is* related to personality development). However, the Japanese concern with precedence which we discussed earlier in terms of sex order ("ladies first" *vs.* "men first") is also manifested in attention to birth order. In the feudal past, a first-born son held special privileges of inheritance and corresponding responsibilities of leadership for the larger family, embraced by the entire set of siblings (younger brothers as well as sisters until they were married off into other men's families). The technical name for this system is primogeniture (literally meaning *first born*). It is well adapted to a densely populated agrarian society where average land holdings are so small that chopping them up into equal parts would spell starvation for all. Primogeniture preserves the family estate intact as a base of support for the eldest son's wife and children, a base to which other family members can return for refuge in emergencies, financial and otherwise.

One day a distinguished Japanese sociologist took us to dinner in a *sukiyaki* restaurant overlooking the Tamagawa River and told us his troubles as an eldest son. His family had been *samurai* soldiers for a feudal *daimyo* lord in a remote prefecture. The family estate had been maintained in the same place for 500 years. With the death of his father, he had just inherited the responsibility for maintaining the family home and shrine. Before the occupation, this would have been easy because landed estates yielded rental income from tenant farmers. But the Land Reform deprived landlords of their lands so that now the house was a white elephant that would have to be maintained from his modest faculty salary. Financially he wanted to get rid of the burden, but he would be severely criticized by his relatives if he did. Nor was he sure he could live with his own conscience if he brought the 500-year history of his family to an end. Yet being family patriarch felt strange to one who always made "modern" recommendations to others at the family court where he served as a conciliator.

Even in "Amerika-Mura," a fishing village that has exported half of its population to Canada, the concept of eldest son as head of the larger "family" persists:

> There has been no change in the idea that eldest sons are to inherit "families" and that it is their exclusive duty to support their parents in their old age. Some parents opposed the expatriation of eldest sons while approving that of second and third sons. Many people came back from abroad after the war driven by the feeling that, being eldest sons, they had a responsibility for the property they had received from their parents, the tombs of their ancestors to look after and their parents to take care of. (Fukutake, 1962.)

In the old days, an elder brother's headship of the larger family (the *ie*) included authority over the lives of his siblings even in adulthood. He played a key role in arranging marriages for his younger siblings and later for their children. In anticipation of this authoritative role, eldest sons were taught from birth to lead the sibling group and were given precedence in eating, bathing, and so forth.[1] Siblings in turn were taught to look up to the elder brother, obey his orders, and pay him the respect and deference due his station.[2]

Postwar reforms introduced by the American occupation and the new Japanese government sought to abolish this special status as a remnant of feudalism. Primogeniture was officially abolished in the new civil code that guaranteed equal inheritance rights to all children—even daughters.[3]

Nevertheless, traditions being what they are, more often than not it *is* the eldest who occupationally succeeds his father. This is true not only for farmers but also for urban proprietors and even professions in private practice (where sons are expected to take over the father's patients or clients).

Because the men in our sample were born well before the postwar reforms were instituted, we should expect a continuing impact of the traditional discrimination. The combined influences of childhood training in the family of orientation and of current occupational and familistic status advantages should make both partners in an eldest son's marriage act differently. The

1. Dore (1958) describes "the general tendency to give precedence to the eldest son in all matters of daily life. He is early given a sense of his own importance as heir designate; he has the use of the family bath before his brothers; he is given the most tasty part of the fish; he is generally indulged more than his younger brothers . . . ; if money for education is scarce, he would have a superior claim."

2. Ezra Vogel informs me that even the PTA was known before the war as the "fathers' and elder brothers' organization." Younger brothers, by contrast, were called "cold-meal eaters" (*hiyameshikui*) or "hangers on" because of their marginal position in the stem-family (Koyama, 1961).

3. However, equal inheritance is no more practical in rural Japan today than in the past, with the result that younger siblings usually surrender their inheritance rights rather than force foreclosure of the family farm to get their share. To be more precise, it is not so much the younger siblings as the nonagricultural siblings who surrender their rights, for it is no longer taken for granted that the eldest son will necessarily be the one to stay home and follow in his father's footsteps.

husband should conceive of himself as superior and the wife should look up to him. Younger sons' marriages, by contrast, should be more equalitarian because their advantage over their sisters is not so great.

Table 6–2—The Marital Imprint of the Japanese Husband's Birth Order

	HUSBAND'S BIRTH ORDER	
	First born	Other
Pre-engagement Discussion		
Discussed traditional and modern husband-wife relationships	1.74	1.49
Power Structure		
Husband's power score	5.30	5.12
Wife-dominant power structure	9%	17%
Division of Labor		
Wife's task performance	4.69	4.33
Feels like a servant to her husband	0.50	0.39
Precedence		
Wife's precedence in taxi	3.16	3.04
Marital Dynamics		
Kinship companionship (visits per year)	14.4	12.6
Therapeutic utilization of the wife	2.26	2.32
Therapeutic utilization of the husband	3.07	3.00
Evaluation		
Wife's satisfaction with companionship	3.77	3.82
Husband's satisfaction with companionship	4.20	4.00
Comparative marital satisfaction		
Both satisfied	35%	39%
Neither	31	32
Husband only	22	15
Wife only	12	15
Total	100%	101%
Minimum Number of Cases	198	244

Table 6–2 shows that eldest sons treat their wives differently and in turn receive different responses in many dimensions of marriage. (Only comparative term of address and the husband's expression of appreciation fail to differentiate the two types.)

Even before marriage, eldest sons discuss traditional as contrasted with modern husband-wife relationships more often than their younger brothers. This could be caused by the girl's fear that an eldest son will be predisposed to a traditional marriage. Such fear is likely to focus especially on whether the couple will have to live with the husband's parents. Although our sample is restricted to those who manage to escape this fate, their frequent kinship companionship shows that they are still deeply involved in their kin networks. This involvement is likely to be reciprocal, with visits initiated by parents and siblings as well as by the couple themselves, because both generations ascribe central importance to this household in the kin network.

Within the eldest son's household, the girl's fears of a more traditional marriage are borne out. The couple have a more patriarchal power structure (with correspondingly rarer wife-dominant deviance). The wife plays the servant role more extensively in the division of labor and recognizes this in feeling like a servant.

On the other hand, this does not mean that the husband demeans her to the extent of getting into the taxi first in feudal style. On the contrary, we have already noted that he expresses appreciation as much as other husbands and we now find that he is even more chivalrous. Perhaps the special training of eldest sons includes the new deference for female weakness implied in chivalry alongside the old presumption of female weakness implied in the patriarchate. Chivalry and male dominance are psychological companions rather than opposites.

Masculine strength and superiority are manifested not only in opening taxi doors but in refraining from burdening the wife with the husband's troubles. She, on the other hand, leans on him correspondingly more in their asymmetrical relationship.

The subjective effect of asymmetry disappoints the wife with her failure to achieve an entirely modern marriage but pleases the husband with the extra prestige, authority, and service that his childhood and contemporary status in the larger family give him. There may be extra burdens for first-born sons in contemporary Japan, but one bonus is the kind of old-fashioned marriage that some men prefer.[4]

EDUCATION

The effect of education on marriage patterns is likely to be ambiguous. On the one hand, education liberates men from tradition. It acquaints them with other ways of life, broadens their horizons, and undermines their acceptance of old ways as inevitable and right. It also trains their minds in the communication processes essential to the new psychological emphasis in marriage.

On the other hand, insofar as one partner's education exceeds the other's, education becomes a source of power. In such cases, introducing more education unilaterally may reinforce the traditional pattern rather than dilute it.

The great emancipator—First let us examine the emancipating effect of education, concentrating on women since they are the sex once held in feudal bondage. For Japan, the pattern is clear in Table 6-3. Higher education turns the wife away from domesticity toward involvement in her external environment. College alumnae are the most skeptical about wanting to be born again as women in Japanese society. A remarkably large proportion of them are employed outside the home at the present time. However, their employment

---

4. Extra burdens produce an overrepresentation of eldest sons among psychotic patients in Japanese mental hospitals. Attempting to interpret this finding, Caudill (1963) comments:

It may be that the eldest son continues to carry many special responsibilities, but in the modern world his privileges in this position are less than in the past. If this is true, the net effect is to make this role a more difficult one to fulfill.

will soon be disrupted as they begin bearing and rearing children. But their educated interest in careers reduces the number of children they desire. In these respects they resemble America's fierce feminists of the 1920's—a remarkable generation of career women, with many Ph.D.s and few children. Since then the winning of feminine rights has lessened the challenge of vocational pioneering, and earlier marriages have reduced the proportion of women studying for advanced degrees. Hence lifelong careers have gone out of style. But early marriage and early child-bearing also mean early completion of child-rearing. So American alumnae are now turning to continuing education, refresher education, and careers begun or resumed in middle age. Perhaps this same trend to a two-phased life (child-rearing first and career later) will occur in Japan in the future. At the moment, however, Japan is a generation behind the United States and its feminists are in full revolt.

Table 6–3—The Emancipating Effect of Women's Education

		Wife's Education			
		HIGH SCHOOL		COLLEGE	
		Non-graduate	Graduate*	Non-graduate	Graduate
Cross sex preference	Tokyo	38%	32%	35%	44%
Division of Labor					
Employed outside the home	Tokyo	33%	24%	43%	69%
	Detroit low income	30%	42%	22%	33%
	high income	9%	11%	21%	29%
	Detroit Total	24%	23%	21%	30%
Marital Dynamics					
Talks to husband's friends	Tokyo	2.48	3.05	3.16	3.38
Friendship companionship	Tokyo	3.4	7.2	9.7	9.2
	Detroit	98.7	74.6	74.4	69.0
Dating companionship	Tokyo	12.4	19.6	22.2	28.9
Child-bearing					
Preferred number of children	Tokyo	2.57	2.48	2.46	2.40
	Detroit	3.30	3.29	3.25	3.30
Comparative Satisfaction					
Both satisfied		19%	36%	38%	54%
Neither satisfied		44	32	30	22
Husband only		25	19	20	5
Wife only		12	13	11	19
Total		100%	100%	99%	100%
N	Tokyo	21	279	96	48
	Detroit	174	179	28	20

* In Japan, graduation occurred after eleven years of schooling under the old educational system, after twelve years under the new. This column includes those with eleven or twelve years of education in Tokyo, but only those with twelve years in Detroit.

Education orients women externally not only to jobs but to activities. Table 6–3 shows that educated wives have more good times outside the home (just as educated Japanese men date more, too).

The particularly rare leisure activity which involves getting together with other couples (friendship companionship) also appeals to educated women in

Japan (while they get together correspondingly less with relatives). Finally, when the husband's friends come to call, women emancipated by education are less hesitant to join in the conversation. Such boldness is especially understandable in this group where most husbands (and presumably most of their friends) are college graduates themselves.

In general, then, the emancipating effect of education is particularly visible in Japan where women are just now emerging into the limelight. In the United States, women's rights have been taken for granted longer, so there is less to emancipate women from. Economic affluence also creates opportunities for volunteer service. As a result, American college alumnae are more domestically oriented than their Japanese counterparts, especially during these early years of marriage. Perhaps our concluding generalization should be that education has a potentially liberating effect, but someone must first be enslaved for its impact to be visible.

In rejecting their traditional feminine role, do emancipated Japanese women destroy both their own and their husbands' marital satisfaction? Do they emancipate themselves at the expense of their marriages? The concluding segment of Table 6–3 shows that, on the contrary, they improve their marriages. So committed are the men and women in our sample to a modern way of life that emancipation of the woman is prerequisite to achieving the style of marriage they prefer. To be sure, there are a few deviant cases—a few old-fashioned couples mutually satisfied with an uneducated wife and even more in which the husband is satisfied but the wife is not. Conversely, at the other extreme, a few emancipated wives have dissatisfied husbands. But the modal categories are diametrically opposite: only when the wife has finished college are both partners satisfied, while wives with the least education have the least satisfactory marriages for themselves or for their husbands.

Communication skills—We have already seen that educated women talk more with their husband's friends. While this is a source of personal satisfaction, the major marital benefit of the wife's education is to facilitate conversation with her husband. The internal dynamics of marriage are strengthened by training in communication skills. Education should increase male communication skills too, but less dramatically because men have not been restricted by social taboos, inside or outside the home.

Table 6–4 shows that education raises communication levels in both countries. However, its impact is almost always greater on wives than on husbands. Education for women provides both skill-training and emancipation. On men, however, there is no need for emancipation as they have always been "top dogs." Indeed, education for men has contradictory effects insofar as skill-training is nullified by creating greater distance between husband and wife. In other words, higher education will lead a man to communicate with his wife chiefly if she is educated too, and therefore she both invites and understands his communications. Because college men marry either equally or less-educated women, their communication patterns are ambiguous. College women, however, seldom marry uneducated men as neither party is attracted to the other. Women almost always marry men at least as well educated.[5] So the effect of education on women is triplicated—not only are women personally emancipated in their expectations and skilled in communication processes, but they acquire equally skillful husbands. Education of both sexes increases their frequency of discussing the news—a particularly intellectual form of companionship. College graduate husbands express their affection for their wives appreciably more, but smaller educational distinctions matter little in this sample.

Table 6–4—Educational Training and Marital Communication Skills

		Education			
		HIGH SCHOOL		COLLEGE	
		Non-graduate	Graduate	Non-graduate	Graduate
Intellectual Companionship (discuss news)					
by husband's education	Tokyo	157	160	176	177
by wife's education	Tokyo	130	170	182	198
Husband Expresses Affection					
by husband's education	Tokyo	120	118	120	142
Informative Companionship Husband tells events					
by husband's education	Tokyo	177	156	178	177
	Detroit	174	191	179	212
Wife listens					
by wife's education	Tokyo	122	171	178	209
	Detroit	174	185	199	214
Therapeutic Utilization Wife tells troubles					
by wife's education	Tokyo	2.66	3.00	3.07	3.30
	Detroit	2.19	2.60	2.75	2.42
Husband listens					
by husband's education	Tokyo	2.80	2.91	2.82	3.14
	Detroit	2.30	2.47	2.80	3.56
Husband tells troubles					
by husband's education	Tokyo	1.60	2.06	2.27	2.38
Wife listens					
by wife's education	Tokyo	1.71	2.27	2.26	2.73
Number of husbands	Tokyo	10	66	93	275
	Detroit	194	131	41	33
Number of wives	Tokyo	21	279	96	48
	Detroit	174	179	28	20

Informative companionship and therapeutic utilization of the husband provide clear-cut international comparisons. The husband's reporting of the day's events increases with his wife's education in both countries, but increases with the husband's education only in the United States.

5. This statement applies with particular force to countries like Japan where relatively few women have been to college. It does not apply, however, to groups like American Negroes where boys tend to drop out of school earlier than girls, so that better-educated wives are fairly common.

Therapeutic utilization of the husband increases with education of both partners in Japan, but especially with the wife's. This contrasts with the situation in the United States where education makes wives more discriminating in their behavior (college-educated wives especially often telling their troubles half the time). Perhaps selectivity and sensitivity to the husband's receptivity come later in the evolution of marriage. Newly emancipated wives—as in Tokyo—welcome the opportunity to communicate their troubles to their husbands.[6] Only in later generations, perhaps, do women discover that husbands have problems too, and sometimes deserve to be left alone rather than bothered with small problems. If this interpretation is correct, the apparent contradiction between Tokyo and Detroit may be resolved in a larger historical perspective.

For the reverse direction (husbands telling their troubles), our data come only from Japan. In that sample, education of both partners strongly increases the husband's likelihood of turning to the wife for help. Presumably education increases both his ability to express inner feelings and her ability to listen and respond. In any case, education of both partners increases therapeutic utilization in both directions in Tokyo.

In general, more often than not education promotes higher levels of communication. Particularly in a modernizing country like Japan, education loosens women's tongues and enables them to create marriages that are not only equalitarian in structure but interactive in dynamics. In the United States, where the emancipation of women and the modernization of marriage have already been consolidated, education has more subtle effects. Instead of further increasing the volume of communication, it introduces greater perceptiveness and empathy so that it limits communication of negative information at the point of diminishing returns—i.e. where the net effect leaves both partners unhappier than before. Educated men and women are more capable of self-therapy in small crises, though still dependent on one another when their own resources are exhausted. Marriage in this stage of history becomes less intensely interactive than in the pioneering days of first-generation equalitarianism. This is a loss, perhaps, as far as the meaningfulness of marriage is concerned, but it may be a gain as far as the totality of life is concerned. Burdened less often with the partner's petty problems, the American spouse may be freer to pursue his other roles as wage-earner, citizen, and hobbyist. If marriage in the individual case is never quite so exciting as when it is new, so marriage collectively is never quite so absorbing as when a new pattern is being worked out for the first time in a society's history. In Tokyo today, modern marriage is on its honeymoon.

The husband's willingness to listen, on the other hand, increases with advanced education in both countries. Hence the American wives' increased selectivity in telling their husbands results from their own considerateness and not from any inconsiderateness of the husbands themselves. Thus education

6. William Caudill reports in a personal communication that the greater the education of female psychiatric patients in contemporary Japan, the greater their self-indulgence (*wagamama*).

increases both partners' altruism—the husband's willingness to be burdened and the wife's willingness to keep her burdens to herself. In this sense, what appears at first glance to be an asymmetrical effect of education on American marriages as gauged by frequency of therapeutic communication turns out at a deeper level to be a symmetrical increase in concern for the partner's welfare.

Comparative education and marital symmetry—We have several times suggested that the effect of education on marriage depends partly on who gets it. If both do, the balance of resources between the partners is not altered (even though the sum of their resources rises). If only one partner goes to college, however, resources are added to one side of the partnership and the balance can be expected to shift in his direction.

Inequalities should appear in any area of marriage where one partner's gain is the other's loss. Such "zero-sum games" include the balance of power and the division of labor as we have defined them. What one partner doesn't decide, the other does. The work one doesn't do, the other must.

Inequality has other effects that are more subtle. It introduces a sense of distance into relationships. Couples with equal resources feel particularly chummy. But when one partner has more than the other, he feels a bit above the other and she (for it is usually the woman who has less, especially in Japan) feels correspondingly inferior. Inferiority feelings make for clinging-vine dependence but not for a sense of intimacy. Hence there is frequently less ease of access, less communication flow in one or both directions, in asymmetrical marriages.

Our resource theory of power is nicely confirmed in Table 6–5. In both Tokyo and Detroit, the partner who has more knowledge and skill at his finger-tips makes more decisions—even though we used diverse lists of decisions in the two cities.

The division of labor, however, is more complicated. In neither country is it related to comparative education in the straightforward manner of power. In both cases, the hardest working wives are not those who are most inferior but rather those rare creatures who are superior. The master-servant relationship shows up only secondarily at the opposite end while the least housework is done by wives in more equally matched marriages. How does this extraordinary combination of superior education, superior power, and extra housework occur? Could these be mother- rather than servant-wives? Do they rule the roost over henpecked husbands and at the same time manage the household? Are they omnivorous "Moms" who delegate neither power nor responsibility to their husbands?

This pattern is reversed in the external employment of women. Servant-wives seldom venture forth to work nor do mother-wives. Both take their domestic roles too seriously to neglect them that much. Only in equalitarian marriages is the wife free to work outside if she needs to (as in the Tokyo sample generally and in low-income Detroit households).

What kind of men do mother-wives marry? Little boys, of course! My guess is that most of these wives do not dominate their husbands for the fun of it. Nor do they appear to get much satisfaction from carrying the housework burden. Rather they have the misfortune to be married to men who shirk their duties, forcing their wives to assume them. Which came first is difficult to say— the relationship is inevitably reciprocal, a vicious circle liable to lead to increasing asymmetry. For neither partner is it very satisfying. In both samples, these are the unhappiest wives and our Tokyo data show that these are also the unhappiest husbands. The wives feel neglected and the husbands browbeaten. Perhaps this is the inevitable result when the rules of mate-selection are broken and women marry their educational inferiors.

Table 6-5—Comparative Education and Marital Symmetry

		Comparative Education			
		HUSBAND MORE			WIFE
		4+years	1–3 years	EQUAL	MORE
Balance of Power					
Husband's power	Tokyo	5.39	5.11	5.07	4.88
	Detroit	5.81	5.61	5.37	4.90
Division of Labor					
Wife's task performance	Tokyo	4.46	4.66	4.23	4.88
	Detroit	5.38	5.12	5.21	5.45
Wife employed	Tokyo	24%	32%	50%	32%
	Detroit	22%	18%	29%	24%
Intellectual Companionship	Tokyo	168	175	182	172
Therapeutic Utilization of Spouse					
Husband's	Tokyo	2.12	2.23	2.39	2.21
Wife's	Tokyo	3.07	3.00	3.03	2.93
Net difference		—0.95	—0.77	—0.64	—0.72
Wife's	Detroit	2.38	2.48	2.55	2.29
Selected Therapeutic Responses					
Sympathy					
Wife	Tokyo	30%	30%	29%	29%
Husband	Tokyo	3%	4%	9%	0
	Detroit	32%	31%	36%	26%
Dismissal					
Wife	Tokyo	10%	12%	14%	25%
Husband	Tokyo	28%	22%	18%	32%
	Detroit	16%	8%	4%	8%
Aggregate Marital Satisfaction					
Husband's	Tokyo	5.61	5.88	5.55	5.03
Wife's	Tokyo	5.20	5.26	5.50	4.92
	Detroit	4.89	5.01	5.09	4.58
Minimum Number of Cases	Tokyo	172	145	99	28
	Detroit	41	96	126	140

Severe strains are produced by educational asymmetry when the husband is inferior. Both partners experience the social repercussions that come with violating cultural norms—gossip, ridicule, and loss of selfesteem. Lack of education handicaps the man occupationally. It doesn't take very much education to be able to keep house. But a man without much education suffers in the competition for employment and promotion.

At the opposite end, men with superior educations may not suffer in the outside world but find their relationship to their wives altered. Table 6–5 shows that intellectual companionship diminishes the greater the gap between husband and wife.

Marital asymmetry is revealed most clearly from information on reciprocal interaction between partners. Husbands and wives come closest to telling their troubles to each other equally often in homogamous marriages. The greater the educational heterogamy, the greater the discrepancy in therapeutic utilization rates. Superior husbands depend on their wives least of all, whereas wives depend most on such talented husbands. Conversely, wives turn for therapeutic relief least to husbands who are educationally inferior. For both sexes, individuals who marry down have less to lean on in crises. On the other hand, only wives depend more heavily on superior partners. In our Tokyo sample inferior men do not turn to their mother-wives as often as homogamous men—partly because they are not sufficiently educated in the art of telling their troubles and also because these mother-wives are more dominantly than nurturantly maternal.

The latter inference may be drawn from the therapeutic responses made by superior Tokyo women. They often conspicuously dismiss the husband's problems as inconsequential and neither help him solve them nor forget about them.

Dismissal and sympathy are usually inversely related. Husbands in both countries express sympathy most for similarly educated wives and least for those whose education exceeds their own. Conversely, both sets of husbands are least apt to dismiss the troubles of equally educated wives.

In general, then, marriages are most symmetrical when they are educationally homogamous but tend to be skewed whenever one partner is better educated. That partner tends to dominate the other in decision-making, to dismiss troubles unsympathetically but to be saddled with extra housework, and in the Japanese case besieged with the spouse's complaints. Such asymmetry is most marked when the wife's education exceeds the husband's. No wonder women find such marriages particularly unsatisfactory despite (or should we say because of?) their greater power.

The marital satisfaction of our Tokyo couples differs between men and women. Whereas wives in both Tokyo and Detroit are most satisfied with equalitarian husbands, Japanese men prefer inferior wives—up to a point. However, even they find wives whose educations are more than a few years below their own less able to meet their needs.

Disappointed with their marriages, superior Japanese wives often turn to external companionship to fill the domestic vacuum. Because they dominate their husbands, they can manipulate their leisure in compensatory directions. Table 6–6 shows that they sometimes get their husbands to take them out for commercial entertainment. Differences are even sharper for sociability with others. Presumably inferior husbands make wives eager to meet other couples through this rare form of Japanese social activity. Inferior wives, by contrast, are more content to stay home and hand their husbands the proverbial slippers.

Dominant wives are less clearly externally oriented in the United States and this response fails to appear in either country for kin contact. Perhaps this is understandable however. Wives can choose where to go on dates and pick out congenial friends for getting together. Relatives, however, are not chosen, and are likely to dislike the son or daughter-in-law. The husband's family may be as uncomfortable with a domineering woman and her superior education as she is with his poorly educated parents and siblings. On the other hand, her family is likely to criticize her inferior husband and discourage his contacts with them. Educational differences strain kin ties, making visits with relatives less comfortable than in homogamous marriages where both partners feel at home with each other's relatives.

Table 6–6—Comparative Education and External Sociability

		Comparative Education			
		HUSBAND MORE YEARS			WIFE MORE
		4+ years	1–3 years	EQUAL	
Annual Frequency					
Dating companionship	Tokyo	20	21	23	24
Friendship companionship	Tokyo	6	8	10	11
	Detroit	80	92	77	86
Kinship companionship	Tokyo	12	13	16	13
	Detroit	63	97	84	87
Minimum Number of Cases	Tokyo	172	145	99	28
	Detroit	41	96	126	140

To summarize, education increases the verbal skills of both men and women and emancipates women raised in a quasi-feudal society. Insofar as education benefits only one partner, however, it alters the couple's resource balance with similar effects on their balance of power regardless of which partner has the greater education. For career purposes, education is more important for husbands than for wives, so men with less education than their wives have their sense of resourcelessness compounded and retreat into marginal roles in marriage which satisfy neither partner. From the wife's viewpoint the most satisfactory relationship is homogamy—where both partners contribute the benefits of education. Japanese men, on the other hand, not fully ready to abandon old prerogatives, still prefer a modest educational advantage.

FOREIGN TRAVEL

To go abroad is educational, too. It broadens one's horizons, bolsters one's self-confidence. It provides contact with alien ways of life. Usually these are modern ways— for educational institutions in backward foreign countries have little to attract a Japanese student. (To guarantee precision, we confined our definition of foreign travel to visiting the United States or Europe.)

Visitors encounter Western attitudes toward women and Western styles of marriage. Japanese girls should be particularly attracted by what they see abroad and by what they experience in dating Western men. (Indeed Japanese men often fear this presumed emancipation; see Blood, forthcoming.) Their susceptibility to emancipation gave them the courage and initiative to go abroad in the first place, only to be reinforced once they got there.

For Japanese men, the impact of Western travel is ambiguous. A clearer picture of Western marriage will be gained, to be sure. But given their doubts about modern marriages at home, they are liable to dislike what they see abroad. Perhaps their reaction depends on how positive their foreign experience is in other respects. In any case, the net effect on their own marriages seems less likely to be unidirectional than for girls.

Table 6–7—The Effects of Foreign Travel on Japanese Marriages

| | FOREIGN TRAVEL | | | |
	Neither Partner	Husband Only	Wife Only	Both Partners
Marital Dynamics				
Wife currently employed	31.6%	25.9%	(66.7%)*	(71.4%)
Dating companionship (per year)	21	17	(22)	(28)
Wife converses with husband's visiting friends	3.09	2.85	(3.22)	(3.43)
Husband expresses appreciation	2.58	2.89	(3.22)	(3.71)
Husband expresses affection (per year)	129	157	(218)	(189)
Comparative Marital Satisfaction				
Both satisfied	36.0%	47.8%	(66.7%)	(50.0%)
Husband only	17.5	13.0	(16.7)	(50.0)
Wife only	13.8	17.4	(0.0)	(0.0)
Neither	32.6	21.7	(16.7)	(0.0)
Total	99.9%	99.9%	100.1%	100.0%
Minimum Number of Cases	325	23	6	6

* Numbers in parentheses are based on less than 10 cases.

We discovered in Chapter 2 that men who study abroad are apt to have marriages arranged for them on their return. The consequences of reactionary mate selection and of elevated status derived from travel appear in a conservative pattern of marriage where only the husband has been abroad. The first three characteristics of modern marriages listed in Table 6–7 are lower for traveled men than for those who stay home. This is offset somewhat, however, by increased expressiveness toward stay-at-home wives.

Foreign travel, like education, has a greater impact on women than men, especially women just emerging from a feudal past. The most direct consequence of travel by women is employment after marriage. This results from the fact that most women travel in order to take graduate training at foreign universities. Once a woman secures advanced professional training abroad, she is not likely to revert to domesticity.

Experience abroad is reinforced by the emancipating effect of continuous employment at home. Not surprisingly the marriages of traveled Japanese women are extraordinarily modern in form.

The most interesting feature of Table 6–7 is what happens when both partners go abroad. Here another kind of reinforcement occurs. With few exceptions, jointly traveled couples are the most Westernized of all. Men who travel abroad behave quite differently if they return to marry a stay-at-home bride or bring back a girl they met abroad (as we suspect often happened in the early postwar era).

I have already mentioned my companion study of Japanese men at the University of Michigan who shy away from marrying girls who study abroad. Table 6–7 suggests the correctness of their predictions that such girls have very modern marriages. They are incorrect, however, in concluding that emancipated marriages are unsatisfactory. At least for the dozen brave men in our sample who were willing to marry Westernized Japanese girls, life is extraordinarily satisfactory for both partners. Perhaps further Westernization of Japanese marriages will produce more satisfaction than Japanese men realize.

For both Japan and the United States, our international comparisons of the effects of pair discrepancies in age and education suggest considerable validity in the theory that the comparative resources which the partners bring to marriage from previous experiences shape their relation to one another. Experience may be acquired in various places—in school, in foreign countries, in the childhood family, even in sheer existence this side of the womb—but in every case the partner with more experience tends to dominate the marriage whereas couples with equal resources have companionable marriages.

If premarital experiences make such consistent impressions on marriage, the immediate participation of husband and wife in external systems should have an even more direct impact.

Contemporary External Participation

In Detroit, the comparative church attendance and organizational membership of husbands and wives affect their marriages in similar ways. However, these external resources are so distinctively American that they could hardly be studied in Japan (or very many other countries). Americans are avid churchgoers, whereas only the tiny Christian minority in Japan attend regularly. Americans are notorious "joiners," using voluntary organizations to accomplish more purposes than most societies have dreamed of. The married clubwoman or "clubman" is too rare in Tokyo to be studied easily.

EMPLOYMENT

In both countries, however, work is a live option for married women. Not only is employment a legitimate activity for urban wives in this emancipated era, but economic pressures on the Tokyo sample and the poorer half of the Detroit sample encourage wives to increase the family's economic resources.

The economic benefit of dual incomes is obvious. Less obvious is the fact that employment as well as churchgoing and club activity result in the broadened horizons, increased information, and *savoir-faire* which come from activities ouside the home. The impact of employment on the wife increases her resourcefulness in so many ways that we should not overemphasize the economic factor.

Our most important comparison is between those wives who work and those who don't. However, more detailed analysis is possible by the partners' degrees of participation in the occupational system—i.e. the number of hours worked—and by the nature of the wife's working role—whether she works with the husband or separately.

Wife's economic role—History is full of wives who worked with (or more precisely for) their husbands. In contemporary Japan, peasant wives work alongside their husbands in the rice paddies. Although there is a rough equalitarianism in peasant marriages (characterized by the fact that they traditionally had more love matches than higher-status couples), the husband is the chief farmer and his wife the assistant. Similarly in the city, working for the husband is very different from working for someone else. Only when the wife has a separate employer is she truly independent of her husband.

In our Tokyo sample, only five wives assist their husbands. Despite the small size of this group, their situation is so different from that of independently employed wives that they deserve special attention.

Table 6–8—The Marital Imprint of the Contrasting Economic Roles of Japanese Wives

	WIFE'S ECONOMIC ROLE		
	Housewife	Collaborator	Independent
Balance of Power			
Husband's power	5.27	(5.00)*	5.05
Internal Companionship			
Intellectual companionship	167	(220)	187
Informative companionship			
Husband tells events	171	(170)	182
Wife tells events	231	(220)	230
External Sociability			
Dating companionship	20	(14)	26
Friendship companionship	7	(9)	9
Kinship companionship	12	(14)	16
Satisfaction with Companionship			
Husband's	4.0	(3.0)	4.4
Wife's	3.7	3.4)	4.0
Minimum Number of Cases	281	4	134

*Numbers in parentheses are based on less than 10 cases.

Contrary to our expectations, the husband's power is more depressed in collaborative Japanese households than where the wife is independently employed. However, the cases are so few and the difference so small that we can only say that our hypothesis is unsupported rather than that it should be revised. Our chief conclusion is that employed women gain power regardless of whether they work for the husband or for someone else.

Given the urban separation of place of work from residence, most city couples are apart during the day. Collaborative couples are uniquely excepted in going out to work at the same place. (Elsewhere in Tokyo many couples combine work place and residence in cottage industries and home shops, but they are excluded from our apartment-house sample.) Collaborative couples have a unique opportunity for togetherness. This is reflected in discussing the news extraordinarily often. However, informative companionship suffers because it depends on telling events that happen to each separately. Collaborative couples are together so much that they observe most events simultaneously and have less opportunity for separate experiences.

After being together all day, collaborators have less incentive to date. When they do go out, they are more apt to add new social dimensions to their experience. Collaborative couples add either friends or relatives to 62 per cent of their external sociability, compared to only 49 per cent for either conventional couples or independently employed couples.

Despite long hours of working together and intense intellectual companionship, collaborative couples are dissatisfied with their companionship. We need to remember that our definition is "companionship in doing things together." This phrase has a leisure-time connotation to which common work is no more relevant than washing dishes together would be for American couples. Good companions enjoy recreational activities together. Hence the lesser dating of collaborative couples strikes at the core of companionship satisfaction.

Curiously, wives resent this deprivation less than husbands. Apparently the opportunity to collaborate with the husband gives the woman a sense of importance and usefulness which mitigates the loss of leisure-time enjoyment. Collaborative men, on the other hand, apparently bemoan their lack of escape from the burdens of work. Small entrepreneurs and private practitioners, they can hardly forget their responsibilities even when not working, short of "getting away from it all" in the nightlife of the big city.

The husband's working hours—Time is a resource not yet mentioned. Some activities occur so rarely in Japan that they can be fitted in around the edges no matter how much the husband works. For example, the holidays that dot the Japanese calendar offer opportunities for getting together with friends even for men who ordinarily work seven days a week.

Other forms of companionship, however, are disrupted if the husband works long hours (especially because the usual workweek in Japan is substantially longer than in the United States). Leisure is a resource that one contributes to marriage by *not* participating in the occupational system. In this sense it contrasts with our general theory about the resources which external involvement promotes. For this reason we will not examine the impact of the husband's working hours on his domestic power, but concentrate on participation in leisure-time activities. Table 6–9 shows that several types of companionship decline in Tokyo as the husband's working hours lengthen. Particularly at the extremes (under 40 hours per week and over 60) the time available makes a substantial difference. However, long working hours interfere more with the husband's ability to be a good companion than with the wife's. Perhaps because they fatigue him, long hours wear down his readiness to go to the trouble of sharing news with his wife of his life apart. On the other hand, no such straightforward effect appears on the wife's reporting. Indeed one gets the impression that beyond 40 hours the longer the husband has been away the greater the wife's need to talk to him. Hence informative companionship in long-separated marriages becomes curiously one-sided, the wife pouring her heart out while the husband rests his weary bones, half-listening but hardly replying.

Table 6–9—The Impact of the Husband's Working Hours on Leisure-time Companionship

		HUSBAND'S WORKING HOURS PER WEEK			
		<40	40–50	51–60*	61+
Internal Companionship					
Intellectual companionship	Tokyo	181	175	177	165
Informative companionship					
Wife tells events	Tokyo	238	228	231	238
Husband tells events	Tokyo	197	174	178	165
	Detroit	171	197	183	—
External Sociability					
Kinship companionship	Tokyo	15	14	13	13
	Detroit	84	86	92	—
Dating companionship	Tokyo	32	22	20	19
Shared Leisure Decision Making					
Radio-TV programs	Tokyo	36%	35%	34%	20%
Holiday outings	Tokyo	50%	46%	47%	14%
Vacations	Detroit	72%	70%	76%	—
Satisfaction with Companionship					
Husband's	Tokyo	4.20	4.17	4.07	3.93
Wife's	Tokyo	4.28	3.87	3.66	3.60
	Detroit	3.84	4.01	3.78	—
Minimum Number of Cases					
	Tokyo	21	190	129	70
	Detroit	202	105	74	—

* For Detroit this category is 51+.

Decision-making is sharply altered in seldom-together Japanese marriages. Wives are so glad to have the husband home that they defer to his preferences for domestic or external entertainment. Joint decision-making gives way to husband dominance in what little free-time he has. Perhaps it is only fair for the husband to be able to control his scarce leisure hours, but the couple's sense of companionship is impaired thereby.

For both partners, the husband's working hours interfere with the satisfactoriness of companionship. Men who work more than 60 hours a week allow the demands of subsistence or success to overshadow their marriage roles. By contrast, men working less than 40 hours foreshadow in their companionable marriages the mutuality that rising standards of living in Japan will promote. To our surprise, however, the American pattern is less clear-cut. Partly because our data fail to distinguish men who work extremely long hours (over 60), we fail to find some types of companionship encroached upon at all. Informative companionship and satisfaction with companionship decline only after the husband's work load passes 50 hours. Perhaps companionship is possible in spite of long working hours if people try hard enough. Because Americans value companionship so much, they often manage to surmount the obstacles of occupational involvement. In Japan, on the other hand, commitment to companionship is so fragile and occupational responsibilities so compelling that companionship occurs only when a couple's weekly calendar permits it.

Marital relationships may be impaired not only by excessively long working hours but by awkward schedules. In Detroit, wives of dayshift men are significantly more satisfied with their marriages than wives of men who work evenings, preventing normal sociability.[7]

Comparative work load—For the wife who works, the allocation of time between husband and wife is drastically altered. If both work fulltime, they are evenly matched. If he works overtime, his occupational role eclipses hers. Correspondingly, the sharpest contrast between marital roles occurs for wives at home all the time with husbands who work more than normally. This series of categories ranging from extreme inequality toward equality is labeled "comparative work load."[8]

As might be expected, the division of labor outside the home balances the division inside. Table 6–10 shows that in both countries the shares of time allocated to employment determine the proportion of housework done by each spouse. The husband's readiness to assist his working wife makes her correspondingly more satisfied with his helpfulness.

The balance of power situation, however, is more complicated. In both countries, working wives are more powerful than housewives. This confirms our resource theory. However, husbands who work overtime are not consistently more powerful than those who work fulltime. This means that time is not the only resource affecting the balance of power. Power is contingent on income, occupational prestige, and knowledge of the external world—factors that are only marginally related to working hours.

The equalitarianism of dual-income households is not only visible structurally but in the dynamics of marriage. We will use the ordinarily asymmetrical therapeutic function to illustrate this shift.

Japanese men usually keep their problems to themselves. But when the wife is employed, the husband finds it more appropriate to share his feelings (perhaps especially those springing from occupational problems), sensing that she is better able to understand them. Her comprehension of his troubles shows in such unladylike responses as advice and active help in solving the husband's problems. By contrast, stay-at-home wives often feel baffled by his problems and unable to do more than simply listen.

---

7. Unfortunately we have no information on shift work in our Japanese data.

8. Overtime is defined relative to societal norms as more than 40 hours in Detroit and more than 50 in Tokyo. This has advantages in splitting our samples into equal subgroups, but complicates the task of interpreting international comparisons.

Table 6–10—Comparative Workload and Marital Symmetry

| | | Comparative Workload | | | |
| | | WIFE NOT EMPLOYED | | WIFE EMPLOYED | |
		Husband Overtime*	Husband Full time	Husband Overtime*	Husband Full time
Division of labor					
Wife's Task Performance	Tokyo	5.19	4.32	4.00	3.73
	Detroit	5.74	5.39	4.73	3.68
Balance of Power					
Husband's Power	Tokyo	5.33	5.48	4.77	5.03
	Detroit	5.65	5.44	4.35	4.42
Therapeutic Interdependence					
Husband Tells Troubles	Tokyo	2.10	2.35	2.47	2.45
Wife responds with advice	Tokyo	7%	9%	11%	15%
Wife helps solve the problem	Tokyo	10%	11%	15%	19%
Wife passive	Tokyo	13%	10%	9%	8%
Wife Tells Troubles	Tokyo	3.03	3.01	2.85	3.11
	Detroit	2.36	2.39	2.55	2.73
Husband responds with advice	Tokyo	31%	35%	42%	45%
	Detroit	18%	19%	42%	30%
Husband passive	Tokyo	8%	8%	0	5%
	Detroit	21%	26%	11%	15%
Satisfaction with Understanding					
Husband's	Tokyo	4.04	4.15	4.35	4.53
Wife's	Tokyo	4.22	4.24	4.47	4.49
	Detroit	3.59	3.60	3.73	3.42
N	Tokyo	143	136	55	73
	Detroit	133	151	37	34

* Tokyo, over 50 hours; Detroit, over 40 hours.

Although a wife's increased resources might be expected to decrease her reliance on her husband for emotional support (by increasing her self-reliance), the fact that employment inducts her into the husband's world makes for mutual understanding. She now has problems similar to his, so he can offer more helpful advice than when her problems are confined to the domestic world. Masculine helplessness in response to the wife's problems correspondingly dwindles.

The net result is greater satisfaction with the partner's understanding for both sexes in Japan. However, in Detroit increased understanding is mitigated for some employed wives by decreased marital satisfaction. There, Blood and Wolfe found working wives and housewives about equally satisfied with their marriages. However, when each group was split into those whose husbands earned less than average ($5,000) or more than average, contradictory trends appeared. When the husband's income was low, additional income produced a happier marriage. On the other hand, when the husband's income was high, the reverse was true.

Whether in the latter case the wife's employment causes marital dissatisfaction or results from it is impossible to prove in a cross-section study. Possibly such wives escape from an unhappy home into outside activity. On the other hand, the fact that low-income working wives are *more* satisfied suggests that employment may also influence marriage. When family income is inadequate, the wife's employment is needed. The husband's appreciation of her working strengthens the marriage bond.

> As the husband's income rises, however, the wife's income becomes steadily less useful. Eventually a point of diminishing returns is reached, where what she adds to the standard of living is more than offset by the loss of her services at home. (Blood and Wolfe, 1960, p. 102.)

The question for Japan is whether income in our Tokyo sample ranges high enough to reach a point of diminishing returns. We already know that husbands of working wives lose power and are pressed into domestic service in Tokyo (as in Detroit) when wives go to work. But the lower level of economic development in Japan (combined with high economic aspirations) may make wifely employment a net gain even in families that are relatively well to do by Japanese standards (but not by American standards).

Table 6–11—Marital Satisfaction in Single- and Dual-Income Households by Husband's Income

		Husband's Income			
		LOW*		HIGH	
		Single-Income	Dual-Income	Single-Income	Dual-Income
Marital satisfaction					
Husband's	Tokyo	5.57	5.73	5.48	6.28
Wife's	Tokyo	5.31	5.47	4.96	5.85
	Detroit	4.64	4.72	5.14	4.17
N	Tokyo	115	95	181	53
	Detroit	141	71	162	25

* Low income in Tokyo is less than 360,000 yen ($1,000) per year. In Detroit, it is less than $5,000 per year.

Table 6–11 shows that the decline in marital satisfaction with employment at high income levels in Detroit does not occur in Tokyo. On the contrary, dual employment is even more beneficial at high-income levels than at subsistence levels in Tokyo. Both husbands and wives are especially pleased with their marriages under these circumstances.

Perhaps sometime in the future the Japanese standard of living will reach the place where high-income couples can afford the luxury of leaving the wife at home. At the moment, however, the fact that dual-income marriages are even more satisfactory at $1,000-plus income levels than below that figure suggests that any point of diminishing returns is a long way off.

Detailed analysis of specific facets of marriage shows that nonworking wives in both samples are more satisfied with the standard of living provided by high-earning husbands. However, in Tokyo, this gain in the standard of living comes at the expense of the interpersonal intimacy both partners (especially wives) prefer. Thus stay-at-home wives of affluent Japanese men are least satisfied with the companionship, love, and understanding they receive from their husbands. For them, the husband's occupational rise and their own domesticity produce the unhappy traditional Japanese pattern. By contrast, working wives of affluent Japanese men have the best of both patterns—a high level of material consumption combined with a modern style of interpersonal living.

External participation by husband and wife in the economic system brings psychological as well as economic resources into the marriage. These gains are not without costs, however—the main one being time subtracted from household functions. These costs are most clearly revealed in the altered division of labor in the home. They may explain the lesser marital satisfaction of high-income dual-income Detroit homes where the increased social cost of the wife's employment outweighs the increased gain in resources even to her (to say nothing of her presumably resentful husband).

HIGH INCOME—NET GAIN OR LOSS?

We have already seen that absorption in the occupational system reduces leisure time so drastically that marital companionship is damaged. This loss may be offset, however, if extra work produces extra income. The two factors pull in opposite directions: occupationally involved husbands bring home extra financial resources at the expense of depleted leisure time. The net effect of these countertrends is difficult to predict.

We have already seen differences between America and Japan in the gain/cost ratio. The average Detroit husband earns five times as much money in 20 per cent less time than our Tokyo men. Hence, Detroit occupations are both less costly and more rewarding. The net result should be that extra income damages marital relationships less in Detroit than in Tokyo.

Table 6–12 shows the expected contribution of income to the husband's power in both cities, further bolstering our resource theory. However, the costs to the wife (and to the husband) are also apparent in the table. In both cities, the extra work required of the husband in making extra income is matched by extra work required of the wife inside the home.

Neither the wife's loss of power nor her extra housework should be interpreted as entirely uncompensated. Increased satisfaction with the standard of living purchasable through the husband's income is evidence of that (though it is intriguing to note that in both cities the next-to-the-top income bracket wives show their envy of the top group through lessened satisfaction).

Though the standard of living rises, extra income is bought at the expense of other aspects of marriage. Aggregate satisfaction sooner or later declines for wives in both countries. As our previous reasoning suggested, the declines are more drastic and occur earlier in Japan than in the United States. Extra effort brings less pay-off in Japan. Whereas marital satisfaction for the wife falls at moderate income levels in Japan, it is only in the top bracket in America that any decline is visible and even then the drop is small.

The specific satisfactions listed in the table show that high-income marriages suffer most in companionship and to a lesser extent in understanding. Similar declines occur above low-income levels in Tokyo wives' satisfaction with the husband's love and his role performance as father to their children. These losses reflect the separation of husband from wife and children to acquire occupational success. Success on the job comes only at the expense of marriage and family living.

Table 6–12—The Marital Repercussions of the Husband's Income

| | | Husband's Income | | | | |
		Very Low*	Low	Moderate	High	Very High
Balance of Power						
Husband's Power	Tokyo	5.1	5.1	5.5	5.7	—
	Detroit	4.8	5.0	5.6	5.9	6.1
Division of Labor						
Wife's Task Performance	Tokyo	4.1	4.8	5.2	5.2	—
	Detroit	4.7	5.2	5.2	5.9	6.3
Aggregate Marital Satisfaction						
Husband's	Tokyo	5.6	5.8	4.8	5.8	—
Wife's	Tokyo	5.4	5.5	4.5	4.5	—
	Detroit	4.4	4.8	5.1	5.2	5.0
Wife's Satisfaction with Husband's Income						
	Tokyo	3.5	4.2	4.0	4.6	—
	Detroit	3.0	3.2	3.8	3.6	3.8
Satisfaction with Companionship						
Husband's	Tokyo	4.1	4.2	3.7	3.9	—
Wife's	Tokyo	3.7	3.6	3.1	2.7	—
	Detroit	3.6	3.9	3.9	4.1	3.8
Satisfaction with Understanding						
Husband's	Tokyo	4.2	4.4	3.7	4.0	—
Wife's	Tokyo	4.4	4.4	4.0	3.9	—
	Detroit	3.3	3.5	3.8	3.7	3.6
Satisfaction with Courtesy and Respect						
Husband's	Tokyo	4.4	4.6	4.5	4.3	—
Wife's	Tokyo	4.5	4.4	4.0	4.2	—
N	Tokyo	210	161	43	27	—
	Detroit	64	148	119	43	25

* Annual Income: Tokyo <$1,000 $1,000+ $1,333+ $1,667+   —
Detroit <$3,000 $3,000+ $5,000+ $7,000+ $10,000+

For Japanese men, however, the situation is more ambiguous. At high income levels, the man gains power and domestic services from his wife. He also earns direct psychological as well as financial rewards through his occupational success. Perhaps these compensating rewards explain why he is less consistently and less acutely dissatisfied than his wife. These diverse trends produce increasing asymmetry in the couple's comparative satisfaction with rising income. Perhaps the wife's dissatisfaction produces the husband's decreased satisfaction with her courtesy and respect even though his power increases. Apparently she can't manage to defer to him gracefully, even though defer she must when he brings home so much "loot."

OCCUPATIONAL STATUS

The final source of marital resources to be examined is occupational status. To be more specific, our high-status occupations are white-collar jobs and our low-status jobs are blue-collar jobs. There are hardly any of the latter in the Tokyo sample. Nevertheless, a few seem beneath the dignity of the remaining clerical, executive, and professional occupations. They include five company chauffeurs, two boilermen, two printers, one fireman, one policeman, one newspaper mailer, one drug factory employee, and one leader of a jazz band. In Detroit, blue-collar workers are numerous: craftsmen, factory workers, service workers, and unskilled laborers. They outnumber white-collar workers and provide a solid basis for analyzing the consequences of occupational status for American marriages.

The Tokyo blue-collar sample is not only small but hardly a cross section of that segment of Japanese society. Living in the same apartment houses with our white-collar workers, they are better off financially than the average blue-collar man. They are also at a disadvantage in prestige compared with their immediate neighbors—which seems likely to leave them defensively "touchy."

Occupational status is a compound of several factors. White-collar occupations require more education and yield more pay per hour. As a result of these dual characteristics, they acquire high prestige in their own right.

Insofar as white-collar workers earn at a higher rate per hour, their income should boomerang less than income earned the hard way—by extra hours of work. Instead we may expect white-collar jobs to provide greater resources to the husband at less cost to the marriage.

Table 6–13—The Marital Contributions of Occupational Status

| | | HUSBAND'S OCCUPATION | |
		Blue-Collar	White-Collar
Balance of Power			
Husband's Power	Tokyo	5.38	5.19
	Detroit	5.07	5.70
Division of Labor			
Wife's Task Performance	Tokyo	4.79	4.49
	Detroit	5.23	6.52
Marital Interaction			
Kinship Companionship	Tokyo	16	13
	Detroit	97	67
Friendship Companionship	Tokyo	5	8
	Detroit	85	82
Dating Companionship	Tokyo	13	21
Intellectual Companionship	Tokyo	122	177
Informative Companionship			
Wife Tells Husband	Tokyo	200	232
Husband Tells Wife	Tokyo	144	176
	Detroit	172	202
Aggregate Marital Satisfaction			
Husband's	Tokyo	4.73	5.68
Wife's	Tokyo	4.69	5.28
	Detroit	4.73	5.08
N	Tokyo	14	430
	Detroit	257	148

To our surprise, the expected contribution of occupational status to the husband's power and the expected decrease in his housework fail to appear in Tokyo. On the contrary, our low-status Tokyo husbands are more domineering and do even less housework than their superiors. Could they be reacting against inferiority feelings generated by their high-status environment? Does threatened masculinity lead them to assert power through excessive demands in decision-making and to crack the whip in the division of labor? Another possibility is that blue-collar husbands in Japan are not emancipated from old-fashioned styles of marriage. Such an interpretation is consistent with the fact that poorly educated men in the Tokyo sample—who according to our resource theory should be powerless at home—are also more domineering than better educated men. One advantage of the nonenlightenment theory is that it fits both the structural and the dynamic differences between the two occupational groups in Tokyo.[9]

Table 6–13 shows that in every type of companionship except one, white-collar husbands outstrip blue-collar men. The one exception—getting together with relatives—is a traditional duty and therefore hardly classifiable as emancipated. Dating, however, and every communicative form of companionship, increase markedly with higher occupational status in both Japan and the United States. Personal interaction and verbal expression are skills intrinsically demanded of white-collar men in their work. No wonder such men are skillful communicators at home.

Contradictions there may be between Japan and the U.S.A. in the impact of occupational status on the objective aspects of marriage, but there is complete unanimity subjectively. Tokyo men and women and Detroit women all agree that white-collar marriages are more satisfactory than blue-collar ones.

SUMMARY

The outside world impinges on marriage in three ways.

In a country where tradition preserves marriage patterns in a feudal mold, experiences and training outside the home broaden the perspective of both sexes, especially for that sex which was previously confined to the home. The emancipating effect of external experience is particularly apparent in the impact of education on Tokyo women. Presumably the new ideas that women learn are the crucial influence.

Secondly, external experience provides men and women with training that carries over into marital interaction. Improved verbal skills are the best example and education again is a prime source.

Finally, external experience provides a variety of resources which the two partners contribute to marriage. These include money, knowledge, prestige and self-confidence. These resources ordinarily determine the balance of power

9. Papers presented by André Michel and Constantina Safilios-Rothschild to the 1966 Evian meetings of the International Sociological Association show that resource theory applies to metropolitan France but not to underdeveloped, highly feudal Greece, where rural, uneducated men are more patriarchal than urban, educated husbands.

between husbands and wives. At least they do so once the feudal pattern has been replaced by an individualistic instead of a sexlinked (i.e. male-dominant) balance of power. The resource theory of power must be limited in its application to modern, emancipated social conditions.

There is also a limitation imposed by the balance between costs and rewards. Involvement in the outside world costs time which is subtracted from the individual's share in the domestic division of labor. Extra work need not, however, interfere with companionship between husband and wife except where it becomes excessive or one sided. Raising the wife's external involvement to the level of the husband increases their equality and comradeship. But overparticipation in the external system by the husband alone widens the resource gap between the partners and separates them physically so that their comradeship is doubly reduced.

Additional resources, then, strengthen marriage when they either raise the resourcefulness of both partners in parallel or improve skills required for intimate personal interaction. On the other hand, noncommunicable resources such as the husband's birth status or hard-earned cash strengthen his position in marriage at the expense of the wife's, undermining the satisfactoriness of marriage in her eyes and perhaps even secondarily in his.

In any case, although the form of impact may vary from country to country and case to case, involvement both before and after marriage in various hierarchically ordered social systems affects the shape of marriage. Our major generalization is that bilateral external participation produces symmetrical marriages, whereas unilateral participation alters the structure of marriage in favor of the partner participating in the external system.

THE IMPACT OF TIME

AND CHILDREN ON MARRIAGE

Couples the world over begin marriage with high hopes. At least in societies where they establish separate households, they start with the enthusiasm and *élan* that characterize new ventures of all kinds. In most cases they have recently discovered each other—and in the case of our *miai* marriages are still getting acquainted. Regardless of how well they know each other, after the wedding they embark on the new experience of keeping house together and functioning for the first time as a married couple. Because their collectivity is limited to two people, they can concentrate their attention on each other (except for outside involvements) and share domestic experiences. It is a time for exploring the mysteries of many firsts in married living. Moreover, the fact that both partners are younger than they will ever be again supplies physical and psychic vigor for living this new life to the fullest. Though technically the honeymoon may have ended, excitement and joy persist.

But not forever. The task of this chapter is to trace changes in marriage as time passes and children arrive.

Time undermines the twin assets of the honeymoon phase of marriage—novelty and youthfulness. With their loss, the pace of marital interaction slows down. The partners grow accustomed to each other and accustomed to their tasks. Tasks are done more perfunctorily and performed alone by whichever partner proves more efficient or convenient. Optional activities based on desire for each other's company wane as the partners take each other for granted. Activities requiring energy disappear from their repertoire as physical capacities dwindle. In short, time corrodes the voluntary interaction patterns from which modern marriages are constructed.

170

What about children? Certainly they introduce new experiences, thereby stimulating new interests. They are also prized possessions—at least in limited numbers. But though most husbands and wives would say that children bring net gains, they have their costs. The chief cost for our purposes is the transformation of men and women from husbands and wives into fathers and mothers. The marriage relationship is replaced in large measure by parent-child relationships. Not completely, to be sure, but inevitably. The helplessness of the newborn infant sees to that. He *must* be fed and diapered or else he will die. Suddenly, abruptly, the marital dyad is transformed into a triad whose central focus is Junior. The husband no longer enjoys his wife's complete attention. He is lucky to be left with anywhere near half. Subsequently the larger the number of children, the greater the attention they pre-empt, leaving less time and energy for the husband.

Many parents would say: "Good riddance. That was an immature, egocentric relationship anyway." We are not concerned here with evaluating the two philosophies—our concern is simply to document the changes that children introduce. However, early child-bearing and lengthening life-expectancies for most couples combine to create a period subsequent to child-bearing as well as one preceding it. Indeed in the United States the postparental period is typically ten times as long as the honeymoon period (Glick, 1955). If those years are to be meaningful, the marital tie somehow needs to survive the child-rearing years.

THE FAMILY LIFE CYCLE

Ordinary marriages go through stages that can be compared for purposes of unraveling the effects of time and children. Since our Japanese couples are concentrated in the early stages of marriage, our main groups are honeymoon couples (married less than four years and still childless), those with preschool children, and those with preadolescent children.[1] One other group is a deviant one—those married four to five years or more but still childless. Since most of these are involuntarily childless, they differ from parents chiefly in the subtle physical causes of infertility rather than in major psychological ways—except that in Tokyo slightly more wives (41 as contrasted with 31 per cent for the rest of the sample) would rather be males if they could have their choice. Disregarding such potential complications, the later-childless group provides an opportunity for comparison of the effect on marriage of the sheer passage of time versus the effect of time plus children.

The chart on the next page shows how our tests of the effect of time and children are derived from our family life-cycle data.[2]

Because the number of cases in all tables in this chapter are the same, it will simplify matters to list them here, together with the precise defining characteristics of each stage in the family life cycle in the two samples.

1. In the Tokyo sample a few of the latter actually were young teenagers, but we kept them anyway because we had so few preadolescents to start with.
2. Because the data are complicated, we present them in the Appendix in the same order.

General Model for Tables on Time and Children

EFFECT OF TIME AND/OR CHILDREN

COMPARISON GROUPS	Time Only (Children Absent)	Time Only (Children Present)	Children Only (Time Constant)	Time Plus Children
	From Honeymoon to Later Childless	From Preschool to Preadolescent	From Later Childless to Child-Rearing*	From Honeymoon to Child-Rearing

* The child-rearing group consists of the preschool and preadolescent groups combined, since the later childless group spans an equivalent length of marriage.

Classification of Families Into Life-Cycle Stages

	DEFINING CHARACTERISTIC			NUMBER OF CASES	
STAGE		Tokyo	Detroit	Tokyo	Detroit
Honeymoon	Years Married	<5*	<4*	167	30
Preschool	Age of Oldest Child	<6	<6	176	152
Preadolescent	Age of Oldest Child	6–11†	6–12†	74	167
Later Childless	Years Married	5–15	4–15	27	56
			Total	444·	405

* The honeymoon lasts a year longer in Tokyo than in Detroit because Japanese couples postpone their child-bearing longer under their less favorable economic conditions. Only with the fifth year of marriage does the proportion of childless couples in the Japanese sample shrink to 20%, when it can be assumed that at least half are involuntarily childless. The honeymoon stage is therefore defined as the normal period of voluntary childlessness preceding the child-bearing stage. The later childless group is a deviant group; most of its members would like to have children but are physically unable to. Only 3 of our 444 Tokyo women say they prefer childlessness.

† The category 6–11 is our recommended definition of preadolescence because it corresponds to the elementary school years. Unfortunately our Detroit data were coded into the less satisfactory interval 6–12 years. Were we to repeat our research, we would use 6–11 years for both samples.

It is apparent from the frequency distribution that the child-rearing groups in Tokyo (preschool and preadolescent stages combined) are skewed toward briefer marriages than in Detroit. Comparisons with the later childless groups can therefore be only loosely labeled "time constant." Nevertheless, comparing these groups should give some idea of the impact of time and children on marriage in the two samples, at least on those variables where that impact is heavy.

Power Structure

The advent of children interferes with the wife's access to contemporary external resources of power. Confined to the home, particularly before the children start school, she can be expected to depend more on her husband. In short, children should shift the balance of power in the husband's direction.

We have remarked before that couples initially share experiences, including decision-making. As time goes on, we expect sharing to give way to specialized decision-making for the sake of convenience.

However, the effect of time on the balance of power is more difficult to predict. As children become less dependent, the wife's power is likely to recover. But should we expect wives without children to become more powerful or less so, the longer they live with their husbands? Lacking an hypothesis, it will be safer to turn to the data first and then attempt an ex post facto interpretation.

Table 7-1—The Impact of Time and Children on the Marital Power Structure

| | EFFECTS OF TIME AND/OR CHILDREN | | | |
	Time Only (Children Absent)	Time Only (Children Present)	Children Only (Time Constant)	Time Plus Children
Husband's Power				
Tokyo	+	−	−	+
Detroit	−	−	+	+
Specialization (number of unilateral decisions)				
Tokyo	+	+	+	+
Detroit	+	+	+	+

Table 7-1 shows the expected increase in the husband's power in both countries when the honeymoon ends with the birth of the first child (time plus children). He also loses power in both samples as the oldest child reaches school age, freeing the wife from total confinement to the home (time only, children present). The remaining comparisons are contradictory because in Tokyo the later childless group is the most husband-dominated of the four groups, whereas in Detroit it is the least husband-dominated. This reverses the direction of comparisons which involve that group.

Much of this discrepancy may result from the differing decisions surveyed in the two countries. On the only common item (deciding whether to buy life insurance) childless men in both cities are less powerful. Moreover, the differences in Detroit are substantially greater than in Tokyo (perhaps because the span of years in Detroit tends to be greater). Childless Detroit women who have been married four to fifteen years conspicuously control their own employment. Secondarily, they are appreciably more involved in choosing the family car, a new house or apartment, and vacation destinations. These decisions have major economic implications and are understandably affected by the resourcefulness of these lifelong career women. If we had more economic decisions in Tokyo, the results might be more like Detroit.

It may be, however, that childlessness affects women differently in the two countries. Presumed fertility is a prerequisite for marriage in Japan. To find oneself infertile must be profoundly disillusioning. Perhaps the domineering behavior of childless Japanese husbands reflects contempt for unworthy wives who accept their "guilt." American women may be less willing to take all the blame for what, after all, is a joint failure. Feeling less ashamed, they carve out a vigorous career-oriented life which includes equally vigorous participation in family decisions.

We expected time more predictably to increase specialization in decision-making. Table 7–1 confirms this hypothesis. Both time and children, taken separately and together, produce autonomous decision-making in both samples, regardless of shifts in direction of the balance of power. This confirms our American findings—despite the difference in measuring instruments. Hence we can generalize crossculturally that the family life-cycle involves progressive specialization of decision-making (at least in these early stages of the cycle).

We have already suggested possible reasons for the growing autonomy of the partners: (1) They become less interested in doing things together as their initial joy in companionship wears off. (2) Their roles are differentiated by the mother's preoccupation with her children, leaving less time for discussing issues to be decided. (3) In addition, they often discover through early joint deliberations which partner is more knowledgeable, more interested, or otherwise more competent than the other. Gradually he takes over responsibility for that area, relieving the spouse of his share of the burden. Joint decisions may be "nice" but they take time and energy. Because energies gradually dissipate with age or are gobbled up by other roles (parental and occupational), efficiency is needed and appreciated. Nevertheless, separate decision-making estranges the partners.

The Division of Labor

If decision-making, ordinarily equalitarian and shared, becomes specialized over the life cycle, the same process should affect the division of labor. Decision-making is not very time-consuming. Many decisions are made only once in a lifetime or at long intervals. Even rather busy couples can consult each other occasionally. But housekeeping is laborious and repetitive. Therefore the benefits of specialization should be even greater.

Chapter 6 stated that the wife's housework is inversely geared to her external participation. Children should increase not only the amount but the proportion of housework she does (by tying her down to the home). Because housework is predominantly a feminine province, the passing years should erode men's initial willingness to help out, leaving wives stuck with routine chores.

In Table 7–2, children dramatically retire their mothers from external employment. However, the data in the Appendix show that "maternity leaves" are more prolonged in the United States where the man's greater earning power enables the family more easily to survive the expense of having children and losing the wife's earnings. This applies primarily to high-income couples in Detroit for whom employment drops almost to zero in the preschool stage. By contrast, women whose husbands earn less than $5,000 per year stay with their jobs as much as Tokyo wives. To be sure, $4,999 is a great deal more than the Japanese families have. But pressure to work is only partly a matter of money as such. Employment results from the desire to close the gap between the husband's earnings and the couple's wishes—a highly relative matter.

Time has less effect on feminine employment. When children are present, time decreases their dependence and frees the wife to return to work. In this sense, the second comparison is the reverse of the third, i.e., it involves subtracting children instead of adding them. With the absence of children, the impact of time is similar. Wives go to work as they discover they are unable to have children.

Table 7-2—The Impact of Time and Children on the Division of Labor

		EFFECTS OF TIME AND/OR CHILDREN			
		Time Only (Children Absent)	Time Only (Children Present)	Children Only (Time Constant)	Time Plus Children
Wife Employed					
	Tokyo	+	+	−	−
	Detroit	+	+	−	−
Wife's Task Performance					
	Tokyo	+	+	−	+
	Detroit	+	+	+	+
Task Specialization (number of unilateral tasks)					
	Tokyo	+	+	−	+
	Detroit	+	+	+	+

Both time and children increase the wife's housework in Detroit and in three of the four comparisons in Tokyo. The one exception is that Tokyo mothers get more help from their husbands than childless Tokyo women. This reversal also appears in task specialization—reflecting the fact that Tokyo fathers share more than Detroit fathers in housekeeping activities (as measured by our instruments).

As with insurance decisions, however, the only comparable task in the two interview schedules fails to reflect the aggregate reversal. Repairs around the house are made by more fathers than nonfathers in both samples. Indeed, detailed analysis of individual items in both questionnaires suggests that the addition of children (time constant) generally increases the husband's responsibility for masculine tasks (in Detroit, not only repairs but keeping track of money and bills; in Tokyo, repairs plus carrying heavy objects, shopping for his own favorite foods and underwear, and putting away his own clothes). In all these areas, the young father takes more responsibility for himself and for tasks he is especially qualified to perform by reason of superior musculature or financial competence. The wife meanwhile is absorbed in her traditional tasks of providing food, clothing, and shelter for her small needy children and, incidentally, for her great big husband. In Detroit, this involves grocery shopping, cooking, dishwashing, and living-room straightening, and for Tokyo mothers putting away the *futon* bedding.

Two apparent exceptions to this pattern occur in Detroit where mothers also do more snowshoveling and lawnmowing. On the basis of physique, we would expect fathers to volunteer for these tasks. However, Detroit snowfalls are rarely heavy, more often requiring a flick of the broom than a heave of the shovel. Similarly, the increasing motorization of Detroit lawnmowing makes muscles less important than they used to be. These are still predominantly male tasks, however, and the exceptional shifts in the female direction with the advent of children may occur when mothers stay home all day.

Apparently, then, time and children increase the wife's task load in both cities. However, Tokyo mothers become so preoccupied with serving their children that they are less able to wait on their husbands in the husband-oriented fashion implied in our Japanese questions. A more carefully equated list of tasks might straighten out the discrepancy in favor of the Detroit pattern as far as basic housework is concerned. If so, the impact of time and children on the division of labor would be to increase the proportion of housework done by the wife and the proportion done separately by the partners. Since the latter generalization applies to decision-making as well, we can make a second-order generalization that the role structure of marriage becomes more segregated under the twin impact of time and children.

The impact of children on marriage depends, of course, on the number of children involved. In both cities, the wife's task performance and the couple's task specialization increase progressively as successive children arrive. (See Appendix.) However, in Detroit—where there are enough families with four or more children so we can study oversized families, a curious reversal occurs. Beyond three children, the wife is unable to keep up with the increased load. So the husband is pressed into service to help out. By coming to his wife's rescue, he reduces her share in the division of labor and reduces the number of tasks she has to do all by herself.

This qualifies our previous generalization about the effects of children on the division of labor. Children increase the wife's share and the partners' separateness only up to a point. If enough children are added, the wife's ability to carry extra loads is exhausted and the husband is redrafted into domestic service—not because he enjoys it (as in honeymoon days) but because otherwise the household will break down (and perhaps the wife too).

The point of overload in the Detroit sample is the fourth child. Presumably breaking points depend on the burdensomeness of the children (e.g., how closely spaced they are), the resources of energy and equipment at the mother's disposal, and the draftability of the father. Japanese men are so involved in the occupational system that they are undraftable even in families of three or more children. The larger the Japanese family, the harder the husband works *outside* the home, making him less available for the help his wife needs.

Marital Courtesy

We discovered earlier that Japanese husbands are extraordinarily chivalrous —especially *miai* husbands who continue courting their wives after marriage. American men, on the other hand, are impressed by the extraordinary deference of Japanese women.

Does this courtesy between contemporary Japanese men and women survive the humdrum of marriage? Do Japanese men keep on courting their wives very long? Are Japanese women eternally courteous?

We have already discovered enough changes in Japanese marriages to make us skeptical. Couples make increasingly autonomous decisions rather than consulting one another and do tasks separately rather than helping one another. These effects of time and children on the structure of marriage hint that chivalry may not long endure either.

Table 7–3—The Impact of Time and Children on Japanese Marital Courtesy

	EFFECTS OF TIME AND/OR CHILDREN			
	Time Only (Children Absent)	Time Only (Children Present)	Children Only (Time Constant)	Time Plus Children
Husband Carries Heavy Objects	−	−	+	−
Wife Gets Bus Seat	−	−	+	−
Wife Gets in Taxi First	−	−	−	−
Husband Expresses Appreciation	−	+	−	−
Wife Expresses Appreciation	=	−	−	−

Table 7–3 shows that chivalry is indeed undermined after marriage. The combined effect of time and children is always negative. Purely symbolic precedence (getting into the taxi first) suffers from time and children, separately or together. Obviously our modern Japanese men tend to revert to ancient form—or at least toward unchivalrous equalitarianism—after the honeymoon ends.

Exceptions occur when chivalry is functionally useful. Wives burdened with children are less able to carry other burdens or offer their husbands the remaining bus seat. Japanese mothers strap babies on their backs. They seat older children on their laps to protect them from the crush of overcrowded public vehicles. Hence it is only fair that husbands should behave more chivalrously.

However, the effect of time when children are present shows how temporary this increase is. Indeed our appendix data show that only bus chivalry increases absolutely from the honeymoon to the preschool stage of the life cycle (and barely perceptibly at that). The effect of children (time constant) is primarily to brake the decline which normally occurs after the honeymoon. Because childless wives have no such needs, their treatment deteriorates more rapidly.

Childless wives not only get less chivalry but behave peculiarly in return. The first column of Table 7–3 shows that although nonmothers are treated less courteously after the honeymoon, they are the only wives who remain steadfastly courteous. Do they feel so guilty about their failure to bear children that they try extra hard to mollify the husband by expressing appreciation for his favors? At least this is consistent with their extra deference in decision-making.

Japanese men are not accustomed to expressing appreciation very often to their wives. What little appreciation they manage during the honeymoon slumps badly after the first child arrives. Wagatsuma suggests that the husband's modest recovery of appreciation as children get older represents

> . . . an attempt to set an example for their children who are growing older. That is, the husbands want their growing children to respect and behave properly to their mothers and, in setting an example, the husbands hope their children will learn also this appreciative attitude toward the mother.

It should be noted, however, that wives meanwhile become *less* appreciative, less courteous, and less submissive. The Japanese saying that "Mother is strong" applies with particular force to the mothers of older children. They seem disinclined to "set a good example."

With few exceptions, the picture shows dwindling courtesy after marriage. The evidence later in this chapter about dwindling American companionship and understanding suggests that marital courtesy is no more long-lived in this country than Japan (if not less so!). Were we to trace the pattern from courtship to marriage we would probably find that chivalry passes its peak when couples move from the tentativeness of mutual pursuit to the certainty of marriage.

In any case, courteous as Japanese may be compared to Westerners, their brand of courtesy is no more immune to corrosion by time and children than anyone else's.

Companionship

Children should interfere with their parents' leisure for engaging in joint activities. In this sense they are a distraction and an intrusion.

Time, on the other hand, may diminish the couple's desire to concentrate on each other and increase their participation in external forms of companionship that bring refreshing contact with outside relatives and friends.

Internal companionship presents an overwhelmingly consistent picture in Table 7–4. Both time and children undermine these purest forms of companionship in Tokyo and the one form of internal companionship that was measured in Detroit. There is no reason to doubt that the remaining types of internal companionship decline progressively in Detroit. (The one exception is that children give wives something new to talk about.)

Table 7–4—The Impact of Time and Children on Husband-Wife Companionship

| | EFFECTS OF TIME AND/OR CHILDREN | | | |
	Time Only (Children Absent)	Time Only (Children Present)	Children Only (Time Constant)	Time Plus Children
Internal Companionship				
Dating Companionship				
Tokyo	−	−	−	−
Intellectual Companionship				
Tokyo	−	−	−	−
Informative Companionship				
Husband tells events				
Tokyo	−	−	−	−
Detroit	−	−	−	−
Wife tells events				
Tokyo	−	−	+	−
External Companionship				
Kinship Companionship				
Tokyo	+	−	−	−
Detroit	−	−	−	−
Friendship Companionship				
Tokyo	+	−	−	−
Detroit	+	+	+	+
Organizational Companionship				
Detroit	+	+	+	+*

* Organizational companionship declines when children are small, but rises as children reach grade-school age to heights surpassing any other stage in the family life cycle (see Eberts, 1963).

These minus signs dramatize the nearly inevitable deterioration of husband-wife relationships under normal conditions. The only way of insulating marriage against attrition is to end it abortively—before children arrive and especially before the honeymoon glow fades. This is one motive for the serial polygamy practiced by movie stars and other romantics in pursuit of eternally youthful relationships. Or one can end relationships even sooner, heeding the warning that "marriage is the death of love"—and pursue lover after lover, only to abandon each once he surrenders and thereby falls in danger of being taken for granted.

These, however, are rare and deviant solutions to the problems of time and children. The common American solution is for partners who earlier devoted themselves to each other to turn their attention outward. By joint ventures into external social circles and formal organizations, they introduce elements of novelty into lives too familiar to provide novelty any longer from within.

Organizational involvement is more than a permitted American solution to internal boredom. It is a direct consequence of having school-age children. Preschool children are so immobile that they tie mothers down, reducing their participation in formal organizations. Adolescents, on the other hand, are so mobile that they abandon their parents for their peers. Preadolescents, however, are old enough to go to school and take part in community activities but need parental sponsors. They transform mothers into PTA members and fathers into little league coaches. Nor is this entirely initiated by the child. Personal concern for their children's welfare leads many American parents into civic betterment campaigns.

Kin companionship, however, fails to follow the rising trend of other external pursuits. Ties with parents and siblings (the chief targets of kinship interaction) are strongest in childhood. To marry successfully requires loosening kin ties and forging ties with the spouse. This transfer occurs gradually and has not been completed during the honeymoon stage. Hence kin interaction is most intense at the beginning of marriage and declines subsequently.

Joint visiting with friends and joint membership in organizations are modern forms of sociability. They function quite differently in Japan than in the United States. In Japan, increased external sociability is a possible solution to internal boredom only for childless couples. Once children arrive, the isolation that used to be the fate of every *wife* still becomes the fate of every *mother*. Unlike Americans who increase their external sociability, Japanese couples progressively withdraw from contact with the outside world.[3]

Why the difference? Probably children strain the resources of Japanese families beyond their ability to surmount them. Money, space, and time for activities with other people are insufficient. Automobiles for easy transport with or without children are rare.

But even if the economic boom increases the average family's material resources, external sociability in the child-rearing years may not rise. It is hindered by the tie between Japanese mothers and children. The strength of that tie is manifested in the shocked tones with which Japanese parents in a department-store auditorium asked me what would happen if an American baby got sick during the night. Sleeping in a separate bedroom, the baby might die without the parents' even knowing it!

If Japanese parents can't let their baby out of sight at night but must snuggle it between them under the *futon*, how much less can they entrust it to a babysitter! The American custom of bringing complete strangers into the home to care for children while parents go out and have a good time shocks Japanese ears. It violates the Confucian emphasis on parents' duty to sacrifice personal pleasures for the sake of bringing children up properly. It violates, too, the Japanese dependence on close personal ties and formal introductions. Americans learn to be sociable early by being left with strange teenage custodians. A generation later it enables the grown-up child to abandon his own children to similar novices.[4]

3. Some modern couples, immediately after marriage, proudly go to movies, plays, and concerts together and sometimes attend parties with friends. Yet, in most Mamachi families this visiting stops abruptly shortly before the first child is born. While some young couples talk of going out occasionally afterward, they rarely do, except perhaps for visits to relatives. (Vogel, 1963.)

4. Upper-middle-class Americans sometimes import European girls to live in so the mother can be free for a career. Vogel (1963) reports that Japanese mothers with live-in maids rarely abandon their children to them, much less to outside babysitters:

The vast majority are not even interested in hiring a stranger for a few hours a week. The gap between family member and stranger is too great to be bridged by mere

The scarcity of civic organizations in Japan restricts this form of sociability—though it might be congenial to community-oriented mothers were it more available. Their sense of duty to their children largely terminates the few external contacts with adults which couples have during courtship and the honeymoon period. Henceforth the wife's chief opportunities to get away from home are with her children. In infancy, a child can be strapped to her back for easy maneuverability. On Sundays, her husband can join in family trips to the zoo, chrysanthemum exhibit, or department store to see the sights. On such occasions, the wife has some companionship with her husband, to be sure, but no longer the exclusive kind involved in internal companionship. Now marital companionship is subordinated to family togetherness, unrelieved by the adult forms of companionship that Detroit couples enjoy when they leave their children at home.

The most common experience in the family life cycle, then, is declining companionship. But in a society overflowing with material and human resources, internal losses can be balanced by new forms of external sociability. These provide potential dynamic infusions to otherwise flagging marriages.

When these declines in internal companionship (and in Japan in external companionship, too) are added to the declining share in decision-making and task performance, married couples become progressively disengaged: they do less and less together, more and more apart.

Emotional Therapy

We have often described emotional interdependence as a subclassification of one form of internal companionship (informative companionship). We should therefore expect to find it, too, declining over the family life cycle.

Table 7–5 shows a general pattern of decline. But there is one exception in the Detroit sample and the Appendix shows that children alone cause a barely perceptible decline in the Tokyo data as well. Apparently children do not appreciably interfere with therapeutic utilization of the partner. Indeed children often *cause* troubles for wives to tell their husbands. This potential upsurge in motivation for therapy is reminiscent of the upsurge in Tokyo mothers' informative companionship as opposed to childless wives. In both cases, children interfere with communication processes, but if enough voltage builds up, the extra resistance is more than offset and communication flows.

The effect of children on therapeutic utilization depends partly on how many children are involved (see Appendix). Detroit wives utilize their husbands most when they have their first child, declining steadily with additional

---

contractual arrangements. A mother's relationship with the children is considered so special that even other members of the family are rarely left to care for children. The mother is irreplaceable.

children (and, we must remember, the additional time required to produce those children). By the time three children are added, mothers rely on their hubands less than childless wives married equally long, while mothers of four or more children are conspicuously reserved. Apparently for Detroit wives, therapeutic utilization is benefited only by one or two children.

In Tokyo, however, children consistently interfere. No upsurge occurs in response to the first child. Instead, each partner relies on the other less and less with each successive child.

Table 7–5—The Impact of Time and Children on Therapeutic Interaction

		EFFECTS OF TIME AND/OR CHILDREN			
		Time Only (Children Absent)	Time Only (Children Present)	Children Only (Time Constant)	Time Plus Children
Therapeutic Utilization					
Husband Tells Troubles					
	Tokyo	−	−	−	−
Wife Tells Troubles					
	Tokyo	−	−	−	−
	Detroit	−	−	+	−
Therapeutic Response					
Help in Getting Away					
Wife's	Tokyo	−	+	−	−
Husband's	Tokyo	−	+	−	−
	Detroit	+	−	−	−
Help in Solving					
Wife's	Tokyo	−	−	−	−
Husband's	Tokyo	−	−	+	−
	Detroit	−	+	+	−
Advice					
Wife's	Tokyo	+	−	−	+
Husband's	Tokyo	−	−	+	−
	Detroit	−	+	−	−
Sympathy					
Wife's	Tokyo	−	+	+	−
Husband's	Tokyo	+	+	−	−
	Detroit	−	+	−	−
. . . .*					
Passivity					
Wife's	Tokyo	−	+	+	+
Husband's	Tokyo	−	−	+	+
	Detroit	+	−	+	+
Criticism					
Wife's	Tokyo	−	+	+	+
Husband's	Tokyo	=	+	+	+
	Detroit	+	=	+	+
Dismissal					
Wife's	Tokyo	+	+	+	+
Husband's	Tokyo	+	+	+	+
	Detroit	+	+	+	+

* The dotted line divides the four best methods from the three worst (see Chapter 8).

In general, then, children interfere in both countries with the ability of men and women to turn to the spouse—the larger the number of children, the greater the barrier. The sole exception is that American marriages accommodate a small number of children more easily than Japanese marriages. New American mothers become more dependent therapeutically, the barrier presented by one or two children not yet being sufficient to block the wife's desire to share her new troubles.

We have already observed the lesser toll of children on American marriages. Given greater resources and a correspondingly larger ideal family size, American marriages are less threatened by the advent of children than today's fragile Japanese marriages.

Time unambiguously undermines therapeutic interdependence in both samples. And time divides couples so much more than children unite them that the combined effect of time plus children depresses trouble-telling in America as well as in Japan. Here, once more, the course of marriage involves increased self-reliance and autonomy, and decreased dependence on one another for relief of personal needs.

Changes in therapeutic responses are complicated because we have not tabulated frequencies of response but proportions, so gains in one category are necessarily balanced by losses in others. Generally speaking the top four responses in Table 7-5 are therapeutically effective in both societies, whereas the last three are less satisfactory (as we shall see in more detail in the next chapter).

First let us compare how time and children affect male methods of dealing with wives in the two samples. In general, helpful methods tend to decrease (22 minus signs in 32 cells) and poor methods increase (19 in 24). This downward trend is particularly marked in the last column where the combined effect of time and children is almost entirely negative.

Exceptions to this trend occur chiefly in the second column where men respond more helpfully to maturing children than they had to the incomprehensible problems of infants. With school-age children, American husbands give more helpful advice and practical help, Tokyo wives are freer to be taken away from their troubles, and both sets of husbands find it easier to be sympathetic.

We suggested earlier that children increase the wife's need for emotional relief because of the problems they provoke. In both samples, the domestic locale of these problems makes them accessible to the husband's practical help, but wives in both societies can less easily be bodily removed from their troubles than women without dependents.

Children increase negative responses in every comparison. Young fathers seem baffled by the problems of babies and toddlers. Moreover, they are burdened by heavy expenses and frequently by loss of the wife's income. As we have already suggested, the more children they acquire, the longer Tokyo husbands have to work to make ends meet. No wonder their patience wears thin and they give way more often to passivity and negativism.

Children overtax the average husband's ability to relieve his wife's problems. Life-cycle changes may intensify the husband's problems too, but they do not change their nature so much. He still brings home the same occupational problems, but because his wife's problems have altered, she is less capable of responding therapeutically. Burdened by very tangible problems, she is less able to muster enough resources to come to his rescue.

Generally speaking, time and children affect our Japanese wives' responses the same way they do the men's. One exception is the differential effect of children on women and men. Children make Japanese wives less able to help their husbands directly, whereas husbands in both samples are better able to help their wives after children arrive. Time, on the other hand, makes Japanese wives bolder about giving advice than when they were first married, whereas male advice-giving decreases from the confident involvement of newlywed husbands. With few exceptions, however, feminine therapeutic responses change in the same direction as masculine ones.

These qualitative changes over the life cycle indicate that husbands and wives not only drift farther apart but on those steadily less frequent occasions when they reach out for emotional support, they are liable to be rebuffed or actually jumped on. These are marginal tendencies, of course, but visible even in the early stages of marriage. They intensify in later years so that for an increasing minority of couples, marriage leads either to divorce or to conflict, bitterness, and disappointment. For such couples, at least, marriage is indeed the death of love.

Love and Sex

Just how often does love die in marriage? When it dies so completely that marriage ends, our study of still-existing marriages loses sight of it. Only a longitudinal follow-up study could catch such utter dissolutions. Nevertheless, even marriages that endure deteriorate. We have suggested before that love wilts especially in love-match marriages in both countries. Now the time has come to test this interpretation explicitly.

Table 7-6 shows love constantly declining, especially in Japan, and especially under the impact of time. The overt expression of love by Japanese husbands ebbs in every comparison. A common Japanese myth is that though Japanese men don't express much affection, they nevertheless love their wives and the wives know it without needing to be told. Our analysis punctures that myth. The declining expression of affection results from a cooling off of love and produces less satisfied wives. Being human, Japanese wives like to be shown that they are loved.

The cooling is mutual. Wives as well as husbands love their partners less. Husbands detect this decline and become less satisfied too. However, the appendix data show that wives are more sensitive than husbands. The decline in both love and satisfaction is greater for wives than for husbands. Male insensitivity, then, may explain the one exception in Table 7-6 to the universal decline of love in Japan, the plateau for fathers during the child-rearing years contrasted with the normal decline for mothers.

Table 7–6—The Impact of Time and Children on Love and Sex

| | | EFFECTS OF TIME AND/OR CHILDREN | | | |
		Time Only (Children Absent)	Time Only (Children Present)	Children Only (Time Constant)	Time Plus Children
Husband Expresses Affection					
	Tokyo	—	—	—	—
Love for Spouse					
Husband's	Tokyo	—	—	—	—
Wife's	Tokyo	—	—	—	—
Satisfaction with Spouse's Expressed Love					
Husband's	Tokyo	—	=	—	—
Wife's	Tokyo	—	—	—	—
	Detroit	+	—	+	+
Length of Foreplay					
	Tokyo	—	—	+	—
Frequency of Intercourse					
	Tokyo	—	—	+	—
Sexual Satisfaction					
Husband's	Tokyo	—	+	—	—
Wife's	Tokyo	—	+	—	—

When we compare across national boundaries, however, a marked contrast appears. Whereas both time and children undermine love for Japanese wives, time occasionally and children consistently increase the love satisfaction of our American wives. So sharp a contrast deserves the further exploration presented in Table 7–7.

Table 7–7—Wife's Satisfaction with Love by Number of Children and Husband's Annual Income

| | | NUMBER OF CHILDREN | | | | |
		Zero	One	Two	Three +*	Four +
HUSBAND'S ANNUAL INCOME						
Low (Under 30,000 Yen)†		5.09	4.51	4.09	3.50	—
Moderate						
(Over 30,000 Yen)		4.97	4.56	4.71	3.94	—
(Under $5,000)		3.81	3.93	4.23	3.79	3.26
High (Over $5,000)		4.00	3.94	3.59	3.92	3.25
N						
Tokyo	Low	123	63	22	2	—
	High	71	79	66	17	—
Detroit	Low	58	46	48	29	27
	High	18	51	69	36	12

* Three children in Detroit, three or more in Tokyo.
† 30,000 Yen = $834.

The purpose of Table 7–7 is to test whether the difference between wives in the two countries is due to differing abilities to afford children. By demonstrating a marked correlation between income level and the most "satisfying" number of children *within* each country, the table supports our international hypothesis. For low-income families in Japan, each succeeding child undermines the wife's love satisfaction. Under stringent circumstances only complete childlessness is entirely compatible with love. As income rises, however, a secondary rise in satisfaction occurs for Japanese mothers of two children; and for low-income American families those are the most satisfied women of all. At high-income levels, the secondary rise occurs still later (at three children) though it fails to reach the childless level. The picture is not quite perfect but the trend is highly suggestive: the higher the resource level, the greater the ability to maintain love or even increase it in the face of additional children.

This international contrast is yet another manifestation of the difference in living standards in Japan and the U.S.A. Children are more financially burdensome in Japan and tie the mother down far more. For both partners they terminate the love-match phase of marriage and plunge them back into feudalistic sex segregation and estrangement. Children bring dating and other socializing almost to a halt in Japan (but not in the United States). Given greater resources of money and leisure, American parents can cope with children more successfully. Indeed, given their larger child-bearing preferences, they even respond positively to the advent of children—at least as far as feelings are concerned. As in Japan, American marital interaction generally suffers from the intervention of children. But unlike our modern urban Japanese parents, Americans often find their total morale rising as they become parents the first few times. Eventually, however, even American resource levels fail to cope with the extra costs of more children, so their morale suffers, too, in "oversize" families.

Returning to Table 7–6, we see that children are more positively related to Japanese sexual experience than to love. The positive effect of children (time constant) might better be described as the negative effect of childlessness on sexual activity. Or perhaps it works the other way around. Perhaps some couples engage in intercourse so seldom that they fail to conceive. In any case the sharpest contrasts are between the honeymooning group who are most active sexually and the later childless couples who are least active. Frequency of intercourse drops especially fast from an average of 72 times per year for honeymooners to about forty for all other life-cycle categories. The greatest force, then, in sexual activity is time: newly married couples are intensely sexual, but this preoccupation fades as the honeymoon phase ends and they become old-married couples.[5]

The recovery of sexual satisfaction as children grow older may reflect emancipation from being chaperoned by the baby. We have already mentioned the custom of placing the baby between the parents on the sleeping pad. This arrangement symbolizes the concern of both parents (especially the mother) with the physical welfare of her sleeping child. It also symbolizes the pre-

5. Many studies in the United States and Japan show declines in length of foreplay and frequency of intercourse as time passes. For example, Shinozaki 1957, finds foreplay averages nearly 10 minutes among young wives (age 20–24), declining to less than 7 minutes after age 35. Frequency of intercourse declines even more sharply from 2.2 times per week at age 20–24 to 1.1 at 35–39. Kinsey, 1953, reports higher levels but a similar decline (from 3.0 to 2.0) for the same age groups in the United States.

eminence of the mother-child dyad over the marital dyad. This is hardly a physical environment or psychological atmosphere conducive to sexual arousal and enjoyment. It suggests why the subjective evaluation of both parents (especially of wives) is lowest during the preschool stage.[6]

In every facet of marriage that we have examined, husbands and wives drift apart over time, interact less, and love each other less. The extra requirements of children generally accentuate this disengagement and disenchantment. However, the impact of children varies with the parents' resourcefulness. In Japan that impact is more severe because there is less time, machinery, and personal help for coping with children's needs. In the division of labor this pressures Japanese husbands into increased service and damages the partner's love for one another. In affluent America, the reverse is true in each instance.

Children then *can* have compensatory advantages even for husband-wife relationships provided they come in limited enough quantities into homes prepared to cope with them. Few homes the world over, however, are so well equipped. Hence the usual effect of children as well as time is to undermine any wishes the parents may have to create modern companionable marriages.

General Satisfaction with Marriage

The impact of time and children on marriage depends not only on the couple's resources for coping with these objective stresses but on whether they prefer a comradely or a traditional marriage. Our Tokyo data offer a nice chance to observe such differences because the two sexes in contemporary Japan hold conflicting values. Men cling to old ways (which burden them less than new ones) while women reach for new ones which burden *them* less. We therefore expect today's Japanese women to take the onslaught of children harder than out-of-the-home husbands. Men may even welcome the reversion to conventional patterns that children bring. Besides, Japanese women should

6. Caudill, 1961a, contrasts the American and Japanese woman's preoccupation with the role of mother:

> . . . the American mother . . . is often seen as in conflict over how much time she should give to various outside activities . . . and how much time she should devote to her children. If she decides the balance should fall in favor of her children, she still rather explicitly reserves certain periods of time off "for herself." Psychologically, this tends to mean time off to express those aspects of her individuality which she feels are separate from her role as mother. . . . Such behavior is less characteristic of the social role or psychological attitude of the Japanese mother.

Presumably sex is one of the nonmaternal activities that more easily survives the invasion of children in the American context.

Caudill, 1962a, also points out that "in general people wish to sleep side by side [in Japan] more than is true in the United States." To American readers, this implies a preference for double beds designed for occupancy and specifically sexual use by married couples. In Japan, however, the phrase *in general* diffusely extends beyond married couples to whole families. Family togetherness dissolves the privacy boundaries of the marital dyad and depresses sexual activity. In short, sexual intercourse may be restricted by too much separateness in an American twin-bed room or too much togetherness in a Japanese "family-bed" room.

feel more disillusioned when normal taken-for-grantedness sets in after the couple become accustomed to each other. The husband's external preoccupation should leave him less sensitive to such losses.

Because our measure of marital satisfaction not only summarizes each partner's evaluation of several facets of marriage, but gives extra weight to his most valued facets, sex differences in value systems as well as in evaluation of particular functions are reflected in the total.

Table 7–8 shows that progressive disenchantment occurs for both sexes in

Table 7–8—The Impact of Time and Children on Marital Satisfactions

		EFFECTS OF TIME AND/OR CHILDREN			
		Time Only (Children Absent)	Time Only (Children Present)	Children Only (Time Constant)	Time Plus Children
Aggregate Satisfaction					
Husband's	Tokyo	−	−	+	−
Wife's	Tokyo	−	−	−	−
	Detroit	−	−	+	+
Specific Satisfaction					
Love					
Husband's	Tokyo	−	=	−	−
Wife's	Tokyo	−	−	−	−
	Detroit	+	−	+	+
Spouse as parent					
Husband's	Tokyo	(−)*	−	(−)*	(−)*
Wife's	Tokyo	(−)*	−	(−)*	(−)*
Understanding					
Husband's	Tokyo	−	+	−	−
Wife's	Tokyo	+	−	−	−
	Detroit	−	−	+	−
Sex					
Husband's	Tokyo	−	+	−	−
Wife's	Tokyo	−	+	−	−
Companionship					
Husband's	Tokyo	−	−	−	−
Wife's	Tokyo	−	+	−	−
	Detroit	−	−	+	−
Courtesy and respect					
Husband's	Tokyo	−	+	−	−
Wife's	Tokyo	−	−	−	−
Husband's income					
Wife's	Tokyo	+	−	+	+
Standard of living					
Wife's	Detroit	+	−	−	+
Wife's financial management					
Husband's	Tokyo	+	−	−	−
Wife's home management					
Husband's	Tokyo	+	−	−	−
Husband's helpfulness					
Wife's	Tokyo	−	−	−	−
Own share in decisions					
Husband's	Tokyo	−	−	−	−
Wife's	Tokyo	−	−	+	−
Spouse's interest in decisions					
Husband's	Tokyo	−	−	+	−
Wife's	Tokyo	−	−	−	−

* One or both cells involves hypothetical satisfaction.

Japan and for wives in both countries. The impact of time is apparently inexorable. Children, however, present an interesting contrast. Whereas women in the Tokyo sample like marriage better without children, their husbands and American women find their lives partially protected against the corrosion of time by the intervention of children. Japanese fathers are less disappointed than childless men. For American women, children are so highly valued that early child-rearing stages are even more satisfactory than the honeymoon. These differences are related to income levels the same way as satisfaction with love alone in Table 7–7. Aggregate marital satisfaction is highest for childless Japanese men and women but rises secondarily for high-income parents of two children. In Detroit, the most satisfied poor couples have two children and the most satisfied higher-income couples have three. In short, total marital satisfaction is related even more dramatically to number of children and ability to cope with them than satisfaction with love alone (see Appendix Table 7–8).

The impact of time and children can better be understood by observing the precise aspects of marriage where satisfaction rises or falls. We have already seen in Table 7–6 that children decrease satisfaction with love in Tokyo but not Detroit. The remainder of Table 7–8 shows what happens to other facets of marriage. Both sexes in Japan are disillusioned by the partner's performance as parent. Children in the flesh reveal the partner as less adequate than had been hoped. Time increases both real dissatisfaction and the expected (hypothetical) dissatisfaction of childless couples. The latter is a halo effect of disillusionment with other aspects of marriage when honeymoon euphoria ebbs into sobriety and naïve optimism gives way to experienced realism. The fact that most parent-role comparisons pit expectations against actualities illustrates the process of disillusionment. The picture is not very pretty.

No other facets of Japanese marriage are as unrelievedly negative as these most subjective ones. Though the impact of time and children elsewhere remains predominantly negative, the exceptions are worthy of comment.

Also rather psychological is the individual's satisfaction with the partner's understanding of his problems and feelings. This is the only place where the impact of time is consistently positive for any one of our three comparison groups. Japanese wives find their husbands relatively unsatisfactory at the beginning of marriage (perhaps because young men in a segregated society have had little opportunity to learn about the opposite sex). Wives do better at first— perhaps because in feudal and postfeudal societies, women devote themselves to the study of masculine psychology. In any case, Japanese men gradually overcome their initial handicap and gain accumulative understanding of feminine problems. We attribute the fact that American men are not similarly benefited to their headstart from growing up in an integrated society. Their superior understanding is demonstrated by their willingness to listen to the problems their wives face in becoming mothers. The superior satisfaction of American mothers is a tribute to American men's ability to transcend role differentiation with empathy and therapeutic responsiveness.

We saw in Table 7–6 that children interfere with sexual satisfaction but both partners enjoy sex more as children grow older and require less attention. Similarly modest revivals of satisfaction occur for Japanese wives with respect to companionship and for husbands regarding courtesy and respect. Mothers of older children feel less alienated from their husbands even though the objective data in Table 7-4 reveal no increases in any companionable activity. Perhaps they become better adjusted to the loss of their initial companionship. Or the loss of companionship with the husband may be counterbalanced by increased companionship with preadolescent children (old enough to do things with the mother but not old enough to abandon her for peers). Whatever the reason, it is important to remember that time increases subjective satisfaction but not the objective intensity of marital companionship. (The effect of children on Detroit wives is too small to deserve comment.)

The husbands' increased satisfaction with courtesy and respect over the child-rearing years is more tangible in origin. When children are small, Japanese men are forced to be chivalrous (see Table 7-3). However, as wives become less burdened with small children they can become more deferential. The husbands' increased satisfaction therefore reflects a real shift in the balance of deference.

The remaining satisfactions concern the role structure of marriage: earning and spending money, housework, and decision-making. We have little American data for these aspects of marriage but the Japanese responses form a reasonably consistent pattern of improvement after the honeymoon. In a fashion somewhat analogous to Japanese men's improved understanding, these aspects of marriage benefit from experience. Unlike love, sex, and companionship which crest in the honeymoon, the practical skills of household economics improve with practice.

Take, for example, the standard of living. Married couples start out financially "from scratch." Unendowed with house or goods, they must earn the money to equip their households. Not only is their initial stock of capital goods zero, but the husband's earning capacity is lower than it will ever be again. (In Japan even more than in the United States, seniority brings automatic pay raises.) Hence the man's initial income is heavily taxed to provide the equipment necessary for married living.

The husband's honeymoon earnings may be bolstered significantly if the wife works. Loss of that income may account for the American wife's lessened satisfaction with the standard of living after children arrive. In Japan our question focused more specifically on the husband's income, enabling wives to express increased appreciation in spite of loss of their own income and the added cost of children.

The honeymoon period is a time of strenuous earning with meagre returns and of strenuous purchasing with the money earned. At the same time, wives trying to learn how to keep house are handicapped by the perennial inefficiencies of Japanese shopping and the time pressures of employment. Most wives quit work with the birth of their first baby, but the extra time released is absorbed by the baby's care and feeding. Children, then, consistently depress masculine satisfaction with feminine managerial functions. But older childless wives become veterans whose increased competence is reflected in growing masculine satisfaction.

For decision-making, the influences are reversed. Time decreases satisfaction as shared decision-making gives way to more efficient but less satisfying specialization. However, children increase the wife's power over our domestically oriented decisions (see Table 7–1), with the result that mothers are more actively involved in these decisions than childless wives of the same age. There is a reciprocal increase in the wife's own satisfaction with her decision-making role and in the husband's appraisal of her interest in decision-making.

To summarize, the chief effect of both time and children on all three groups is negative. However, there are exceptions. In Japan, the exceptions more often involve time, whereas in Detroit they are concentrated in positive responses to children. This difference between the two countries is essentially reciprocal. Time benefits Japanese marriages by relieving parents of the burdens of young children as they grow older. By contrast, Detroit wives (and presumably their husbands) are more familistically oriented (i.e., value larger families) and better equipped to absorb children into on-going patterns of marriage. This value orientation and readiness for children make possible more positive responses to the arrival of children—especially in moderate numbers.

We have not shown in Table 7–8 but need to remember that aggregate marital satisfaction is composed not only of the specific satisfactions listed but of the ability to have the desired number of children. Our Tokyo men do not want any more children than their wives, but their marriage goals are less threatened by children than the wives' goals. For wives, children mean reversion to a role too reminiscent of the feudal past. For husbands, children bring fewer losses, and the inability to have children in a patrilineal society creates greater sorrow. For these dual reasons, our Japanese fathers are more satisfied than older childless men, whereas for their wives the situation is reversed.

Table 7–9—The Effect of Children on Marital Satisfaction by Type of Introduction

Type of Introduction	Childless Couples	Parents	Net Difference
Love Match			
Husband's satisfaction	5.93	5.29	−0.64
Wife's satisfaction	5.86	5.06	−0.80
Arranged Marriage			
Husband's satisfaction	5.70	6.06	+0.36
Wife's satisfaction	6.18	4.55	−1.63
Minimum N			
Love Match	72	109	
Arranged Marriage	40	66	

Table 7–9 shows that husband-wife differences in response to children are concentrated in arranged marriages. Husbands who resort to the traditional system of mate-selection are the only ones who collectively find parenthood more satisfactory than marriage without children. Their wives, by contrast,

are acutely disillusioned as they move from the intensive courtship of early marriage to the feudal patterns of later marriage following a *miai*. Both objectively and subjectively these wives swing from one extreme to the other in what must be a painful transition.

In their subjective evaluations of the impact of children on marriage, then, our three groups (Tokyo husbands, Tokyo wives, and Detroit wives) differ from each other. The Tokyo men might be labeled traditional, clinging to old patterns of male dominance and welcoming children to carry on the family line and to bring their wives home as conventional housewives. The Detroit wives are not traditional in the sense of clinging to the past, but neotraditional. On the surface they resemble Tokyo husbands, but their appreciation stems from different motives—an affluence-based enjoyment of children as temporary additions to the home, as the fulfilment of feminity, yet without prejudicing their ability to resume work in the future, to continuing a substantial (though reduced) amount of external sociability, with no threat of feudalistic familism.

Tokyo wives, however, are in a difficult spot. They are still attempting to win their way in an erstwhile patriarchal society. Their feminist gains have yet to be consolidated. Indeed they may be labeled *feminists*. For them, the home-confining burden of children threatens hard-won gains and threatens their sense of identity as human beings equal in importance and dignity with men. Motherhood thrusts them back into a servant role with painful connotations. It terminates their brief escape from feudalism into modern equalitarianism during the honeymoon stage of marriage. They look back with nostalgia on courtship as an idyllic time, and find little to relieve their despair in finding their own marriages so much like those of the parents they have revolted against.[7]

As might be expected, wives whose sex-role preference is masculine or uncertain are hit especially hard by the arrival of children (see Appendix, Table 7-Y). For them, marital satisfaction plummets farther with the arrival of children than for the majority who prefer the feminine role. It is important to emphasize, however, that in contemporary Japan even feminine role-oriented wives suffer substantially reduced satisfaction rather than find an American upsurge of marital feeling. Indeed, under contemporary Japanese conditions, it is only childless feminine-oriented wives who are able to hold on to the satisfaction of early marriage. In short, even feminine-oriented women (to say nothing of masculine-oriented ones) are so "feminist" that children ruin the structural basis for marital happiness.

---

7. This does not mean that Japanese women dislike children. On my first visit to Japan, I was struck by the pleasure that Japanese parents of both sexes find in their young children. In a comparative study, Caudill and Weinstein (1966) find that Japanese mothers leave their babies alone less, and spend more time rocking them. Japanese custom requires mother and baby to bathe together and sleep together. The intensity of mother-child togetherness in Japan is one reason why children interfere with husband-wife togetherness in Japan more than in America.

The question at issue is the relative strength of the husband-wife bond as compared to the parent-child bond. My contention is that women in my Tokyo sample are eager to maintain their relationship to the husband, and that children prevent them from achieving that goal.

In America, by contrast, the feminist revolt was only a phase. Once a sense of equality with men had been achieved, it was no longer necessary to struggle so hard to imitate them. Women could devote the best years of their lives to bearing and rearing children. Parenthood could even become a time of fulfilment, blessing marriage and enriching the couple's sense of love for each other.

Because this change has occurred in the United States, sooner or later it may in Japan as well. Eventually, Japanese women may lose their fear that men will lord it over them. Eventually both sexes may take for granted the respect that women are now struggling to achieve. Eventually, too, the rising standard of living will ease the resource-burden each child presents. Perhaps even the tightly knit social structure will give way to a more informal, more sociable, less duty-bound way of life that will blend motherhood and modern marriage more smoothly.

To arrive at postfeminism, however, demands changes in both sexes. Japanese men will have to surrender their remaining claims to special privileges. They will have to accord their wives the respect they crave even when saddled with children. Wives will have to become better able to retain their individuality and to entrust their children to mother-substitutes if their marriages are to survive the crisis of parenthood with minimal damage.[8]

Both sexes, then, will have to change if the conflict of interest between men and women is to be resolved. In many Japanese marriages, that conflict has not yet come to the surface. Indeed my original plan to study the presumed war of the sexes had to be abandoned when I discovered how rarely it breaks out into the open. Nevertheless, underground tension is detectable in the contrasting evaluations of marriage by the two sexes. Perhaps that tension will have to erupt in open conflict before it can be resolved. In the meantime, the "cold war" is restrained by the success with which Japanese couples limit their child-bearing to the modest proportions their limited resources can bear. Were they to have the king-sized families of contemporary Americans or prewar Japanese, wives would be even more miserable. Then, perhaps even husbands would find parenthood a net loss.

By conscientiously practicing contraception, and—failing that—abortion, today's Japanese urbanities pursue their goals of material prosperity and marital happiness with reasonably balanced success. With fewer children per family, there is more room for individuality—not only for mothers but for children. If the ideal city family today (like the ideal American family during the Depression) consists of one boy and one girl, there is no structural basis for precedence to an eldest son. Similarly a brother and sister are forced into closer partnership when they are the only siblings than when they can pair off into sex-segregated cliques within the family. These changes in family composition provide the foundation for an equalitarianism that can resolve the conflicting

8. Caudill believes contemporary Japanese rarely prefer autonomy or individuality: "It strikes me that, loosely, *everybody* 'wants to be taken care of' in Japan." I am writing in rather long-range terms when I suggest that the impact of children on Japanese marriages may eventually resemble the American situation.

interests of the sexes and consolidate the modernization of Japanese marriages.

Time, however, is another matter. No differences between traditionalists, feminists, and neotraditionalists alter its effect on marriage. With hardly an exception (save for those aspects of marriage where cumulation occurs, as in understanding), time wears away both marital interaction and the partners' satisfactions with their marriages. The corrosive effect of time, therefore, is unambiguously confirmed by our international comparisons.

THE REPERCUSSIONS

OF MARITAL INTERACTION PATTERNS

T HUS far we haven't reached the heart of the evaluation of marriage. We have look at forces outside the partners that shape their relationship—events which happen before marriage, involvement in external systems, the impersonal march of time, and the children whom parents produce but who henceforth become *outside* (in the sense of *objective*) forces in their own right. But we have yet to test what difference it makes how the partners treat each other. We have made many assumptions. We have assumed that intensive interaction makes marriages strong and that specialization weakens them. We have inferred that patriarchal authority alarms Japanese women while nurturant service gratifies Japanese men. But these have been only inferences, drawn secondhand from clues suggested in correlations between external forces and marital phenomena.

Now the time has come to move from inferences to tests—to examine directly the consequences of alternative styles of marriage. Is interaction valued by both sexes and in both countries? Is one sex's gain the other's loss in Japan as far as the division of labor and balance of power are concerned? Do men in our Tokyo sample really like old-fashioned wives better than modern ones? And do women in both countries really prefer the same kinds of husbands?

These are questions which can be answered by examining the consequences of marital interaction patterns. Primarily we are interested in the subjective consequences, i.e., how well certain acts satisfy the partner who is the beneficiary (or victim!) of those acts. Along the way, however, some objective consequences will be of interest—ways in which one set of acts conditions (or at least correlates with) others. These findings will answer the *so what* practical questions within marriage. Regardless of whom you married or how you met, how long you've been married or how many children you have, if you treat your partner a certain way, what consequences can you expect?

The Repercussions of the Power Structure

The power structure forms a crucial element in the structure of marriage. Hence it should have important consequences for other aspects of marriage and for marital satisfaction.

Power structure has two main facets. (1) The balance of power may favor the husband at one extreme, the wife at the other, or be evenly balanced in between. (2) Within the equalitarian middle range, decisions may be made jointly (syncratically) or separately (autonomously). In the latter case, the partners may take turns making the same decisions or—more often—divide marriage up into different spheres of influence. The husband then rules supreme in one half of marriage, the wife in the other.

Our four decision-making patterns combine these two facets of decision making into one series of categories. The impact of the balance factor may be seen by contrasting husband-dominant and wife-dominant patterns of decision making by only one partner. The effect of sharing versus dividing-up decision making may be seen by comparing syncratic with autonomic patterns, both of which are equally balanced.

Table 8–1—Marital Repercussions of Decision-Making Patterns

		DECISION-MAKING PATTERN			
		Syncratic	Autonomic	Husband Dominant	Wife Dominant
Intrinsic Satisfactions of Decisions					
Husband's satisfaction with					
Wife's interest	Tokyo	4.56	4.25	4.46	4.59
Own share in decisions	Tokyo	4.60	4.33	4.56	4.61
Wife's satisfaction with					
Husband's interest	Tokyo	4.03	3.62	4.21	3.68
Own share in decisions	Tokyo	4.61	4.06	4.60	4.16
Wife's Task Performance					
	Tokyo	4.33	4.67	4.21	4.83
	Detroit	4.94	5.54	5.08	5.42
Relevant Satisfactions					
Wife Feels Like Servant	Tokyo	0.28	0.47	0.70	0.31
Courtesy and Respect					
Husband's satisfaction	Tokyo	4.44	4.26	4.49	4.37
Wife's satisfaction	Tokyo	4.64	4.30	4.30	4.46
Companionship					
Husband's satisfaction	Tokyo	4.32	3.91	3.97	4.11
Wife's satisfaction	Tokyo	4.06	3.51	3.86	3.74
	Detroit	4.13	3.77	3.92	3.82

		DECISION-MAKING PATTERN		Husband	Wife
		Syncratic	Autonomic	Dominant	Dominant
Therapeutic Interrelationship					
Husband's Utilization of					
Wife	Tokyo	2.47	2.19	2.28	2.24
Wife's Utilization of					
Husband	Tokyo	3.16	2.89	3.14	3.00
	Detroit	2.71	2.40	2.36	2.36
Wife's Response (selected)					
Help husband away	Tokyo	19%	16%	24%	7%
Dismissal	Tokyo	12%	15%	10%	22%
Passive	Tokyo	7%	17%	13%	2%
Husband's Response (selected)					
Advice	Tokyo	43%	34%	33%	36%
	Detroit	19%	26%	20%	22%
Sympathy	Tokyo	5%	4%	3%	5%
	Detroit	40%	23%	31%	26%
Help wife away	Tokyo	9%	6%	4%	5%
	Detroit	6%	3%	2%	4%
Dismissal	Tokyo	18%	27%	27%	31%
	Detroit	6%	8%	10%	5%
Passive	Tokyo	6%	6%	10%	3%
	Detroit	12%	21%	20%	22%
Length of Foreplay (minutes)					
	Tokyo	10.1	9.6	10.5	7.9
Expected Number of Children					
	Tokyo	2.20	2.15	2.39	2.11
	Detroit	2.63	2.82	3.03	2.68
Aggregate Satisfaction					
Husband's	Tokyo	5.80	5.31	5.79	5.67
Wife's	Tokyo	5.83	4.62	5.55	5.00
	Detroit	5.19	4.90	4.89	4.58
Comparative Satisfaction (Tokyo)					
Both		45%	29%	38%	37%
Neither		25	41	24	35
Husband Only		13	20	20	21
Wife Only		17	10	18	8
		---	---	---	---
Total		100%	100%	100%	101%
N	Tokyo	142	127	90	61
	Detroit	64	111	103	67

As expected, both partners in Tokyo are satisfied with the other's active interest in decision making when he dominates the marriage. Contrary to expectations, however, satisfaction with one's own share in decision making is not inversely related. Dominant husbands are not the most satisfied but nearly the least satisfied with their own share, while dominant wives also rank next to last and rate their satisfaction conspicuously low. Apparently, for both sexes, to dominate the power structure is to have too much of a good thing. Both would be happy to sacrifice some of their own power to gain an interested colleague. For both sexes dominance is not so much a prized possession as a burden assumed by default. The weaker partner, on the other hand, welcomes the other's strength. Especially wives who depend on their husbands (but dependent men almost as much) are more satisfied with the balance of power than "top dogs." We should beware of assuming that dominant husbands are tyrants who enjoy cracking the whip (save, perhaps, full-blown neurotics) or that dominant wives feel privileged to have so much power. Both feel let down and unsupported by contemptible, dependent spouses.

This does not mean that they would feel any better to transfer half their burden entirely to the spouse and thereby achieve an autonomous relationship. Bad enough to have a dependent spouse, but worse yet an independent one! From every angle, autonomic power is the least satisfactory of the four structures. It not only has the same disadvantage of unilateral decision making as the asymmetrical forms, but it involves unilateral implementation by the same partner. Separate spheres of influence are separate spheres of action. Thus contact between the partners dwindles as nearly to zero as possible for people living in the same house.

We had expected patriarchal husbands to issue orders for wives to carry out, but we were wrong. In both countries, feminine task performance in husband-dominant marriages is low. This means that patriarchal husbands are responsible not only for decisions but for housework. No wonder they wish their wives were more involved! Conversely, dominant wives fail to enlist their husbands in the housework—so Casper Milquetoast should hardly be portrayed wearing an apron. For both sexes in both countries, dominant partners carry heavy responsibility for the dependent partner.

Why then do Japanese wives of dominant husbands feel like servants? Apparently they perceive their inferior position in the family stratification system—a position comparable to a maid's—even though their role in the division of labor is not nearly so active. Their low power position makes them dissatisfied with the husband's respect, whereas men in the same marriages find dependent wives correspondingly respectful.[1] It is interesting to note, however, that wife-dominant marriages are not the obverse of husband-dominated ones. Japanese wives (like American ones, we suspect) feel most respected not when their husbands relinquish all power to them, but when they share power syncratically.

If decision-making is to be equalitarian, Tokyo respondents clearly prefer it to be syncratic rather than autonomic. Syncratic partners' efforts do not deserve as enthusiastic commendation as dominant partners who decide "beyond the call of duty," but they are nevertheless ranked second. And satisfaction with one's own voice fully matches that of dependent husbands and wives.

For maximum satisfaction, then, one may choose between sharing power with the partner or turning it over to him. The secondary consequences are not the same, however, as the balance of Table 8–1 shows. For most of the remaining comparisons, advantages lie with the syncratic pattern.

1. Vogel's description (1963) of his six families must be limited to husband-dominant families:

> The father's power . . . contributes to the emotional distance between him and the rest of his family. Because the wife and children know that the father may become firm or demanding, they are cautious, reserved, and rarely completely at ease in his presence.

Shared decision-making understandably produces sharing in other ways. Both sexes in Japan and wives in both countries are most satisfied with companionship in syncratic marriages.

To illustrate what happens in many facets of marriage, I have selected the therapeutic interrelationship of the partners. Men find dependent wives too far beneath them, dominant wives too far above them, and autonomous wives too far away to bother them with their troubles. On the other hand, couples who share decision making also share their troubles. The two asymmetrical power structures are not mirror images. Men seldom turn to dominant wives for therapy, but dependent women seek out strong husbands almost as often as syncratic wives. Following tradition, the wife not only leans on the man's leadership and relies on his task assistance, but cries on his shoulder when she feels overwhelmed. There is no conventional parallel for men—which may be why they tell their troubles only in modern interdependent marriages.

Wives of dominant husbands respond traditionally by helping them get away from their troubles (which we assume includes such feminine services as a hot bath and massage, as well as the sex play listed in Table 8–1).

Dominant wives, on the other hand, often dismiss the husband's troubles as unimportant, while distant (autonomic) wives make no response at all. (Note the depressed sexual activity of both groups.)

In both countries, syncratic men specialize in helping the wife forget her troubles. In each they excel at the modal response—in Japan by giving more advice and in America by giving more sympathy. In neither does the shared context of syncratic power allow dismissal or passivity.

Conventionalism appears in the child-bearing expectations of husband-dominated marriages. These men cling to old-fashioned large-family patterns—but this cannot be blamed on Japanese feudalism because it is just as characteristic of dominant American men. Perhaps the crucial feature of these marriages is the wives' dependence. They lean on their husbands precisely because they are resourceless (having cut themselves off from the outside world). Domestically oriented, they seek fulfillment through children. Not just husbands but wives too prize children in old-fashioned marriages (as evidenced by the fact that they *prefer* as well as expect the largest number of children).

We have in these four authority structures, then, the elements of two marriage ideals—conventional (husband dominant) and modern (syncratic). Autonomic and wife-dominant decision-making are both deviant types. It is to be expected therefore that these deviant types will be the least satisfactory in the aggregate for both partners. The latter part of Table 8–1 confirms this reasoning.[2]

2. The unpopularity of autonomic decision making in our sample contrasts with the vigorous defense of autonomy described by Vogel (1963) for his six executive families in a Tokyo suburb:

> . . . at present, the families' efforts are directed at maintaining the principle of decentralized authority. The wife in particular has developed subtle means of preserving her autonomy. . . . She prefers to avoid questions altogether, and to this end she practices concealment and evasion.

Such tactics may well succeed in preserving the wife's autonomy, but our data suggest the toll exacted of the marriage.

The best marriages (particularly from the feminine viewpoint) are syncratic. Next best (and a close second for our Tokyo men) is husband dominance. Whether autonomy or wife dominance is worse is not clear from the international comparison, but it is entirely clear that neither satisfies either sex as much as the more popular forms.

Although there is international agreement on the satisfactoriness of syncratic power, the two countries differ in evaluating patriarchal marriages. In postfeudal Japan, this is not only a close rival for male popularity but a popular alternative for unemancipated Japanese women. American women, however, would rather be independent than dominated.

In general, then, both sexes in both samples find shared decision making the most satisfactory. For any who regret the impending demise of Japanese patriarchy we can offer the consolation that its successor is at least as satisfactory for the man and appreciably more satisfactory for the woman. There are specific losses, to be sure, in surrendering the caresses and deference of a dependent wife, but shared decision-making yields companionship and mutual respect which more than make up for those losses.

The Repercussions of the Division of Labor

Housework is nearly synonymous with *women's work*, but not quite—otherwise there would be no division of labor within the home. Some tasks men usually do and others they sometimes assist with. But any count of the total work done at home not only in conventional marriages but even in dual-income marriages shows wives doing the great majority even in the United States—to say nothing of Japan (see Blood and Hamblin, 1958).

Hence, differences between family patterns of housework do not cover as wide a range as power structures. For all practical purposes, there is no such thing as a husband-dominant division of labor, save the one-case-in-a-million where roles are completely reversed. Rather, the variance lies between homes where the wife does it all and those where she gets enough help from the husband so that they become colleagues in housework.

The former are servant wives in the literal sense of the term. We expect them to be more common in Tokyo than Detroit because Japan has a surviving servant-wife tradition but the U.S.A. does not. But since our measures of the division of labor are not identical, we cannot establish arbitrary cutting points and say with assurance: "These are the servant wives." We can, however, explore the question indirectly by the three following steps:

(1) The proportion of Tokyo wives who feel like servants rises steadily with the proportion of housework done. However, it rises particularly steeply in the last three categories (see Table 8–2, scale 8–10). Hence these seem properly designated the servant wives. They are 11 per cent of our Tokyo families.

Table 8–2—Marital Repercussions of the Division of Labor

		DIVISION OF LABOR*		
		Colleagues	Moderates	Servant Wives
Intrinsic Satisfactions				
Wife feels like servant	Tokyo	0.26	0.46	0.86
Wife's satisfaction with husband's helpfulness	Tokyo	4.33	3.51	1.98
Husband's satisfaction with wife's home management	Tokyo	4.18	4.15	4.00
Satisfaction with courtesy and respect				
Husband's	Tokyo	4.55	4.38	4.53
Wife's	Tokyo	4.64	4.36	3.98
Aggregate Satisfaction				
Husband's	Tokyo	6.00	5.48	5.23
Wife's	Tokyo	5.97	5.17	3.65
	Detroit	5.10	4.82	4.37
Comparative Satisfaction (Tokyo)				
Both		48%	34%	14%
Neither		25	32	49
Husband only		13	18	34
Wife only		14	15	3
Total		100%	99%	100%
N	Tokyo	158	231	44
	Detroit	143	202	26

* Cutting points on division-of-labor scales in Tokyo are 0–3, 4–7, 8–10; in Detroit, 1–4, 5–8, and 9 only.

(2) As Table 8–2 shows, these same Tokyo wives are markedly dissatisfied with their marriages as a whole (as well as with the husband's courtesy and helpfulness).

(3) In the Detroit data, only the last category in our 9-point American scale is significantly low in marital satisfaction. We infer that those are the servant wives in Detroit. They represent 7 per cent of the Detroit sample. These few Detroit wives resemble the Tokyo servant wives in carrying so heavy a burden of housework that their total marriage suffers in satisfactoriness.[3]

Conversely, if we ask not simply what proportion of work the wife does but how many tasks are shared equally with the husband, we find that wives in both cities are more satisfied the larger the number of shared tasks. This is reminiscent of syncratic power structures (which also produce the happiest marriages).

3. It is important to remember that Japanese servant wives are more "serviceable" than American ones; i.e., they perform more intimate services. Therefore, a given amount of service in Japan produces less resentment than it would in the United States:

A few [Japanese] wives feel burdened because they must work so hard in the home, but most take if for granted that husbands, like children, cannot look after their own possessions or prepare their own food. Almost every household has at least one story of a time when the husband tried to do something for himself such as prepare a meal or find his clothes, only to make a bungling mess which the wife had to resolve. (Vogel, 1963.)

We found, however, in our examination of the repercussions of power structure that husbands who dominated their homes were almost as satisfied with their marriages as those whose wives joined them in making decisions. The division of labor involves similar ambivalence for men. This can be seen in the ups and downs of more detailed tables summarized in Table 8–2. Arrayed by the wife's task performance, the husband's satisfaction with her home management is especially irregular and his general marital satisfaction fluctuates, unlike the regular and larger correlations for wives. Masculine ambivalence is strikingly revealed in comparative satisfaction. Although servant-wife marriages rarely satisfy both partners and even less often the wife alone, over one-third of them *do* satisfy the husband. Here, apparently are true patriarchs, the true "tyrants" in the Tokyo sample. A small group, to be sure—only a dozen—these men are tyrannical in the sense that they enjoy being waited on despite the wife's dissatisfaction with her servitude. Indicating obsolescence of the servant-wife pattern in contemporary urban Japan is the fact that so few wives find this situation satisfactory. It has been rejected almost completely by our young wives and is clung to by only a few die-hard men.

Here perhaps even more than in power structure we see intrinsic strains pushing Japanese marriages toward modernization. For a dependent wife, there are compensating advantages in submissiveness—to surrender power to the husband is to surrender responsibility. But in the division of labor, servant-wives have not less responsibility but more. No wonder their evaluation of marriage is black.

Perhaps we should say that there is ambivalence for both sexes with respect to power structures, but no longer any ambivalence regarding household tasks for young Japanese women. To be a scullery maid is no longer an honorable profession. Some measure of help from the husband is now expected, desired, and appreciated. Indeed, the more help the merrier as far as these women, their Detroit counterparts, and even many Tokyo husbands are concerned. Although housework is normally segregated, in the best marriages in both countries thoughtful husbands cross sex lines to aid the wife when she is hard pressed.

The Consequences of Courtesy

Japanese husbands and wives address each other in half a dozen major ways and a dozen rarer terms. So wide is the variety and so complex the semantic problems for non-Japanese-speaking persons that I have despaired of being able to master the subject, much less communicate it successfully to my readers. Nevertheless, some features of the situation are apparent.

In feudal days, terms of address emphasized status differences between people. Inferiors used honorific terms to convey deference and respect to superiors. Women acknowledged inferiority by speaking deferentially to their husbands.

The radical transformation of social relationships in Japan has largely destroyed those customary forms of speech. Especially in the intimacy of marriage, new terms have appeared.

Today in the happiest Tokyo marriages, wives no longer emphasize their respect but their love. The most enthusiastic husbands are not those whose wives bow and scrape before them, but those who call them almost disrespectfully darling (*omae*) or use intimate pet names. The most enthusiastic wives wear the same appellations. Or the suffix *chan* is added to their names, an affectionate diminutive used with little children.

An alternative pattern makes the wife feel even less like a servant—to address her as "you" (*anata*) with all the formality once reserved for men. Here chivalry turns the linguistic tables and accords the wife the respect traditionally reserved for men. There is a fascinating reciprocity about *anata* (equivalent to the formal French *vous*) and *kimi* (like the informal *tu*). For a husband to be called *anata* is merely customary, signifying nothing special. For a wife, it signifies extra respect. Conversely, for a wife to be called *kimi* seems disrespectful nowadays, but for a husband, it is affectionately intimate.

The most disrespectful methods involve being commandeered with a "Hey!" (*oi*), a "Look here!" (*ne* or *chotto*) or being ignored by not being addressed at all. They are disliked by both sexes. They mean the partner is not addressed as a person granted recognition but as a slave to be ordered about. The impact is understandably offensive.

PRECEDENCE PATTERNS

Japanese men are changing not only the traditional terms of address but also the traditional order of precedence. How does the new chivalry affect the two partners?

Table 8-3 shows that Japanese women appreciate the courtesy of being allowed to step into the taxi first, Western style. Their reaction to the bus situation is not quite so marked, perhaps because precedence in taxis is a purely symbolic gesture, but husbands who are extra tired may successfully argue that they need to sit down at least part of the time.

For men, however, the situation is less clear. Since chivalry is something men perform for women, there is no reason why we should expect the wife to seem either more or less courteous as a result. The surprising feature of Table 8-3 is that husbands who benefit from precedence feel not more satisfied but less so. Could this mean that precedence is not the wife's gift but the husband's seizure? Do men dissatisfied in other respects retaliate by acting selfishly or belligerently in precedence situations? Numerous mutually dissatisfied marriages with taxi-precedent husbands imply as much.

Both symbolic chivalry and practical chivalry produce happily married couples. However, bus-sitting husbands occasionally are unilaterally satisfied. Apparently such men enjoy the dutiful submission of their wives to old patterns. However, this is a handful of cases at best. Nor is this the traditional patriarchate reciprocally re-enacted, since wives who enjoy these duties are even rarer.

Table 8-3—Satisfaction with Precedence Patterns (Tokyo)

PRECEDENCE PATTERN

	Wife Always	Wife Uusually	50/50	Husband Usually or Always
Getting into Taxi				
Satisfaction with courtesy and respect				
Wife's	4.57	4.45	4.30	3.96
Husband's	4.50	4.51	4.53	4.14
Comparative marital satisfaction				
Both	46%	30%	44%	17%
Neither	26	30	27	52
Husband only	14	22	23	22
Wife only	14	17	6	9
Total	100%	99%	100%	100%
N	211	122	47	63
Sitting Down on Bus, Train				
Satisfaction with courtesy and respect				
Wife's	4.49	4.31	4.14	4.14
Husband's	4.52	4.29	4.47	4.21
Comparative marital satisfaction				
Both	40%	34%	27%	8%
Neither	27	38	47	46
Husband only	18	18	13	31
Wife only	15	10	13	15
Total	100%	100%	100%	100%
N	296	113	21	14

Generally speaking, the traditional Japanese wife who supposedly found satisfaction in giving way to her lord and master has disappeared from these precedence patterns. In those rare cases where masculine precedence survives at all, its emotional tone for wives is consistently bitter. And only exceptional husbands manage to find much satisfaction in traditions which provoke so much resentment.

Though we have no data, we assume that American wives also appreciate the courtesy conveyed by chivalrous husbands. Even though husbands derive no direct benefit from surrendered precedence privileges, we would be surprised not to find in America as well as Japan that husbands in the most happily married couples are the most chivalrous. Marital satisfaction and masculine chivalry are two parts of a mutually reinforcing beneficent cycle.

EXPRESSING APPRECIATION

Precedence today is something the average man gives his wife out of consideration for her feelings and welfare. It is mostly one way. Appreciation for the partner's services, however, can be given in both directions. Since service is traditionally the wife's business, husbands take it more for granted than wives when the tables are turned. Nevertheless both sexes in our sample usually express appreciation even for small favors, to say nothing of big ones.

Table 8–4—Consequences of Expressing Appreciation for Small Favors (Tokyo)

| | FREQUENCY OF APPRECIATION EXPRESSED BY SPOUSE | | | |
	Always	Usually	50/50	Seldom or Never
Satisfaction with Courtesy and Respect				
Husband's	4.98	4.18	3.87	3.52
Wife's	4.74	4.56	4.32	3.96
Comparative Marital Satisfaction				
Wife Thanks				
Both satisfied	53%	34%	9%	5%
Neither satisfied	14	35	56	70
Husband only	24	13	17	11
Wife only	10	18	17	14
Total	101%	100%	99%	100%
N	165	126	34	37
Husband Thanks				
Both satisfied	53%	42%	29%	19%
Neither satisfied	17	24	33	53
Husband only	15	22	24	15
Wife only	16	12	13	13
Total	101%	100%	99%	100%
N	102	116	45	101

Courtesy is not only the modal pattern but, as Table 8–4 shows, is unambiguously appreciated by both partners. Unlike precedence where every increase for one partner is the other's loss, mutual appreciation is a fair exchange. The more one person expresses his thanks, the more the other is likely to reciprocate.

Although feminine courtesy is more conventional and more frequent, we hardly find it taken for granted by men. Male satisfaction with courtesy and respect rises steeply as the wife expresses her thanks. And aggregate satisfaction for the man also shoots up.

Feudal survivals appear in the sizable minority of Japanese men who seldom or never thank their wives and in the group of wife-thanked men who are unilaterally happy. In both cases we see the patriarchal bias of a postfeudal society whose patterns of courtesy traditionally benefited men only. In the light of history, however, the notable feature of Table 8–4 is not its feudal survivals but its remarkably modern symmetry in both objective frequency of courtesy and subjective appreciation of it.

In the light of this evidence, no one could contend that Tokyo wives know their services are appreciated without having to be told. The markedly increased satisfaction of both sexes resulting from the partner's expression of appreciation shows that Japanese women as well as men are human. One may guess one's services are appreciated, but it is nicer to be told.

The same can be said for precedence chivalry as well as thanks-giving courtesy: it pays to be courteous. The recipient appreciates the partner's thoughtfulness and the donor finds in return that love and satisfaction increase.

The Consequences of Companionship

Both in making decisions and doing housework, the most satisfied husbands and wives collaborate with each other. If this is true in traditional areas, how much more it should be for leisure-time companionship! Having fun together is the American definition of the essence of marriage. "Ordinary" marriages stick to business and concentrate on making ends meet. "Superior" marriages rise above concern with daily subsistence to engage in verbal exchanges as well as joint activities enjoyable in themselves and symbolic of continued interest in the partner.

INTERNAL COMMUNICATION

Intensive verbal communication of thoughts and feelings is an essential feature of companionship. Many young moderns believe there should be no secrets at all between husbands and wives. Their main concern, however, is not to expunge the last vestiges of privacy but to encourage sharing with each other. Particularly when they are separated during the day, couples want to bridge the gap by communicating their independent experiences. Beyond that is sharing opinions about public events in the world around.

To share opinions is intrinsically a mutual process. One can hardly discuss the news without both partners taking part.

Communicating separate events can be one way, however. In our Tokyo sample, wives communicate more than husbands. Nevertheless even one-way communication requires not only a speaker but an audience. Hence, informative companionship is promoted both by willingness to talk and willingness to listen. The best marriages involve maximum willingness by both partners both to tell and listen because either act encourages the partner to reciprocate.

Table 8–5 shows that internal communication of opinions about the news (intellectual companionship) and of events that have happened during the day (informative companionship) generally promote companionship between the partners. This is especially true for wives. In both Tokyo and Detroit, wives are more satisfied with the husband's companionship and with marriage as a whole the more intense the verbal exchange. For informative companionship this applies to higher frequences of communication both *from* the husband and *to* the husband. For wives therefore we can generalize crossculturally that increased verbal communication strengthens husband-wife relationships.

Table 8–5—The Satisfaction Value of Internal Communication

		FREQUENCY OF COMMUNICATION			
		Daily	Almost daily	Weekly	Less often
Intellectual Companionship (Tokyo)					
Husband's satisfaction		4.52	4.21	3.64	3.64
Wife's satisfaction		4.34	3.85	3.48	2.84
N		85	229	104	25
Informative Companionship					
Husband tells events, wife listens					
Satisfaction with companionship					
Husband's	Tokyo	4.47	4.20	3.90	3.13
Wife's	Tokyo	4.38	3.87	3.44	2.72
	Detroit	4.12	3.98	3.59	3.51
Aggregate satisfaction					
Husband's	Tokyo	6.36	5.83	5.33	3.72
Wife's	Tokyo	6.15	5.36	4.75	3.42
	Detroit	5.07	4.90	4.69	4.52
Comparative satisfaction (Tokyo)					
Both		51%	39%	29%	15%
Neither		19	30	36	61
Husband only		16	19	21	12
Wife only		14	12	15	12
Total		100%	100%	101%	100%
Minimum Number of					
Cases	Tokyo	97	147	87	33
	Detroit	172	88	66	75
Wife tells events (Tokyo)					
Satisfaction with companionship					
Husband's		4.46	3.89	3.36	(3.20)*
Wife's		4.02	3.67	3.33	(3.60)
Comparative marital satisfaction					
Both		45%	34%	16%	(25%)
Neither		22	37	50	(50)
Husband only		20	17	18	(0)
Wife only		13	13	16	(25)
Total		100%	101%	100%	(100%)
Minimum Number of Cases		172	150	38	4

* Numbers in parentheses are based on less than 10 cases.

For Tokyo husbands, however, the pattern is not so strong, even though its main outlines are the same. This sex difference is especially apparent in the failure of male satisfaction to decline farther when intellectual companionship slips below once a week (whereas female satisfaction drops precipitously at that point).

Since the scales are not the same, we cannot precisely compare the effect of informative companionship on wives in our two cities. We can compare the effect on husbands and wives in Tokyo, however. As might be expected, the individual's sense of companionship increases more when the partner is expressive than when he is only passively receptive. Comparing satisfaction with companionship at high and low communication frequencies indicates that expressive partners are important to both sexes in Japan. Expressive wives increase the husband's companionship satisfaction just as much as the reverse.

Although bilateral expressiveness is important to the sense of companionship, the effect of informative companionship on aggregate marital satisfaction is skewed. Perhaps because male fluency is more rare, the husband's contribution to marital satisfaction via informative communication is sharper than the wife's. The wife's ability to talk can more nearly be taken for granted in Japan (as is true in the U.S.A.). The husband who brings home news of the day's activities, however, shows the mark of a thoughtful man in a thriving marriage. To do so less than once a week (and for wives as little as once a week) is to weaken the marriage disastrously.

It is likely that being communicated with is also more important to American wives than to their husbands. At least one study shows that American wives complain about their husbands' silence while husbands complain about feminine noisiness (i.e., "nagging," see Terman, 1938).

This partly reflects constitutional differences in verbal expressiveness. Role factors also seem to involved, however. When wives are confined to the home, their opportunities for adult communication are restricted. Whereas husbands get to talk to people in the outside world, housewives have few opportunities and traditionally looked forward to the time when "the iceman cometh" for fleeting snatches of conversation.

This hypothesis can be tested with data from our two samples. It is confirmed for Detroit wives (whose companionship satisfaction falls 50 per cent farther for housewives than for working wives with identical decreases in informative communication). In the Tokyo sample, however, there is no difference between working wives and housewives—both resent the husband's reticence equally strongly. Could this be an international difference? Could Japanese wives in this new era be particularly sensitive to the husband's behavior whereas American wives, more secure in their companionship, find alternative conversational resources at work? Is there any correlation between the greater openness of the American national character to interaction with strangers (on the job) and the greater reserve of the Japanese personality? Either factor could lead Japanese working wives to be just as dependent as housewives on the husband's expressiveness. Whether either interpretation is sound we cannot say for sure.

Housewives and working wives may or may not differ internationally in their responsiveness to husbandly expressiveness. Wives in general, however, clearly appreciate husbands who take the trouble to report their experiences. And for Japanese husbands, the companionship value of internal communication is almost as great. With the possible exception of couples who discuss world events infrequently, there are hardly any men who enjoy wives so submissive that they say little or nothing to their intellectual "superiors." As for more personal news conveyed by informative companionship, even those rare silence-appreciators disappear.

Given the remarkably equalitarian and highbrow character of intellectual companionship and the nearly reciprocal appreciation of informative companionship, we can see how far our Tokyo couples have departed from the reserve and deference of classical Japanese marriages. No longer the externally oriented patriarch matched with a husband-oriented submissive wife. Today the husband is oriented to the wife almost as much as she to him, and superior-inferior relations have given way to boldly equalitarian discussions of topics outside as well as inside the home. Even internal communication has its external reference point in intellectual companionship, showing how emancipated these marriages have become.

EXTERNAL SOCIABILITY

The role factors that make internal communication more important to wives than to husbands also make external sociability more important. Every man has a daily excuse to get away from home and out into the world. Indeed the excuse is so compulsory (*having* to go to work) that the average man daydreams of being able to stay home and sleep late. For housewives, however, variety comes in reverse. Granted that mothers of small children would be delighted to sleep late, they hardly look forward to opportunities to stay home. *That* is *their* job!

This does not mean that external sociability becomes a net loss for the average man, however. The difference is one of degree, rather than kind. Men, too, enjoy visiting friends and relatives, going out to see the sights and having a good time. We expect external sociability to promote marital satisfaction for both partners—but more for women than for men.

Just as there seems to be a constitutional predisposition to verbal expressiveness in women, so there may be an innate tendency for women to prize sociability. Psychological evidence suggests that men ordinarily lean toward the manipulation of things whereas women prefer interacting with people (Tyler, 1956). If constitutional differences are involved, they reinforce what we expect on the basis of role differentiation alone.

However, external sociability is more complicated than internal communication. The latter focuses exclusively on the partners. When the husband talks with his wife, there is no doubt that this attention is devoted to her. External sociability by definition introduces other people. They may be relatives (either the husband's *or* the wife's and therefore individuals to whom the partners feel differentially close—especially in early marriage). Friends are more apt to be mutual, but again may be childhood or work friends of only one partner. Even dating may involve the partner in activities she doesn't care for. Given such complications, external sociability sometimes demonstrates the individual's *dislike* of the partner rather than his desire for her company. Hence, external sociability should contribute less than internal communication to marital satisfaction.

Table 8–6 shows that external sociability indeed influences satisfaction with companionship and with marriage ambiguously. Some trends are apparent but they are seldom as sharp or consistent as with internal communication.

Relatives are a source of companionship satisfaction for wives more clearly than for husbands (the most satisfied husbands being those who never see them at all). Possibly we should interpret kinship companionship as bimodal for Japanese men (and for American women who see their relatives two or three times a year). The latter groups are generally explainable on the basis of ecology—those who moved so far from relatives that they can see them only during vacations. Perhaps the same factor applies to Japanese couples who move to the metropolis from the provinces. The question arises whether such couples are more companionable *because* they see their relatives so seldom. That interpretation might be consistent with Bott's generalization that migration promotes marital solidarity by severing ties with childhood friends and relatives (Bott, 1957).

Table 8–6—The Satisfaction Value of External Sociability

		FREQUENCY OF EXTERNAL SOCIABILITY BY THE COUPLE					
		Weekly	2–3 Monthly	Monthly	2–3 Yearly	Less	Never
Kinship Companionship							
Satisfaction with Companionship							
Husband's	Tokyo	4.15	4.34	4.06	3.93	3.96	4.45
Wife's	Tokyo	3.84	4.03	3.85	3.66	3.60	3.45
	Detroit	3.92	3.72	3.69	4.03	3.27	—
N	Tokyo	184	107	111	114	52	11
	Detroit	274	57	16	33	11	0
Friendship Companionship							
Satisfaction with Companionship							
Husband's	Tokyo	4.42	4.36	4.23	4.04	4.06	3.66
Wife's	Tokyo	3.95	3.84	4.10	3.71	3.58	3.54
	Detroit	3.88	3.91	3.95	3.52	(3.88)*	(4.75)
N	Tokyo	19	48	116	158	52	50
	Detroit	253	68	41	27	8	4
Dating Companionship (Tokyo)							
Satisfaction with Companionship							
Husband's		4.36	4.15	4.00	3.88	(3.43)	3.50
Wife's		4.22	3.89	3.56	3.69	(2.43)	2.60
Comparative Marital Satisfaction							
Both		51%	32%	35%	36%	(40%)	(14%)
Neither		28	28	35	32	(40)	(43)
Husband only		7	21	21	19	(20)	(29)
Wife only		14	18	9	13	(0)	(14)
Total		100%	99%	100%	100%	(100%)	(100%)
Minimum Number of Cases		81	127	113	31	5	7

* Numbers in parentheses are based on less than 10 cases.

Although in the middle ranges kinship contact seems to promote satisfaction with companionship, at high intensities it interferes with the husband-wife relationship.

For Japanese couples, companionship is impaired when kinship contact exceeds a few times a month. For Americans, the point of diminishing returns is higher—so high it is masked by the collapsed categories presented in Table 8–6. However, more detailed analysis of the Detroit data shows a similar impairment of the marriage bond at high intensities of kinship contact (see my forthcoming kinship paper). In such cases, kin ties eclipse marital ties.

Within Japan, detailed analysis reveals that the effects of kin contact differ sharply according to the husband's birth order. For eldest sons, kin contact is a family responsibility. The most happily married couples (as measured by comparative satisfaction) are those who discharge this obligation most frequently. This pattern is essentially reversed for younger sons. For them the *less* frequent the contact with relatives, the happier the marriage. When contact falls below a few times a year, marital satisfaction decreases, to be sure—but that optimum category is striking less than the weekly peak for eldest sons. Recalling the differences between marriages by husband's family status in Chapter 6, we see further evidence here of the survival of feudal elements in the marriage patterns of eldest sons, whereas younger sons are correspondingly emancipated.

Kinship companionship, then, interferes with marital companionship under special circumstances. Consequently its overall contribution to marital satisfaction is dampened.

Similar (though lesser) ambiguities affect sociability with other people. This too may threaten the dyadic relationship. Wives in both countries find moderate (monthly) contacts with friends beneficial but beyond that point, "three's a crowd." For Japanese men, however, there is no point of diminishing returns. The more the merrier. Perhaps "polygamous" men enjoy intensive contact with other couples whereas insecure wives become jealous. Intimate external involvement by the husband converts merely crowded threesomes into marital triangles.

More detailed analysis of the most intensively sociable Japanese couples suggests however that we should not make too much of the difference between husbands and wives. Of the nineteen wives in this group, all but one are highly satisfied with their companionship (4.17). Significantly these very satisfied women all engage in active conversation with the husband's visiting friends. The one exception (who is so thoroughly disgusted with her lack of companionship that she pulls the average down for the total group) is a woman who seldom or never converses with those visiting friends even though she sees them at least once a week. This is presumably a feudal family in which sociability with friends is so husband-focused that the wife is alienated rather than benefited. No such explanation accounts for the lower satisfaction of Japanese wives in the several-visits-per-month category, however. So ambiguity remains in the relationship between sociability with friends and the wife's satisfaction with companionship.

The relationship between the wife's role and her satisfaction with companionship differs so sharply in the two countries that we can find no binational confirmation of our hypothesis that housewives appreciate friendship companionship more than working wives. In couple-oriented Tokyo, working wives find more companionship than housewives with their husbands. In child-oriented Detroit, the reverse is true. Hence only in Detroit is there any suggestion that housewives find friendship companionship more rewarding than working wives—and this inference must be regarded as indirect at best.

Only dating companionship consistently heightens marital satisfaction for both sexes in Japan. This involves no kinship obligations or occupational interests to confuse the partner's motivation. No third parties (neither relatives nor friends) dilute the couple's companionship with each other. Dating is therefore the only form of external sociability that is purely companionable. Even this, however, correlates less than internal communication with marital satisfaction and satisfaction with companionship. Apparently what a couple do away from home tests their relationship less than what they do when they are alone together. Even though dating involves no interaction with other people, the individual's attention may be on the movie, the floor show, or any other spectacle rather than on the partner. On the other hand, there can be no doubt about the focus of attention during oral communication. The listener receives the full benefit of the speaker's companionship.

Our Tokyo question about who decides where to go on a holiday outing offers a nice oportunity to examine the relation between control over one type of dating activity, dating frequency, and the wife's satisfaction with companionship. In general (as we have seen in Table 8–1) shared control correlates with companionship. In fact, as long as recreational decisions are made' jointly it doesn't matter very much how often a couple go out (i.e., the wife's satisfaction with companionship declines only slightly as dating decreases from once a week to a few times a year). By contrast, the most enthusiastic wives are those whose patriarchal husbands unilaterally decide to take them out every week. Conversely no equalitarian wife so despairs of her husband's companionship as wives of patriarchs who decide to take them out as little as once a month. In the latter case, wives share nothing with their husbands—neither decision making nor recreation. In the former, the absence of shared power is more than offset by the husband's freely given testimonial via his uncoerced decision to date his wife so often that he still enjoys her company.

Here, then, is further testimony that companionship is most satisfying under circumstances that guarantee the purity of motivation. Whenever recreational choices bring husband and wife into unadultered contact with each other, marriage is strengthened. But when extraneous factors intervene, the benefits of pair activities are correspondingly clouded.

The Consequences of Therapeutic Interdependence

Because telling one's troubles to the partner is a form of internal communication, we expect it to produce just as much marital satisfaction as intellectual or informative companionship.

Table 8–7 demonstrates that frequent communication of troubles is highly correlated with marital satisfaction and satisfaction with the partner's understanding of ego's problems and feelings. This general relationship holds for both sexes in Japan and for women in both countries.

Table 8–7—Consequences of Therapeutic Interdependence

		FREQUENCY OF TELLING AND HEARING TROUBLES				
		Always	Usually	50/50	Seldom	Never
Husband Tells His Troubles (Tokyo)						
Wife's Therapeutic Response						
Passive		6%	7%	15%	17%	—*
Wife's Therapeutic Effectiveness		2.44	1.99	1.73	1.59	—
Husband's Satisfaction with						
Understanding		4.75	4.27	4.04	3.94	3.81
Comparative Marital Satisfaction						
Both		53%	42%	38%	27%	13%
Neither		12	26	37	41	52
Husband only		25	16	12	18	22
Wife only		10	16	13	14	13
Total		100%	100%	100%	100%	100%
Minimum Number of Cases		72	105	60	104	23
Wife Tells Troubles						
Husband's Therapeutic Response						
Advice	Tokyo	40%	38%	33%	26%	—
	Detroit	31%	15%	25%	20%	—
Dismissal	Tokyo	20%	27%	29%	33%	—
	Detroit	8%	9%	7%	6%	—
Passive	Tokyo	7%	6%	4%	11%	—
	Detroit	12%	22%	22%	29%	—
Husband's Therapeutic Effectiveness						
	Tokyo	2.60	2.43	2.18	2.09	—
	Detroit	2.56	2.48	2.45	2.04	—
Wife's Satisfaction with Understanding						
	Tokyo	4.58	4.29	3.87	4.07	(2.29)†
	Detroit	3.72	3.68	3.68	3.25	3.19
Comparative Marital Satisfaction (Tokyo)						
Both		44%	33%	30%	31%	(0)
Neither		26	33	35	40	(75%)
Husband only		12	24	32	16	(25)
Wife only		18	10	3	13	(0)
Total		100%	100%	100%	100%	(100%)
Wife's Marital Satisfaction						
	Tokyo	5.93	5.11	4.30	4.27	(3.20)
	Detroit	5.21	4.97	4.88	4.33	4.54
Minimum Number of Cases	Tokyo	164	114	37	45	4
	Detroit	86	97	110	72	13

* Therapeutic response is inapplicable where the spouse never tells his troubles.
† Numbers in parentheses are based on less than 10 cases.

Comparing sexes, therapeutic expressiveness by a man is a surer sign of marital satisfaction than a woman's. Japanese men who always tell their troubles are comparatively rare (as can be seen in the number of cases of men contrasted with women who always do). Any man sufficiently emancipated from traditional masculine aloofness to rely so thoroughly on his wife for emotional relief can be counted on to be an effective partner in other respects, too. For women, on the other hand, emotional dependence is more common and therefore less sharply correlated with marital satisfaction.

The relationship between therapeutic dependence and the partner's therapeutic effectiveness is presumably circular. The more often the individual tells his troubles, the greater the partner's opportunities to acquire skill in relieving those troubles. On the other hand, the more helpful the response, the greater the likelihood of telling troubles again. The latter sequence is suggested by the prominence of passive and brush-off responses to those who seldom tell their troubles. On the other hand, those who often hear about their partners' troubles are in a stronger position to be able to respond with appropriate advice.

Though linear dependent variables such as degree of satisfaction correlate nicely with degree of dependence, this is hardly true of differing kinds of response. Except for unresponsive passivity (which is hardly a *kind* of response), there is great variation between samples, between sexes, and between degrees of dependence in the kinds of response made. Table 8–7 contains only those responses that are related progressively to degree of dependence in at least one sample. We are forced to conclude that frequency of therapeutic reliance is related to marital satisfaction but hardly determines the nature of the response the partner will make.

THERAPEUTIC RESPONSIVENESS

Earlier we have seen sharp sex differences and crosscultural differences in the kinds of responses made to the partner's recital of troubles. For example, the most popular response of Tokyo wives and Detroit husbands is sympathy, whereas Tokyo husbands prefer to give advice. Second-ranking responses differ even more: advice from Detroit husbands, dismissing troubles from Tokyo husbands, and helping husbands forget their troubles (get away from them) from Tokyo wives.

Table 8–8—Satisfaction Value of Therapeutic Responsiveness

		Sympathy	Advice	Helping solve	Helping away	Dis-missal	Passive	Criti-cism
NATURE OF PARTNER'S THERAPEUTIC RESPONSE								
Rank Order of Therapeutic Effectiveness*								
Husband Feels†	Tokyo	4	1	2	3	5	6	7
Wife Feels †	Tokyo	4	3	1	2	5	6	7
	Detroit	2	4	3	1	5	6	7
Rank Order of Satisfaction with Understanding								
Husband's	Tokyo	2	1	3	4	5	6	7
Wife's	Tokyo	1	2	3	4	5	6	7
	Detroit	1	3	2	4	5	6	7

| | | NATURE OF PARTNER'S THERAPEUTIC RESPONSE | | | | | | |
		Sympathy	Advice	Helping solve	Helping away	Dis-missal	Passive	Criti-cism
ank Order of Aggregate								
Satisfaction with Marriage								
Husband's	Tokyo	2	1	4	3	5	6	7
Wife's	Tokyo	1	4	3	2	5	6	7
	Detroit	3	4	2	1	5.5	5.5	7
omparative Satisfaction (Tokyo)								
y Wife's Response								
Rank Order of Mutual								
Satisfaction		1.5	3	4	1.5	5	6	7
Percentage Distribution								
Both		51%	46%	33%	51%	29%	13%	(0)‡
Neither		16	26	31	22	41	51	(100%)
Husband only		24	20	24	13	10	13	(0)
Wife only		9	9	12	14	20	22	(0)
Total		100%	101%	100%	100%	100%	99%	(100%)
N		110	35	42	55	49	37	5
y Husband's Response								
Rank Order of Mutual								
Satisfaction		1	4	3	2	6	5	7
Percentage Distribution								
Both		68%	42%	43%	54%	21%	28%	(0)
Neither		11	22	19	25	48	48	(100%)
Husband only		5	20	22	17	19	12	(0)
Wife only		16	16	16	4	12	12	(0)
Total		100%	100%	100%	100%	100%	100%	(100%)
N	Tokyo	20	159	85	30	107	29	4
	Detroit	116	86	33	13	28	80	25

* See Appendix for data.
† How husband feels about wife's response and vice versa.
‡ Numbers in parentheses are based on less than 10 cases.

Given such striking differences in response patterns, it would be surprising if there were much similarity in evaluating these contrasting activities. Yet Table 8–8 shows remarkable agreement on the three worst responses. Worst of all is to criticize the partner and reject his cry for help. Better to do nothing except listen to the tale of woe. Better yet to try to convince the spouse that troubles aren't worth worrying about—a stratagem which succeeds often enough to rank better than saying nothing at all but is consistently the least helpful of the positive responses. For most men and women, troubles are not so easily brushed aside, and something more is needed to make them disappear than waving a magic wand.

The remaining approaches are clearly better than dismissal but not so clearly distinguishable from each other. Their rank order of immediate effect is about as random as could be imagined. Moreover, the order of the four methods shifts from one criterion to another. Only within the single criterion of satisfaction with the partner's understanding is there much consistency between groups— sympathy best and help in getting away from troubles weakest of the four methods. We can hardly say that there is much cross-cultural or cross-sex generality about the order of the top four methods.

Perhaps one reason for this variability is that therapeutic methods need to vary with circumstances. Some problems can be attacked practically by the spouse—others can't. Getting away from the problem and forgetting about it is sometimes possible but not always. While effective in the short run, it is almost as ineffectual as dismissal in assuring the partner that his problems are understood. It's too escapist for that. Nevertheless escaping is a favorite device in happy marriages, perhaps because going out on a date is a favorite activity. (The previous chapter stated that children reduce both marital satisfaction and reliance on this method.)

Comparison of aggregate satisfaction with the frequency distribution of cases shows that the most satisfied marriage partners receive the rarest forms of therapy—advice from ordinarily submissive Japanese women, sympathy from ordinarily unemotional Japanese men, and help in getting away from it all from ordinarily psychological American men. The Japanese combination is interesting because it reverses the usual sex roles. The best Japanese marriages are those in which wives respond in the usual masculine fashion and men in the usual feminine fashion (or perhaps we should say in the usual American fashion). Presumably this is another manifestation of the principle that the best marriages are based on sharing. Just as we have seen that shared decision-making, shared housework, and close communication occur in the best marriages, so emotional therapy is most effective where men's and women's roles converge. When sex roles are rigidly differentiated, it is hard for men and women to enter into each other's lives, to feel empathy, to understand, and to be helpful. When sex roles converge, however, the gap between the sexes is more easily bridged, and men and women come to each other's rescue more successfully.

Whereas Tokyo husbands consistently rank advice first, they react to the traditionally Japanese womanly help in forgetting their troubles worse than either group of women. This seems to be one area in which men as well as women show a latent readiness to abandon traditional roles for new ones. If we interpret these data correctly, they mean that many Japanese men would welcome a shift from indirect ways of dealing with their problems to more directly helpful and intelligent responses. Even though this is a vanguard segment of the Japanese male population, therapeutic patterns have only begun to shift in that direction. As they proceed further under the impetus of increasingly equalitarian conditions, the male response promises to be positive.

Advice is less appreciated by women than by men, however, perhaps as a legacy of centuries of masculine domination. Because Japan is in the midst of a feminist revolt, we might expect women there to react even more negatively to advice than over here. However, receiving advice seems to be more acceptable in Japan than in America. Marriage conciliation in Japan consists of hearing a couple's troubles and then giving official advice as to what should be done, whereas in the U.S. it is far less directive. Perhaps in this respect Japanese women are not yet fully emancipated from their cultural past.

Those women within our Tokyo sample who are most dissatisfied with the feminine role respond passively to the husband's troubles significantly less often and dismiss his troubles correspondingly more. In this limited way, Japanese feminists shift from a typically feminine response to a more actively masculine one.

When "masculine" women receive the husband's therapeutic responses, their evaluation of his effectiveness differs even more sharply (see Appendix Table 8-8). Whereas role-accepting women rate sympathy the most effective masculine response, role-rejecting women rate it even less effective than sheer passivity. Rather our feminists prefer more practical help—help in solving their problems but more especially help in getting away from their troubles (i.e., in getting away from their role). Conforming women, on the other hand, not only prize sympathy but find the three worst responses—dismissal, passivity, and criticism—therapeutically more effective than their rebellious sisters. Indeed the sharpest contrast of all is between two conformists who feel "much better" and "a little better" after the husband criticizes them and two rebels who feel only "about the same" and "worse." This analysis by sex-role preference reveals the bifurcation of contemporary Japanese womanhood into a relatively emotional, submissive majority and a hardheaded, unemotional minority. The majority are so submissive that they feel more satisfied with the husband's understanding of their problems after he responds critically than those who never tell their troubles at all. For them the husband's criticism is evidence of his understanding. For Japanese men and American women, by contrast, to be criticized for having gotten into trouble in the first place isn't "taken lying down," but resented as evidence of the partner's lack of understanding.

Generally speaking, then, our three groups of respondents agree that dismissal, passivity, and criticism are unsatisfactory responses. However, our quasi-masochistic Japanese women, and especially the most womanly Japanese women, find more satisfaction in such male responses than most American women or (we suspect) men in either country.

The Consequences of Expressing Affection

In our Detroit study, questions on affectionate and sexual behavior were ruled out for public relations reasons by our research superiors. Hence our data on love and sex are confined to the Tokyo project whose university sponsors generously allowed us to probe this controversial subject.

Our sole question on affectionate behavior concerned the frequency with which the husband expresses his love in words, gesture, or facial expression. This communicative act closely correlates with the husband's frequency of communicating other positive messages to his wife. For example, husbands who tell their wives about things that happened to them every day also tell their wives they love them almost every day (mean: 182 times per year), whereas when informative companionship sinks to less than once a week, expression of affection does, too (37 per year).

Table 8–9—Consequences of Expressing Affection

		HUSBAND EXPRESSES AFFECTION				
	Daily	Almost Daily	1–2 Weekly	2–3 Monthly	Less	Never
Wife's Satisfaction with Love	5.25	5.08	4.54	4.37	4.02	3.86
Wife's Satisfaction with Love by Husband's Love						
Intense, powerful	5.48	5.26	5.06	(5.00)	(5.50)	(5.00)
Strong	5.30	5.14	4.74	4.59	4.40	4.31
Considerable	4.62	4.85	4.03	3.85	4.07	(3.13)
Little	(5.00)*	(4.67)	(4.20)	(4.20)	(2.89)	(3.25)
Comparative Marital Satisfaction						
Both	58%	51%	25%	31%	12%	14%
Neither	15	21	40	34	50	54
Husband only	11	15	22	26	19	23
Wife only	17	13	12	9	19	9
Total	101%	100%	99%	100%	100%	100%
N	66	106	99	35	32	22

	WIFE'S LOVE FOR HUSBAND			
	Intense	Strong	Considerable	Little or none
Husband's Satisfaction with Love	5.50	5.03	4.40	4.00
Comparative Marital Satisfaction				
Both	78%	48%	11%	3%
Neither	6	21	49	72
Husband only	8	15	29	16
Wife only	8	16	11	9
Total	100%	100%	100%	100%
N	42	239	126	37

* Numbers in parentheses are based on less than 10 cases.

I have mentioned before the popular notion that Japanese wives know their husbands love them without having to be told. Several informants believe Japanese men are less *expressive* than American men but love their wives just as much—and their wives know it. Table 8-9 suggests, however, that Japanese women fully appreciate being told that they are lovable. At least their satisfaction with the husband's love is nicely correlated with his expressing it. Indeed, a more refined analysis shows that even if we hold constant how much the husband loves his wife, expressing it adds an extra margin of satisfaction for the wife. American women may possibly value expression even more —but certainly the reverse implication cannot be drawn that Japanese women have mysterious powers of discernment. Perhaps wives used to be satisfied with unexpressed love in the feudal past (when wives also supposedly "accepted" the husband's extramarital liaisons). But today's wives have seen too many American movies to be satisfied any longer with inarticulate husbands.

Overt expression of affection is also very much a part of the most successful marriages in Tokyo, especially for wives. Presumably if we asked husbands how affectionate their wives were toward them, we would find a more direct contribution to the husband's marital satisfaction, too. Even though we have seen various hints throughout the study that love means more to women than to men, we should remember that both sexes in Japan rank love as the most important aspect of marriage. Hence it should loom importantly for men too.

The nearest equivalent we have to the husband's expression of love is the wife's self-reported amount of love. As the lower half of Table 8–9 shows, this is closely related to the husband's satisfaction with her love. Apparently she either communicates her love successfully to him or he *does* have those mysterious Japanese perceptual powers!

Because love both makes the partner happy and registers one's own happiness, the wife's degree of love correlates extremely closely with both partners' satisfaction with marriage. Ordinarily in this chapter we have attempted to assess the subjective consequences of objective behavior. The bottom section of the table violates this rule by linking two subjective phenomena and is partly a "spurious correlation." It would not be fair to compare the upper and lower halves of Table 8–9 and deduce that love means more to Japanese men than women—the independent variables are not the same.

We can safely say, however, that love is a crucial aspect of contemporary Japanese marriages—for arranged marriages as well as love matches, for men as well as women. And to be most effective, love must be expressed.

The Consequences of Sexual Activity

In the sexual area, we have three behavioral questions: who makes sexual decisions, how frequent is intercourse, and how prolonged is foreplay?

In earlier chapters, we found sex ambiguous. Traditionally, it was the husband's prerogative and the wife's duty. Hence intercourse may be variously motivated, especially from the wife's viewpoint. Although most shared activities are closely tied to marital satisfaction, this may be less true of sex than of companionship, emotional therapy, or love.

Table 8–10 both objectively and subjectively reveals the advantages of collaboration in sexual decision-making. Foreplay is longest and intercourse most frequent in syncratic marriages. Wives, too, are most satisfied sexually when decisions are made jointly. However, from the men's responses, the greatest sexual satisfaction is derived from wives who are sexually assertive and unilaterally decide half the time to approach their husbands. Such wives are both sexually aggressive and sexually receptive (they allow their husbands to initiate intercourse equally often). Perhaps sexual variety is the

Table 8–10—Consequences of Sexual Decision-Making Patterns

SEXUAL DECISION-MAKING

	Husband Always	Husband Usually	50/50	Shared	Wife Usually	Wife Always
Length of Foreplay (minutes)	9.6	9.9	8.1	10.0	— (7.5) —	
Frequency of Intercourse (per year)	50	54	57	60	50	(35)
Sexual Satisfaction						
Husband's	4.07	4.38	4.68	4.54	4.50	(4.50)
Wife's	3.86	4.04	4.30	4.32	4.08	(3.00)
Comparative Marital Satisfaction						
Both	25%	36%	65%	45%	— 50% —	
Neither	44	31	23	20	30	
Husband only	18	20	12	19	10	
Wife only	13	13	0	16	10	
Total	100%	100%	100%	100%	—100% —	
Minimum number of cases	102	136	17	97	— 8 —	

Table 8–11—Consequences of Frequency of Intercourse

FREQUENCY OF INTERCOURSE

	Less Than Weekly	1–2 Weekly	More Than Twice Weekly
Sexual Satisfaction			
Husband's	3.95	4.37	5.27
Wife's	3.64	4.15	4.62
by Wife's Sex Role Preference			
Feminine	3.81	4.27	4.56
Not feminine	3.33	3.94	(4.83)
Comparative Marital Satisfaction			
Both	27%	37%	61%
Neither	36	31	18
Husband only	17	19	11
Wife only	20	12	11
Total	100%	99%	101%
Minimum Number of Cases	66	266	28

Table 8–12—Consequences of Length of Foreplay

LENGTH OF FOREPLAY (IN MINUTES)

	<5	5–9	10–14	15+
Sexual Satisfaction				
Husband's	3.73	4.08	4.47	4.60
Wife's	3.86	4.13	4.02	4.17
Comparative Marital Satisfaction				
Both	32%	29%	39%	44%
Neither	44	39	27	23
Husband only	16	12	23	19
Wife only	8	20	11	14
Total	100%	100%	100%	100%
Minimum Number of Cases	25	75	85	108

chief boon of taking turns in making decisions. Unlike decision-making generally (where syncratic marriages are more satisfying than autonomic ones), sexual decisions are decisions to approach the partner and therefore involve unilateral initiative but not unilateral execution. In this sense, 50/50 initiative reflects maximal sexual freedom and spontaneity by the women—a rare quality the world round.

The table suggests quite different qualities in matriarchal marriages. Wives who make all the decisions about sex (or about most things) generally use their power to resist the husband's sexual demands. Perhaps we could label them both rigid (i.e., domineering) and frigid. On the other hand, their husbands may be sexually timid as well as decision-wise meek.

At the opposite extreme, husbands who always make sexual decisions are less grateful for that power than disgusted by their wives' passivity. In patriarchal marriages, the wife does her duty, to be sure, but with so little enthusiasm that the husband hardly benefits sexually.

Sex, in short, requires the active participation of both partners to be mutually satisfying. And to be most exciting of all, it requires not even-tenored collaboration but the spicy variety of alternating initiative.

Though husbands generally are more enthusiastic about sex than wives, satisfaction increases for both partners with increased frequency of intercourse. This is another point in our analysis where the flow of influences must surely be reciprocal. If sex is satisfying, then it is repeated more often.

Table 8–11 shows only the slightest hint that a few wives find marriage more attractive without sex. The trend toward "wife only" marital satisfaction with decreased intercourse fails to counterbalance the larger trend toward mutual satisfaction with frequent intercourse.

It is unfortunate that our frequency classifications are so broad. If we had a finer breakdown of the "more-than-twice-weekly" category we might find an upper limit beyond which satisfaction for the wife falls. Within the present limits, however, there isn't the slightest evidence of "excessive" intercourse.

One might hypothesize that feminist wives would be the first to rebel at being "used" sexually. The table shows how inappropriate such a concept is for these Japanese women. Though rebellious wives as a whole find sex less satisfying than conformist wives, their response to variations in frequency is twice as sensitive. Or perhaps we should say they are twice as apt to act out their positive or negative feelings about sex in sexual activity or resistance.

We have suggested before that length of foreplay is more difficult to estimate than frequency of intercourse—both highly variable phenomena. Perhaps unreliability reduces the relationship of foreplay to sexual satisfaction and marital satisfaction. In any case, the relationship is conspicuously weak.

The chief value of Table 8–12 lies in the comparison between husbands and wives. Foreplay correlates surprisingly little with the wife's sexual satisfaction. Perhaps sex manuals that urge husbands to "go slowly" in arousing the partner overestimate the importance of foreplay to women. On the other hand the greater impact of foreplay on male satisfaction may fit in with our earlier speculations about the value to the husband of female initiative and activity.

In general, sexual activity seems less ambiguously related to marital satisfaction than we expected. The more sexually active both partners are, the more satisfactory the marriage in general and its sexual facet in particular. Despite the feudal heritage of Japan, the most submissive females are neither the most frequently "exploited" nor the most satisfying partners. Rather, our tables suggest that the emancipation of women produces in both partners increased enjoyment of the sexual side of marriage.

The Repercussions of Marital Interaction Patterns

Even though it is sometimes hard to know whether acts or feelings come first, the analysis of marital interaction as a whole is easier. Love doesn't grow in a vacuum but reflects the partner's past and future behaviors. The more the partner does for me, the greater my love grows. When love is lost, it can be regained by intensifying acts that create satisfaction more easily than by conjuring up feelings. Once created, positive feelings lead to further positive acts. But the beneficent cycle can be initiated more tangibly with actions than feelings.

What does this chapter tell us about the kinds of actions that strengthen marital bonds? Any act performed *for* the partner is good for something. Acts performed *with* the partner are better. And best of all are activities in which the partner is not only present but the focus of attention. To borrow a popular phrase, it is people-to-people (i.e., person-to-person) interaction that promotes relationships.

Interaction takes many forms: expressing love, sharing troubles, discussing almost anything, making decisions together. These acts meet the partner's needs for recognition and response. More importantly than getting tangible things done, they express the partner's appreciation for me as a person, and mine for him.

One-sided services (the housework of servant wives or the sexual service of submissive wives) may satisfy the partner more than no service at all. But in every aspect of marriage, the happiest couples share and share alike. It takes two to make a good marriage. Wives must receive as well as give. Only when marriage is a reciprocal feedback system does it work best.

Though men are not identical with women in all their needs, nor Americans identical with Japanese in all their preferences, with few exceptions we can conclude that the higher the reciprocal interaction level between husband and wife, the greater their satisfaction. And more often than not, the common human needs of both sexes and both cultures transcend the variations between them.

Appendixes

APPENDIX A
DETAILED TABLES

Table 7–1—Marital Power Structure by Stage in Family Life Cycle

| | | *STAGE IN FAMILY LIFE CIRCLE* | | | | |
		Honey-moon	Pre-school	Pre-adolescent	Child-rearing	Later childless
Husband's power						
	Tokyo	5.15	5.28	5.08	5.21	5.29
	Detroit	5.33	5.48	5.32	5.40	4.67
Unilateral decisions						
	Tokyo	1.66	2.05	2.16	2.08	1.96
	Detroit	3.70	3.91	3.92	3.92	3.76
N						
	Tokyo	167	176	74	250	27
	Detroit	30	152	167	319	56

Table 7–2—The Division of Labor by Stage in Family Life Cycle

| | | *STAGE IN FAMILY LIFE CYCLE* | | | | |
		Honey-moon	Pre-school	Pre-adolescent	Child-rearing	Later childless
Wife employed						
	Tokyo	49%	19%	22%	20%	59%
	Detroit	50%	14%	19%	16%	52%
Wife's task performance						
	Tokyo	4.12	4.55	5.00	4.70	4.92
	Detroit	4.65	5.17	5.58	5.39	4.96
Unilateral tasks						
	Tokyo	3.23	3.66	3.69	3.67	3.74
	Detroit	4.92	5.17	5.30	5.24	4.96
N						
	Tokyo	167	176	74	250	27
	Detroit	30	152	167	319	56

Table 7–3—Marital Courtesy by Stage in Family Life Cycle (Tokyo)

| | *STAGES IN FAMILY LIFE CYCLE* | | | | |
	Honey-moon	Pre-school	Pre-adolescent	Child-rearing	Later childless
Husband carries heavy objects	3.41	3.32	2.96	3.21	3.07
Wife gets bus seat	3.59	3.60	3.50	3.56	3.22
Wife gets in taxi first	3.26	3.05	2.80	2.97	3.07
Husband expresses appreciation	2.78	2.49	2.59	2.52	2.67
Wife expresses appreciation	3.33	3.13	2.76	3.02	3.33
N	167	176	74	250	27

Table 7–4—Companionship by Stage in Family Life Cycle

		STAGE IN FAMILY LIFE CYCLE				
		Honey-moon	Pre-school	Pre-adolescent	Child-rearing	Later childless
Internal companionship						
Dating companionship						
	Tokyo	28.2	18.3	11.8	16.4	26.4
Intellectual companionship						
	Tokyo	189	169	146	162	186
Informative companionship						
Husband tells	Tokyo	194	173	136	162	164
	Detroit	220	185	174	179	184
Wife tells	Tokyo	240	228	218	225	222
External companionship						
Kinship companionship						
	Tokyo	15.5	11.7	11.1	11.4	18.1
	Detroit	115	92	74	83	90
Friendship companionship						
	Tokyo	10.1	6.4	4.4	5.8	11.7
	Detroit	70	86	87	87	78
Organizational companionship*						
	Detroit	0.63	0.55	0.96	0.76	0.73
N	Tokyo	167	176	74	250	27
	Detroit	30	152	167	319	56

* The number of organizations the couple belong to jointly.

Table 7–5—Therapeutic Interaction by Stage in Family Life Cycle

		STAGE IN FAMILY LIFE CYCLE				
		Honey-moon	Pre-school	Pre-adolescent	Child-rearing	Later childless
Therapeutic utilization						
Husband tells troubles						
	Tokyo	2.45	2.25	2.06	2.19	2.22
Wife tells troubles						
	Tokyo	3.18	3.01	2.76	2.93	2.96
	Detroit	2.63	2.53	2.32	2.42	2.34
*Therapeutic response**						
Help in Getting Away						
Wife's	Tokyo	21.9%	12.4%	20.3%	14.9%	15.4%
Husband's	Tokyo	11.4%	3.5%	4.3%	3.7%	7.7%
	Detroit	3.6%	4.2%	2.5%	3.3%	3.8%
Help in Solving						
Wife's	Tokyo	16.6%	13.1%	4.3%	10.4%	15.4%
Husband's	Tokyo	22.2%	19.3%	17.2%	18.7%	11.5%
	Detroit	14.3%	7.7%	10.2%	9.0%	3.8%
Advice						
Wife's	Tokyo	7.3%	13.1%	8.7%	11.7%	19.2%
Husband's	Tokyo	37.1%	36.8%	35.8%	36.5%	34.6%
	Detroit	28.6%	21.0%	22.3%	21.7%	24.6%
Sympathy						
Wife's	Tokyo	35.1%	31.4%	33.3%	32.0%	26.9%
Husband's	Tokyo	4.8%	2.3%	5.7%	3.3%	15.4%
	Detroit	50.0%	26.6%	28.6%	27.7%	35.9%

		STAGE IN FAMILY LIFE CYCLE				
		Honey-moon	Pre-school	Pre-adolescent	Child-rearing	Later childless
Passivity						
Wife's	Tokyo	7.9%	13.1%	14.5%	13.5%	7.7%
Husband's	Tokyo	5.4%	8.8%	5.7%	7.9%	3.8%
	Detroit	0	25.2%	20.4%	22.7%	22.6%
Criticism						
Wife's	Tokyo	1.3%	1.3%	1.4%	1.4%	0
Husband's	Tokyo	0	1.2%	2.9%	1.7	0
	Detroit	3.6%	7.0%	7.0%	7.0%	5.7%
Dismissal						
Wife's	Tokyo	9.9%	15.7%	17.4%	16.2%	15.4%
Husband's	Tokyo	19.2%	28.1%	28.6%	28.2%	26.9%
	Detroit	0	8.4%	8.9%	8.7%	3.8%
Totals						
Wife's	Tokyo	100.0%	100.1%	99.9%	100.1%	100.0%
Husband's	Tokyo	100.1%	100.0%	100.2%	100.0%	99.9%
	Detroit	100.1%	100.1%	99.9%	100.1%	100.2%
N	Tokyo	167	176	74	250	27
	Detroit	30	152	167	319	56

* Omitting those who never tell their troubles and those whose responses are not ascertained

Table 7–6—Love and Sex by Stage in Family Life Cycle

		STAGE IN FAMILY LIFE CYCLE				
		Honey-moon	Pre-school	Pre-adolescent	Child-rearing	Later childless
Husband expresses affection						
	Tokyo	178	111	85	103	133
Love for spouse						
Husband's	Tokyo	3.98	3.68	3.56	3.65	3.77
Wife's	Tokyo	3.86	3.58	3.27	3.48	3.56
Satisfaction with love						
Husband's	Tokyo	5.04	4.66	4.66	4.66	4.85
Wife's	Tokyo	5.08	4.52	4.42	4.49	4.86
	Detroit	3.97	4.20	4.01	4.10	4.04
Length of foreplay						
	Tokyo	10.7	9.5	8.7	9.2	8.3
Frequency of intercourse						
	Tokyo	72	46	42	45	40
Sexual satisfaction						
Husband's	Tokyo	4.56	4.24	4.29	4.25	4.32
Wife's	Tokyo	4.30	3.88	4.11	3.94	4.12
N	Tokyo	167	176	74	250	27
	Detroit	30	152	167	319	56

Table 7–8—Marital Satisfactions by Stage in Family Life Cycle

		STAGE IN FAMILY LIFE CYCLE				
		Honey-moon	Pre-school	Pre-adolescent	Child-rearing	Later childless
Aggregate satisfaction						
Husband's	Tokyo	6.21	5.43	5.36	5.41	4.65
Wife's	Tokyo	5.95	4.89	4.69	4.84	5.17
	Detroit	4.89	5.09	4.81	4.94	4.37
SPECIFIC SATISFACTIONS						
Love						
Husband's	Tokyo	5.04	4.66	4.66	4.66	4.85
Wife's	Tokyo	5.08	4.52	4.42	4.49	4.86
	Detroit	3.97	4.20	4.01	4.10	4.04
Spouse as parent						
Husband's	Tokyo	(4.72)*	4.59	4.18	4.43	(4.50)*
Wife's	Tokyo	(4.67)*	4.58	4.23	4.43	(4.52)*
Understanding						
Husband's	Tokyo	4.43	4.10	4.04	4.09	4.11
Wife's	Tokyo	4.60	4.07	4.14	4.09	4.63
	Detroit	3.62	3.69	3.51	3.60	3.55
Sex						
Husband's	Tokyo	4.56	4.24	4.29	4.25	4.32
Wife's	Tokyo	4.30	3.88	4.11	3.94	4.12
Companionship						
Husband's	Tokyo	4.43	3.94	3.72	3.87	4.18
Wife's	Tokyo	4.26	3.46	3.53	3.48	3.85
	Detroit	4.00	3.92	3.83	3.87	3.86
Courtesy, respect						
Husband's	Tokyo	4.71	4.28	4.33	4.29	4.33
Wife's	Tokyo	4.72	4.25	4.08	4.20	4.63
Husband's Income						
Wife's	Tokyo	3.83	3.95	3.92	3.94	3.85
Standard of living						
Wife's	Detroit	3.33	3.50	3.33	3.41	3.45
Wife's financial management						
Husband's	Tokyo	4.17	4.21	3.74	4.07	4.22
Wife's home management						
Husband's	Tokyo	4.25	4.12	3.84	4.04	4.63
Husband's helpfulness						
Wife's	Tokyo	4.05	3.42	3.36	3.40	3.52
Own share decisions						
Husband's	Tokyo	4.64	4.52	4.26	4.44	4.56
Wife's	Tokyo	4.66	4.22	4.11	4.18	4.07
Spouse's interest in decision-making						
Husband's	Tokyo	4.60	4.46	4.19	4.38	4.37
Wife's	Tokyo	4.19	3.70	3.64	3.68	3.78
N	Tokyo	167	176	74	250	27
	Detroit	30	152	167	319	56

* Hypothetical estimates of satisfaction.

Table 7–X*—Marital Structure, Dynamics, and Satisfaction by Number of Children and Family Income

		NUMBER OF CHILDREN				
		Zero	One	Two	Three†	Four +*
Wife's task performance						
	Tokyo	4.23	4.55	4.67	6.05	—
	Detroit	4.74	5.26	5.35	5.84	5.19
Unilateral tasks						
	Tokyo	3.30	3.60	3.74	3.84	—
	Detroit	3.70	3.44	3.93	4.48	4.15
Therapeutic utilization of spouse						
Husband's	Tokyo	2.42	2.23	2.20	1.84	—
Wife's	Tokyo	3.15	2.95	2.95	2.74	—
	Detroit	2.39	2.67	2.43	2.28	2.10
Satisfaction with love						
Husband's	Tokyo	5.02	4.68	4.70	4.37	—
Wife's	Tokyo	5.04	4.53	4.56	3.90	—
	Detroit	3.94	4.18	4.24	4.09	3.59
AGGREGATE SATISFACTION						
Husband's	Tokyo					
Low income		6.03	5.17	5.14	(6.00)	—
Moderate income		5.96	5.51	5.93	4.29	—
Wife's	Tokyo					
Low income		5.90	4.76	4.52	(4.50)	—
Moderate income		5.74	5.00	5.03	3.93	—
Wife's	Detroit					
Moderate income		4.31	4.96	5.09	4.61	4.28
High income		4.71	5.10	5.00	5.43	5.00
Minimum Number of Cases						
	Tokyo	153	131	78	19	—
	Detroit	74	93	112	64	37

* See Tables 7–2, 5, 6, 8.
† For Japanese respondents this classification means "three or more."

Table 7–Y—Wife's Marital Satisfaction by Sex Role Preference by Stage in Family Life Cycle (Tokyo)

	STAGE IN FAMILY LIFE CYCLE				
	Honey-moon	Pre-school	Pre-adolescent	Child-rearing	Later childless
Wife's marital satisfaction by sex role preference					
Feminine	6.07	5.08	5.00	5.05	6.08
Masculine or uncertain	5.70	4.53	3.95	4.38	4.09
N					
Feminine	104	114	50	164	13
Other	50	58	21	79	11

Table 8–8—Satisfaction Value of Therapeutic Responsiveness

NATURE OF PARTNER'S THERAPEUTIC RESPONSE

		Sympathy	Advice	Help solve	Help away	Dismissal	Passive	Criticism
Therapeutic effectiveness								
Husband feels	Tokyo	1.98	2.26	2.18	2.12	1.89	1.25	0.80
Wife feels	Tokyo	2.50	2.58	2.62	2.60	2.20	1.97	1.50
	Detroit	2.72	2.56	2.61	2.85	2.11	2.05	1.36
Satisfaction with understanding								
Husband's	Tokyo	4.60	4.71	4.38	4.34	3.87	3.28	2.40
Wife's	Tokyo	4.95	4.92	4.62	4.47	4.07	3.36	2.75
	Detroit	3.80	3.64	3.79	3.62	3.43	3.41	3.12
Aggregate satisfaction with marriage								
Husband's	Tokyo	6.46	6.50	6.13	6.15	4.91	3.61	2.80
Wife's	Tokyo	6.57	5.65	5.66	5.73	4.61	3.86	3.25
	Detroit	5.07	4.76	5.22	5.31	4.67	4.67	4.38
Husband's therapeutic effectiveness by wife's sex role preference								
Feminine		2.69	2.60	2.62	2.54	2.30	2.06	(2.50)
Masculine or uncertain		(1.75)	2.55	2.63	(2.83)	2.03	1.83	(0.50)
Minimum Number of Cases								
Wife's response	Tokyo	110	35	42	55	49	37	5
Husband's response	Tokyo	20	159	85	30	107	29	4
	Detroit	116	86	33	13	28	80	25

APPENDIX B

TOKYO INTERVIEW SCHEDULES

TOKYO INTERVIEW SCHEDULES

English Translation

1. When did you meet your husband for the first time?

2. When you first met your husband, did someone introduce you to each other, or not?

3* (IF INTRODUCED) Who introduced him to you? (check one)

    (1) My parent or his friend
    (2) An older sibling or his friend
    (3) A younger sibling or his friend
    (4) My friend
    (5) My employer or superior at work
    (6) My teacher
    (7) An older relative
    (8) A young relative
    (9) My minister or religious leader
  (10) A neighbor
  (11) The leader of an organization I belong to
  (12) Someone else (fill in)

4* (IF INTRODUCED) Was he introduced as a possible marriage partner or not?

5* (IF HE WAS INTRODUCED AS A POSSIBLE MARRIAGE PARTNER) Who first thought that you might be interested in meeting a possible marriage partner?

    (1) I had already said I was interested in meeting a possible marriage partner

1. 御主人と 始めて お逢いに なったのは 何時でしたか.

2. 御主人に 始めて お逢いに なられた時 誰方の御紹介が あったのですか. それとも その他の方法で お逢いに なったのですか.

3. (御紹介が あったの でしたら) 誰方が 御主人を 紹介されたの ですか. (どれか 1つ チェックする事)
    (1) 御両親 又は その お友達
    (2) 年上の きょうだい 又は その お友達
    (3) 年下の きょうだい 又は その お友達
    (4) お友達
    (5) 雇い主 又は 職場の上役
    (6) 先生
    (7) 年上の 親類
    (8) 若い 親類
    (9) 牧師 その他 宗教関係の方
  (10) 近所の人
  (11) 団体関係の 上司
  (12) その他 (具体的に 記入する事)

4. (御紹介が あったの でしたら) 御紹介を受けられた時 御主人は 結婚を予想して 紹介されたのですか. それとも そんなことは なかったのですか.

5. (もし 御結婚の相手として 紹介されたのでしたら) 貴女に 結婚の相手を お世話しようと 最初に 考えられたのは どなたですか.
    (1) 前から 御自分で 結婚したいと 云って 居られた.

---

* Except where otherwise indicated, questions were asked of wives only. Starred questions were asked of both partners. Questions asked of husbands only appear at the end of this list.

5* (cont'd)

    (2) My parents wanted me to meet a
           possible marriage partner

    (3) The person who introduced us (IF
           OTHER THAN A PARENT) wanted me to
           meet a possible marriage partner

(2)御両親が あなたの 結婚を 心配された.

(3)(御両親以外の時) お二人を 紹介して 下さった
方が あなたの 結婚を 心配された.

6. Did you have a formal _miai_?

6. 正式の お見合の 席で お逢いに なったのですか

7. (IF YES) How many were present at the
miai including you and your husband?

7. (そうだとしたら) その場に 列席なさったのは
あなたと 御主人を 入れて 何人でしたか.

8. How many weeks, months, or years went
by from the time you began going with
your husband until you were engaged
(or until you exchanged _yuino_ betrothal
gifts)?

8. 御主人との お話が 始って 御婚約までに
どの位 経って 居りましたか. 御婚約なさら
なかった 場合には 結納を 取り交わされた
時迄の こととして お答え下さい.

9* Prior to your engagement, how many times
altogether did you meet your husband's
family?

9. 御婚約前に 御主人の 家族の方と 全部で
何度位 お逢いに なりましたか.

10* About how many times before your engagement did you meet the fellows who were
your husband's friends?

10. 御婚約前に 御主人の お友達と 何度位
お逢いに なりましたか.

11. How many times before your engagement
did the two of you go out alone together?

11. 御婚約前に 何度位 お二人で お附合を
なさったことが ございますか.

During the period before engagement, we
would like to know whether you discussed
together certain topics.

御婚約前に 貴方々は 御一緒に 色々なこと
について 話し合われたことと 存じます.

12. How often did you discuss national or
international political issues?

12. 国内政治や 国際政治については どの位
話し合われましたか.

        (Card I)

(カード 1)

    Often (3x)***
    Sometimes (2x)
    Seldom (1x)
    Never (0)

よく
時々
たまたま
全然ない

* This question asked of both partners.
*** Numbers in parentheses show weights used in computing mean frequencies.

13. How often did the two of you discuss "traditional" vs. "modern" husband-wife relationships? (Card I)

14. How often did you two discuss his vocation plans and aspirations and the wife's work? (Card I)

15＊ How often did your husband tell you about things which had happened to him between dates? (Card I)

16＊ How often did he tell you about emotional problems facing him? (Card I)

17＊ Now we are interested in the situation which existed at the time you got engaged. Which of the following terms best describes your own attitude at that time toward the idea of marrying this particular man?

      (Card II)

Eager, enthusiastic (5x)＊＊＊
Happy (4x)
Indecisive (3x)
Indifferent, unconcerned (2x)
Reluctant, hesitant (1x)
Opposed (0)

18＊ Which term best describes your father's attitude toward your marrying him? (If had no parents, what was attitude of closest male relative or parent-substitute?) (Card II)

19＊ Which term best describes your mother's attitude toward your marrying him? (Card II)

＊ This question asked of both partners.

＊＊＊ Numbers in parentheses show weights used in computing mean frequencies.

13. 旧式な 夫婦関係や 新しい 夫婦関係については どの位 話し合われましたか.

14. 御主人の お仕事の 計画や 理想や 共稼ぎに ついては どの位話し合われましたか.

15. お二人が しばらく 逢わなかった間 御主人に 起ったことが どの位 話題に上りましたか.

16. 御主人に 起った 心配事や 不愉快な 経験を 御主人は どの位 あなたに お話しになり ましたか.

17. 初. 此処から あなたが 御婚約なさった時の 事について 伺わせて 頂きたいと 思います. 御婚約なさった時の 御主人に 対する あなた の お気持は このカードにある 表現の中の どれに 最も 近かったでしょうか.

    （カード 2）

熱望した
嬉しかった
あれこれと 思い迷った
どちらでも よかった
気乗が しなかった
反対 だった

18. あなたの 御結婚についての お父さんの お 気持は 如何でしたか. （御両親が 居らっしゃ らなかった 場合には 一番近い 親類の方か 親代りの 態度）

19. あなたの 御結婚についての お母さんの お気持は 如何でしたか.

20* As for your father, your mother, and
    yourself, whom would you say had the
    most influence in the decision that
    you would marry this boy? (Lit. who
    was the chief "promoting power"?)

21* Who had the next most influence?

22* At the time of your engagement, how
    much love would you say you felt
    toward your fiance?

    (Card III)

    Intense, powerful (5x)
    A great deal (lit. strong,
    firm) (4x)
    Considerable (3x)
    A little (2x)
    Hardly any (1x)
    None (0)

23* In general, would you classify your
    marriage as an arranged marriage or
    a love-match?

24* Marriage has so many different as-
    pects that sometimes it is difficult
    to say which is most important. Here
    is a list of ten characteristics of a
    good husband. In your opinion, which
    would you say it is most important for
    the husband to be?

    (Card IV for wives)

    (1) Courteous and respectful toward
         his wife
    (2) Compatible in making decisions
    (3) Helpful with household tasks
    (4) A good breadwinner
    (5) Health for having children
    (6) A good father in raising children
    (7) A good companion in leisure-time
         activities

* This question asked of both partners.

20. あなたと お父さん と お母さん のうちで 御主
    との 結婚を 決められるのに 一番 強い
    推進力と なったのは 誰方 ですか。

21. 次に 強い 推進力と なったのは 誰方 です

22. 御婚約 なさった時 あなたは 御婚約者に
    どれ程 愛情を 感じて 居られたでしょうか。

    (カード 3)
    強烈 だった
    強く 感じた
    可成 感じた
    少し 感じた
    殆んど 感じなかった
    全然 感じなかった

23. 一口に 言えば あなたの 結婚は 見合結婚
    恋愛結婚 の どちらに なるでしょうか。

24. 結婚生活には 色々な面が ありますので どれ
    一番 大切かと 言うことは 一概には 言えませ
    比処に 10程 「良い 御主人」の 特性を 引
    き出して あります。 あなたの お考えでは 御
    人に 一番 大切なものは この中の どれに
    あたるでしょう。

    (1) 御主人が 奥さんを 尊重なさること。
    (2) 物事が 円満に 取り決められること。
    (3) 家事も 手伝って 下さること。
    (4) 生活力が あること。
    (5) 子供さんが 出来る程 健康であること。
    (6) 御主人が 子供さんにとって よい 父親で
        あること。
    (7) お仕事のない時 よく奥さんの お相手をして
        下さること

(8) Understanding and sympathetic toward
     wife's problems and feelings
(9) Loving and affectionate
(10) Attractive as a male

(Card IV for husbands)

(1) Courteous and respectful toward
     her husband
(2) Compatible in making family de-
     cisions
(3) A good house-keeper, home-maker
(4) A wise manager in spending money
(5) Healthy for bearing children
(6) A good mother in raising children
(7) A good companion in leisure-time
     activities
(8) Understanding and sympathetic
     toward the husband's problems and
     feelings
(9) Loving and affectionate
(10) Sexually attractive

25* Which would you say is next most impor-
     tant? (Card IV)

26* And which is most important after that?
     (Card IV)

27. When did you marry?

28* What does your husband usually call you
     at home?

29. When you and your husband are taking a
     taxi who usually gets in first?

              (Card V)

Husband always (0)
Husband more often than wife (1x)
Husband and wife equally often (2x)
Wife more often than husband (3x)
Wife always (4x)

* This question asked of both partners.

(8) 御主人が 奥さんの 立場や お気持を よく
    理解して 下さること.
(9) 愛情が 豊かなこと
(10) 男性的な 魅力が あること

(1) 奥さんが 御主人を 尊重なさること.
(2) 物事が 円満に とりきめられること.
(3) 家事の 切り盛りが 上手なこと.
(4) 家計の やりくりが 上手なこと.
(5) 子供さんが 出来る程 健康であること.
(6) 奥さんが 子供さんにとって よい母親であること.
(7) よく 御主人の お相手を して下さること.
(8) 奥さんが 御主人の 立場や お気持を よく
    理解して 下さること.
(9) 愛情が 豊かなこと.
(10) 女性的な 魅力が あること.

25. 次に 大切だと 思われるのは どれですか.

26. 三番目は 如何 ですか.

27. 何時 御結婚に なりましたか.

28. 御主人は あなたを お宅で 普通 何と 呼
    ばれますか.

29. お二人で タクシーに お乗りになる時 どちら
    が 先に 乗りますか.

       (カード 5)

いつも 御主人
たいてい 御主人
御主人の 時と 奥さんの 時と 同じ位の割
たいてい 奥さん
いつも 奥さん

30. When you and your husband board a bus
    or local train, if only one seat is
    left, which of you usually sits down?
    (Card V)

    Now we would like to know how you and
    your husband divide up some of the fam-
    ily tasks.

    (IF NEITHER HAS EVER DONE TASK, ASK ON
    A HYPOTHETICAL BASIS: If you or your
    husband did do it, who do you think
    would do the work?)

31. Who puts away the <u>futon</u> quilts in the
    morning? (Card V)

32. Who repairs things around the house?
    (Card V)

33. When you are out in public together,
    who carries heavy objects such as a
    suitcase or child? (Card V)

34. Which of you shops for the husband's
    special delicacies? (Card V)

35. Who buys ordinary clothes (such as
    underwear, handkerchiefs) for the
    husband? (Card V)

36. Who folds up the husband's clothes
    and puts them away after he takes
    them off at night? (Card V)

37. Who takes the children out on Sunday?
    (Card V)

* This question asked of both partners.

30. 御主人と お二人で 乗物に のられた時 席が
    一つしか なかった様な 場合 どちらが お座
    りに なりますか.

    扨 今度は あなたと 御主人との お仕事の
    分担に ついて 伺わせて 頂きます.

    (まだ したことが ないと すれば 左の 空欄に
    チェックして 仮定として 聞くこと. もし あなた
    か 御主人が なさると すれば どちらが
    なさるでしょうね.)

31. 朝 ふとんを 上げるのは どちらですか.

32. 家の中や 家の廻りの 一寸した 修理や
    手入などは どちらが なさいますか.

33. お揃いで 外に 出られた時 子供さんを
    だかれたり スーツ・ケースの 様な 重い 荷物
    を 持つのは どちらですか.

34. 御主人の 好物を 買いに 行かれるのは
    どちらですか.

35. 御主人の 日常衣類 (下着や ハンカチ など)を
    お買いに なるのは どちらですか.

36. 夜 御主人が 脱がれた 洋服を たたんで
    しまわれるのは どちらですか.

37. 日曜などに 子供さんを 連れて お出に
    なるのは どちらですか.

38. Who disciplines the children? (Card V)

38. 子供さんに 躾を なさるのは どちらですか

39. Who helps the children with their school lessons? (Card V)

39. 子供さんの 勉強を みてあげるのは どちらですか.

Next we would like to ask several questions about how much say you and your husband usually have in various family decisions. Here is a list of different ways of dividing up decisions.

次に あなたと 御主人との間で 色々なことを お決めになる時のことについて 問わせて 頂きます. 比処に カードが あります.

(IF A DECISION HAS NEVER BEEN MADE; ASK ON A HYPOTHETICAL BASIS: "If you did decide it, who do you think would make the final decision?")

(まだ お決めに なったことが ないならば 二重枠の中に 〇印を書いて 決めなければ ならなくなった 時のことを 仮定して 聞いて 下さい.)

40. Disregarding the question of how much you may talk things over ahead of time, who usually makes the final decision about whether or not to buy some life insurance?

40. 事前の 話し合い その他は 一応ぬきにして 物事を 最后に お決めになるのは どなた でしょうか. たとえば 保険等に入る時 最終的に お決めになるのは どちらですか

(Card VI)

Husband always (4x)
Husband more often than wife (3x)
Either of you decides separately and equally often (2x)
You always compromise (between you) (2x)
Wife more often than husband (1x)
Wife always (0)

(カード 6)
何時も 御主人
御主人の方が 多い
お二人が 同じ位の割合で 別々に決める
何時も お二人の間で 妥協なさる
あなたの方が 多い.
何時も あなた

41. Who usually makes the final decision about whether you can buy new Western-style clothes? (Card VI)

41. あなたが 新しい 洋服を お買いになる時は 最終的に お決めになるのは どちらですか.

42. Who usually makes the final decision about how much to spend for an obituary gift or congratulatory gift? (Card VI)

42. お香典の額や お祝の金額を 最終的に 決める時は. どちらですか.

43. Who usually makes the final decision about where to go on a holiday outing? (Card VI)

43. 休みに 何処かに お出になる 様な時の 行先を 最終的に お決めになるのは どちらですか.

44. Who usually decides when sexual rela-
    tions will occur?   (Card VI)

44. 夫婦の交わりを なさる時　最終的に お決め
    なるのは どちらですか.

45. Who usually makes the final decision
    about what radio or T.V. program to
    listen to in the evening?   (Card VI)

45. 夜 聞く ラジオ や テレビ の 番組を 最終的
    お決めに なるのは　どちらですか.

46. Who usually makes the final decision
    about how much money the children may
    have to spend?   (Card VI)

46. 子供さんの お小遣いの額を 最終的に
    お決めに なるのは どちらですか.

47. Who usually decides the children's
    lessons such as music, dancing, cal-
    ligraphy and abacus.   (Card VI)

47. 子供さんに 音楽や 舞踊等の おけいこ事を
    させたり そろばん塾に 通わせたり する時
    最后に お決めに なるのは どちらですか.

48. Who usually makes the final decision
    about what school the children will
    attend?   (Card VI)

48. 子供さんを 入れる学校を 最終的に きめるの
    どちらでしょう.

49* How often does your husband tell you
    about things that happened to him
    during the day?

49. 御主人は その日の 出来事を どの位 あな
    に お話しに なりますか.

(Card VII)

(カード 7)
毎日
殆んど 毎日
週に 1～2度
月に 2～3度
月に 1度
年に 2～3度
それよりも 少い
全然ない

Everyday (300x)
Almost everyday (200x)
Once or twice a week (50x)
A few times a month (20x)
Once a month (10x)
A few times a year (2x)
Less than that (1x)
Never (0)

50. How often do you discuss news events
    with your husband (i.e. things that
    happen outside your family)?   (Card VII)

50. 新聞や ラジオで 知る ニュース（御家庭以外
    を どれ位 御主人と 話し合われますか.

52. How often do you and your husband
    get together with friends?   (Card VII)

52. どの位 御夫婦で 御両親や 親類の
    方々と 往き来を なさいますか.

* This question asked of both partners.

How often do you and your husband go out together just for a good time by yourselves? (Card VII)

How often does your husband tell or show you by a gesture or facial expression that he loves you? (Card VII)

How often do you and your husband have sexual relations? (Card VII)

How often do you feel as though you are like a servant to your husband?

(Card VIII)

Always (4x)
Usually (3x)
About half the time (2x)
Seldom (1x)
Never (0)

'* How often does your husband thank you for little things that you do for him? (Card VIII)

. How often do you join the conversation when your husband's friends come to visit your home? (Card VIII)

'* When you have had a bad day, how often do you tell your husband about your troubles? (Card VIII)

'* (IF EVER TELLS) When you do tell him about your troubles what does he say or do?

(Card IX)

(1) He helps me directly with the problem
(2) He helps me get away from my troubles

This question asked of both partners.

53. どの位 御夫婦で 外に 遊びに 出かけ られることが ありますか.

54. お宅の 御主人は どの位 あなたへの 愛情 を 言葉や 仕事や 表情で お示しに なりますか.

55. どの位 御主人と 夫婦の 交りを なさいますか.

56. どの位 御主人が あなたを 女中の様に あつかわれることが ございますか.

(カード 8)
何時も
大低
半分位
たまに
全然ない

57. あなたが 御主人に 一寸したことを して さしあげた時 御主人は どれ位 お礼を 云われますか.

58. 御主人の お友達が 見えた時 どの位 あなたも 一緒に お話の 仲間に 入られますか.

59. いやなことが あった時 あなたは 御主人 に どれ位 打ち明けられますか.

60. (打ち明ける場合) 御主人は あなたの 問題を 聞いて どの様な 反応を 示されますか.

(カード 9)
(1)問題を 解決する為に 色々と 手を うって 下さる.
(2)あなたの うさを 晴らして 下さる.

(3) He gives me suggestions about how I can solve the problem

(4) He tells me to forget my troubles because they are not important

(5) He says they are my own fault and not to bother him with them

(6) He expresses sympathy or affection for me

(7) He just listens, does not say much

61* Does he usually make you feel <u>much better</u>, <u>a little better</u>, <u>about the same</u>, or <u>worse</u>? (3x, 2x, 1x, 0 respectively)

Now we would appreciate knowing how you feel about certain specific aspects of your marriage. Here is a list of possible feelings you might have. For instance, which of those terms best describes how you feel about...

62* The courtesy and respect your husband shows you as his wife?

(Card X)

Extremely bad (0)
Dissatisfied (1x)
Not dissatisfied but wish there were more   (2x)
Can't complain (3x)
Fairly satisfied (4x)
Satisfied (5x)
Ideal (6x)

63. How do you feel about the help you get from your husband with household tasks? (Card X)

64* How do you feel about the interest your husband takes in making family decisions? (Card X)

65* How do you feel about the share in making family decisions which your husband gives you?   (Card X)

* This question asked of both partners.

(3) 問題の 解決の 方法を 教えて下さる.

(4) 大した ことは ないのだから 気に留めるなと 云われる.

(5) 全ては あなたの 罪だから そんな事で 余り わずらわせないで ほしいと 云われる.

(6) 同情したり 愛情を 示して下さる.

(7) 聞いては 下さる けれども 余り 取りあっては 下さらない.

61. 普通 御主人に 聞いて いただいたら どの様に なりますか. ずっと楽に なりますか 少し楽に なりますか. 大して 変りませんか それとも 却って 辛くなりますか.

今度は あなたの 結婚生活の 色々な面に ついて 少し 立入ったことを 伺わせて 頂きますが このカードを 使って 次の 幾つかの 質問に お答え 願いたいと 思います

62. 御主人は あなたを 妻として 尊重して 居らっしゃるという点では どう お感じになって いらっしゃいますか.

(カード 10)
全然 駄目
不満に 思う
もう少し どうにか なればと 思う
まあまあ という所
可成 満足しています
満足しています
申し分なし

63. 家事の ことなど 御主人は どれ程 手伝って 下さる という点では どの様に お感じに なって いらっしゃいますか.

64. 家庭内で 物事を お決めになる時 御主人が どの程度 関心を もって 居られるか という点では どう お感じになって 居られますか.

65. 家庭内で 物事を お決めになる時 御主人が あなたに 相談を なさるという点 については どう お感じになって 居られますか.

6. How do you feel about your husband's ability as a breadwinner - your place to live, clothes, food, etc.? (Card X)

7* How do you feel about the way your husband functions as a father to your children? (Card X)

8* How do you feel about your husband's understanding of your problems and feelings? (Card X)

9* How do you feel about the companionship you have in doing things together with your husband? (Card X)

0* How do you feel about the sexual satisfaction you experience in your marriage? (Card X)

1* How do you feel about the love and affection you receive from your husband? (Card X)

2* Using this card, which term best describes your affection for your husband?

(Card XI)

Very intense, powerful (5x)
Strong, firm (4x)
Considerable (3x)
A little (2x)
Hardly any (1x)
None (0)

3. Do you expect to have any (more) children?

* This question asked of both partners.

66. 御主人の 生活力という面〔衣食住等〕では どう お感じになって 居らっしゃいますか。

67. あなたの 御主人を 父親として どんな風だと お感じになって いらっしゃいますか。

68. 御主人は あなたの 立場や 気持を よく 理解して 下さるという点では どのように 感じて いらっしゃいますか。

69. 御主人は よく あなたの お相手を して 下さるという点では どの様に お感じですか。

70. 御主人との 夫婦の 交わりについて どの程度 満足なさって いらっしゃいますか。

71. 御主人の 愛情を あなたは どの様に 感じて いらっしゃいますか。

72. このカードに ある 表現の中で あなたの 御主人への 愛情を 一番よく 表わして いる ものは どれで しょうか。

（カード 11）
強烈である
強く 感じている
可成 感じている
少し 感じている
殆んど 感じていない
全然 感じて いない

73. もっと お子さんが 出来ると お思いですか。

74. (IF YES, OR IN DOUBT) Counting those you have now, how many children do you expect to have altogether?

75* We have been talking about the number of children you <u>expect</u> to have. Now how many children would you <u>want</u> to have altogether if you could choose and have just the number you want?

76. If you could have your choice, would you rather be a boy or a girl?

　　(1) I wish I were a boy
　　(2) I am happy I was a girl

77. Do you do any work other than housework?

78* (IF YES) How many hours a week?

79. Do you work with your husband or separately?

80* Before becoming acquainted with your husband, how many men had you ever been introduced to by <u>miai</u>?

81* Not counting your husband, how many young men did you ever go out with for a good time? (e.g. go to a movie, concert or dine together)

82* Have you ever been to Europe or America?

83* What was the last school you attended?

* This question asked of both partners.

74.（まだ 生れるかもしれないとすれば） 今 居らっしゃる お子さんも 入れて 全部で 何人位 欲しいと お考えですか.

75.

75. お子さんは 何人位が 理想的だと 思われますか.

76. もし 出来ることなら 男に 生れたかったと 思われますか. それとも 女であって よかったと 思われますか.
　(1) 男に 生れたかった.
　(2) 女で よかった.

77. あなたは 家事以外に お仕事を 持って 居られますか.

78.（お仕事を 持って 居られるとしたら） 一週間に 何時間位 働かれますか.

79. その お仕事は 御主人と 一緒ですか. それとも 別々ですか.

80. 御主人に お知り合いに なる前に 何人位 他の男の方と 見合を なさった ことが おありですか.

81. 御主人を 数えないで 何人位の 男の方と お附合を なさったことが ございますか （例えば 映画に行くとか 音楽会に 行くとか 食事を なさるなど）

82. ヨーロッパか アメリカに 行かれたことが ございますか.

83. 最終学校は どちらですか.

84* Did you finish or quit this school?

84. 卒業なさいましたか、それとも 中途退学ですか.

85* What year were you born?

84. 何年 生れ ですか.

86. How many children do you have?

86. お子さんは 何人 居らっしゃいますか.

87. How old are they?

87. お子さんは おいくつ ですか.

25** When you have sexual relations with your wife, about how many minutes are usually spent in foreplay?

25. 奥さんと 夫婦の 交わりをなさる時 何分位 前戯を なさいますか.

27** How do you feel about the work your wife does in household tasks? (Card X)

27. 奥さんの 家事の 切り盛りについては どう お感じに なって 居られますか.

30** How do you feel about your wife's management of the money at her disposal? (Card X)

30. 奥さんの 家計の やりくりについては 如何 ですか.

38** Are you the first son?

38. あなたは 御長男 ですか.

45** What is your occupation? (Specify in detail)

45. あなたの 御職業は 何ですか (具体的 に 記入して 下さい)

46** What is your usual monthly income? (If you operate a business, this means <u>net</u> income)

46. あなたの 月収は お幾ら位ですか. (もし 商売をして 居られるのでしたら実 収入額を お書き下さい)

* This question asked of both partners.

** Husbands only.

APPENDIX C

DETROIT INTERVIEW SCHEDULE
(Wives only)

Detroit Interview Schedule
(Wives Only)*

About how often do you folks get together outside of work with any of
the people you or your husband work
with?

(Card I)

Every day (300x)**
Almost every day (200x)
Once or twice a week (50x)
A few times a month (20x)
Once a month (10x)
A few times a year (2x)
Less often (1x)
Never (0)

One way in which some couples spend
their time is in clubs and organiz-
tions. Please look at this list and
tell me which of these kinds of organizations you or your husband belong to, if any.

(IF NECESSARY) 39a. Do you and he
belong to the same club?

(Card IV)

Labor unions
A church
Church-connected groups
Fraternal organizations or lodges
Veteran's organizations
Business or civic groups
Parent-Teachers Associations
Neighborhood clubs or community centers
Organizations of people of same nation-
   ality background
Sport teams
Political clubs or organizations
Neighborhood improvement associations
Women's clubs
Charitable and welfare organizations

45. We would like to know how you and your
    husband divide up some of the family
    jobs. Here is a list of different ways
    of dividing up jobs. Now who does the
    grocery shopping?

    (Card V)

    Husband always (0)
    Husband more than wife (1x)
    Husband and wife exactly the same (2x)
    Wife more than husband (3x)
    Wife always (4x)

46. Who gets your husband's breakfast on
    work days?(Card V)

47. Who does the evening dishes? (Card V)

48. Who straightens up the livingroom when
    company is coming?(Card V)

49. Who mows the lawn? (Card V)

50. Who shovels the sidewalk? (Card V)

51. Who repairs things around the house?
    (Card V)

52. Who keeps track of the money and the
    bills? (Card V)

54. In every family somebody has to decide
    such things as where the family will
    live and so on. Many couples talk such
    things over first, but the final decision

Numbers in parentheses show weights used in computing mean frequencies.

Questions not used in this book have been omitted.

54. (cont'd) often has to be made by the
husband or the wife. For instance,
who usually makes the final decision
about what car to get?

(Card VI)

Husband always (4x)
Husband more than wife (3x)
Husband and wife exactly the same (2x)
Wife more than husband (1x)
Wife always (0)

55. ...about whether or not to buy some
life insurance? (Card VI)

56. ...about what house or apartment to
take? (Card VI)

57. Who usually makes the final decision
about what job your husband should
take? (Card VI)

58. ...about whether or not you should go
to work or quit work? (Card VI)

59. ...about how much money your ramily
can afford to spend per week on food?
(Card VI)

60. ...about what doctor to have when someone is sick? (Card VI)

66. Thinking of marriage in general, which
one of the five things on this next card
would you say is the most valuable part
of marriage?

66. (cont'd)

(Card VII)

(1) The chance to have children
(2) The standard of living--the
kind of house, clothes, car
and so forth.
(3) The husband's understanding
of the wife's problems and
feelings.
(4) The husband's expression of
love and affection for the
wife.
(5) Companionship in doing things
together with the husband.

67. Which would you say is the next most
valuable? (Card VII)

68. Which would you say is the third most
valuable? (Card VII)

70. When you've had a bad day, do you tell
your husband about your troubles:
always, usually, about half the time,
seldom, or never? (4x, 3x, 2x, 1x, 0
respectively)

(IF EVER TELLS HUSBAND) 72. When you do
tell about your troubles, what does he
say or do?

73. After he's done that, do you usually f
much better, a little better, about th
same, or worse? (3x, 2x, 1x, 0 respec
ly)

74. We are also interested in the changing size of American families. To begin with how many children have you had altogether?

(IF ANY) 75. What are their ages?

79. How long have you been married?

80. Do you expect to have any (more) children?

81. (IF YES, IN DOUBT, DON'T KNOW) Counting those you have now, how many children do you expect to have altogether?

2a. We have been talking about the number of children you expect to have. Now, if you could choose and have just the number you want by the time you are 45, how many would that be?

02. Here is a card that lists some feelings you might have about certain aspects of marriage. Could you tell me the statement that best describes how you feel about each of the following? For example, how do you feel about your standard of living--the kind of house, clothes, car, and so forth?

(Card VIII)

Pretty disappointed--I'm really missing out on that. (1x)
It would be nice to have more. (2x)
It's all right, I guess--I can't complain. (3x)
Quite satisfied--I'm lucky the way it is. (4x)
Enthusiastic--it couldn't be better. (5x)

104. How do you feel about the love and affection you receive? (Card VIII)

105. How do you feel about the companionship in doing things together? (Card VIII)

106. When your husband comes home from work, how often does he tell you about things that happened there? (Card I)

Census Data

7.** What was the highest grade of school you completed?

7a.** (IF ATTENDED COLLEGE) How many years of college did you complete?

12. What was your total family income in 1954, considering all sources as rents, profits, wages, interest and so on?

12a. How much of that was income of the head of the family?

13.** What is your occupation?

13a.**(IF WIFE IS EMPLOYED) How many hours do you usually work in a week?

* This question was also asked with respect to the husband.

APPENDIX D
COMPUTATION OF INDICES

The husband's power score was reduced as follows from the sum of the weighted answers shown in the questionnaires:

Tokyo	Detroit
0– 9 = 0 (low power)	
10–11 = 1	0–11 = 1
12–13 = 2	12–13 = 2
14–15 = 3	14–15 = 3
16–17 = 4	16–17 = 4
18–19 = 5	18 = 5
20–21 = 6	19–20 = 6
22–23 = 7	21–22 = 7
24–25 = 8	23–24 = 8
26–27 = 9	25–26 = 9
28–36 = 10 (high power)	27–32 = 10

Power structures were classified by the following cutting points on the reduced scales given above:

	Tokyo	Detroit
Wife dominant	= 0– 3	1– 4
Husband dominant	= 7–10	8–10
Equalitarian	= 4– 6	5– 7

Equalitarian power structures were subdivided according to the number of shared decisions:

	Tokyo	Detroit
Autonomic	= 0–4	0–4
Syncratic	= 5–9	5–8

The wife's task performance score was reduced as follows from the sum of the weighted answers shown in the questionnaires:

Tokyo	Detroit
0–12 = 0 (low task performance)	
13–14 = 1	0– 9 = 1
15–16 = 2	10–11 = 2
17–18 = 3	12–13 = 3
19–20 = 4	14–15 = 4
21–22 = 5	16 = 5
23–24 = 6	17–18 = 6
25–26 = 7	19–20 = 7
27–28 = 8	21–23 = 8
29–30 = 9	24–32 = 9
31–36 = 10 (high task performance)	

Marital satisfaction scores were computed by summing the product of the satisfaction scores (Card X in Tokyo, Card VIII in Detroit) by the weighted importance of that facet of marriage:

$$
\begin{aligned}
\text{First choice} &= 5x \\
\text{Second choice} &= 4x \\
\text{Third choice} &= 3x \\
\text{Not chosen} &= 1x
\end{aligned}
$$

In Tokyo, the satisfaction responses for Questions 64 and 65 were averaged together in order to summarize the respondent's satisfaction with "compatibility in making decisions."

Satisfaction with the couple's expected number of children was inferred by the following scoring of the discrepancy between the expected number and the wife's preferred number:

Tokyo	Detroit
No discrepancy $= 6x$	
0.5 $= 5x$	0 or 0.5 $= 5x$
1.0 $= 4x$	1.0 $= 4x$
1.5 $= 3x$	1.5 or 2.0 $= 3x$
2.0 $= 2x$	2.5 $+= 2x$
2.5 $+= 1x$	Prefer some, expect
Prefer some, expect	none, or vice versa $= 1x$
none, or vice versa $= 0$	

The aggregate satisfaction scores were reduced as follows:

Tokyo	Detroit
0– 45 $=$ 0 (low satisfaction)	
46– 50 $=$ 1	14–29 $=$ 1
51– 55 $=$ 2	30–38 $=$ 2
56– 60 $=$ 3	39–42 $=$ 3
61– 65 $=$ 4	43–46 $=$ 4
66– 70 $=$ 5	47–50 $=$ 5
71– 75 $=$ 6	51–54 $=$ 6
76– 80 $=$ 7	55–58 $=$ 7
81– 85 $=$ 8	59–63 $=$ 8
86– 90 $=$ 9	64–70 $=$ 9
91–114 $=$ 10 (high satisfaction)	

Comparative marital satisfaction (Tokyo) treats aggregate satisfaction of 6–10 as satisfied, 0–5 as dissatisfied.

REFERENCES

Aiken, Michael, and David Goldberg. Monograph on kinship data from the Detroit Area Study. In preparation.

Ariga, Kizaemon. "Contemporary Japanese Family in Transition," in *Transactions of the Third World Congress of Sociology* (1955), **4**: 215–221.

Asayama, Shinichi. "Comparison of Sexual Development of American and Japanese Adolescents," *Psychologia* (1957), **1**: 129–131.

Baber, Ray E. *Youth Looks at Marriage and the Family: A Study of Changing Japanese Attitudes.* Tokyo: International Christian University, 1958.

Beardsley, Richard K., John W. Hall, and Robert E. Ward. *Village Japan.* Chicago: University of Chicago Press, 1959.

Benedict, Ruth. *The Chrysanthemum and the Sword.* Boston: Houghton Mifflin, 1946.

Bennett, John W., and Robert K. McKnight. "Misunderstandings in Communication Between Japanese Students and Americans," *Social Problems* (1956), **4**: 243–256.

Blood, Robert O., Jr. *Marriage.* New York: The Free Press, 1962.

—— "The Husband-Wife Relationship." in F. Ivan Nye and Lois W. Hoffman (eds.), *The Employed Mother in America.* Chicago: Rand McNally (1963), pp. 282–305.

—— "Culture Contact and Social Change: The Impact of Foreign Study on Japanese Marriage Patterns." Accepted for publication in *Asian Survey* (forthcoming).

—— "Kinship Interaction and Marital Solidarity," forthcoming.

—— and Robert L. Hamblin. "The Effect of the Wife's Employment on the Family Power Structure," *Social Forces* (1958), **36**: 347–352.

—— Reuben Hill, André Michel, and Constantina Safilios-Rothschild. "Comparative Analysis of Family Power Structure: Problems of Measurement and Interpretation," a paper presented to the Ninth International Seminar on Family Research. Tokyo: 1965, to be published in René König and Reuben Hill (eds.), *Yearbook of the International Sociological Association*, 1966.

—— and John Yuzuru Takeshita. "Development of Cross-Cultural Equivalence of Measures of Marital Interaction for U.S.A. and Japan," *Transactions of the Fifth World Congress of Sociology* (1964), **4**: 333–344.

—— and Donald M. Wolfe. *Husbands and Wives: the Dynamics of Married Living.* New York: The Free Press, 1960.

Bott, Elizabeth. *Family and Social Network.* London: Tavistock, 1957.

Burgess, Ernest W., and Harvey J. Locke. *The Family: From Institution to Companionship.* New York: American Book Company, 1953.

—— and Paul Wallin. *Engagement and Marriage.* Philadelphia: Lippincott, 1953.

Caudill, William. "Around the Clock Patient Care in Japanese Psychiatric Hospitals: the Role of the Tsukisoi," *American Sociological Review* (1961a), **26**: 204–214.

—— "Some Problems in Transnational Communication (Japan–United States)" in *Application of Psychiatric Insights to Cross-Cultural Communication* (1961b), Group for the Advancement of Psychiatry, pp. 409–421.

—— "Anthropology and Psychoanalysis: Some Theoretical Issues," in Thomas Gladwin and William C. Sturtevant (eds.), *Anthropology and Human Behavior.* Washington: The Anthropological Society of Washington (1962a), pp. 174–214.

—— "Patterns of Emotion in Modern Japan," in Robert J. Smith and Richard K. Beardsley (eds.), *Japanese Culture: Its Development and Characteristics.* Chicago: Aldine (1962b), pp. 115–131.

—— "Social Background and Sibling Rank Among Japanese Psychiatric Patients," a paper presented at the second Conference on the Modernization of Japan (1963).

—— and L. Takeo Doi. "Interrelations of Psychiatry, Culture and Emotion in Japan," in Iago Galdston (ed.), *Medicine and Anthropology.* New York: International Universities Press (1963).

—— and Helen Weinstein. "Maternal Care and Infant Behavior in Japanese and American Urban Middle Class Families," in René König and Reuben Hill (eds.), *Yearbook of the International Sociological Association,* 1966.

Cox, Kozue Tomita. "Dynamics of Marital Disharmony in Japan." Tokyo: Aoyama Gakuin University, unpublished M.A. thesis in Psychology, 1966.

Dore, R. P. *City Life in Japan: A Study of a Tokyo Ward.* London: Routledge and Kegan Paul, 1958.

Duverger, Maurice. *The Political Role of Women.* Paris: Unesco, 1955.

Eberts, Paul R. "Family Life Cycle and Community Involvement," unpublished Ph.D. dissertation, Ann Arbor: University of Michigan, 1963.

DeVos, George. "The Relation of Guilt Toward Parents to Achievement and Arranged Marriage Among the Japanese," *Psychiatry* (1960), **23**: 287–301.

—— and Hiroshi Wagatsuma. *Japan's Invisible Race: Caste in Culture and Personality.* Berkeley: University of California Press, 1966.

Freedman, Ronald, Pascal K. Whelpton, and Arthur A. Campbell. *Family Planning, Sterility and Population Growth.* New York: McGraw-Hill, 1959.

Fukutake, Tadashi. *Man and Society in Japan.* Tokyo: University of Tokyo Press, 1962.

Gibran, Kahlil. *The Prophet.* New York: Knopf, 1923.

Glick, Paul C. "The Life Cycle of the Family," *Marriage and Family Living* (1955), **17**: 3–9.

Goode, William J. "The Theoretical Importance of Love," *American Sociological Review* (1959), **24**: 38–47.

Hollingshead, August B. "Marital Status and Wedding Behavior," *Marriage and Family Living* (1952), **14**: 308–311.

Homans, George C. *The Human Group.* New York: Harcourt, Brace, 1950.

Hoshino, Ikumi. "Apartment Life in Japan," *Journal of Marriage and the Family* (1964), **26**: 312–317.

Kharchev, A. G. "Results of the Investigation of the Motives of Marriage in the USSR," a paper presented to the Eighth International Seminar on Family Research, Oslo, 1963.

Kinsey, Alfred C., Wardell B. Pomeroy, Clyde E. Martin, and Paul H. Gebhard. *Sexual Behavior in the Human Female*. Philadelphia: W. B. Saunders, 1953.

Koyama, Takashi. *The Changing Social Position of Women in Japan*. Paris: Unesco, 1961.

───── ed. *Gendai Kazoku no Kenkyu* (An Investigation of the Contemporary [Japanese] Family). Tokyo: Kobundo, 1960.

Lane, Robert. *Political Life*. New York: The Free Press, 1959.

Lifton, Robert Jay. "Youth and History: Individual Change in Postwar Japan," *Daedalus* (1962), **9**: 172–197.

Matsumoto, Yoshiharu Scott. "Contemporary Japan: The Individual and the Group," in *Transactions of the American Philosophical Society* (1960), **50** (Part 1): 1–75.

Mead, Margaret. *Sex and Temperament in Three Primitive Societies*. New York: Morrow, 1935.

Ministry of Justice. *Statistical Yearbook of the Family Affairs Section of the Ministry of Justice*. Tokyo (in Japanese), 1957.

Ministry of Labor, Women's and Minors' Bureau. *The Life and Opinions of Housewives*. Tokyo (in Japanese), 1957.

Nadler, Eugene B. and William R. Morrow. "Authoritarian Attitudes Toward Woman, Their Correlates," *Journal of Social Psychology* (1959), **49**: 113–123.

Norbeck, Edward. *Takashima, A Japanese Fishing Community*. Salt Lake City: University of Utah Press, 1954.

Plath, David W. *The After Hours: Modern Japan and the Search for Enjoyment*. Berkeley: University of California Press, 1964.

Popenoe, Paul. "Meetings that Lead to Marriage," *Eugenical News*, (1932), **17**: 86.

Shinozaki, Nobuo. "Report on Sexual Life of Japanese," *Research Data* C. No. 11. Tokyo: Ministry of Welfare, Institute of Population Problems, 1957.

Slater, Philip E. "Social Limitations on Libidinal Withdrawal," *American Journal of Sociology* (1961), **67**: 296–311.

Smith, Robert J. *Kurusu: A Japanese Agricultural Community*. Ann Arbor: Center for Japanese Studies, *Occasional Papers*, No. 5, 1956.

Steiner, Kurt. "Postwar Changes in the Japanese Civil Codes," *Washington Law Review* (1950), **25**: 286–312.

Takeshita, Yuzuru. "Socio-economic Correlates of Urban Fertility in Japan," unpublished Ph.D. dissertation, Ann Arbor: University of Michigan, 1962.

Tanino, Setsu. "Family Life," *International Social Science Journal* (1961), **13**: 57–64.

Terman, Lewis M. *Psychological Factors in Marital Happiness*. New York: McGraw-Hill, 1938.

Tyler, Leona. *Psychology of Human Differences*. New York: Appleton-Century-Crofts, 1956.

Vogel, Ezra F. "The Democratization of Family Relations in Japanese Urban Society," *Asian Survey* (1961a), **1**: No. 4, 18–24.

───── "The Go-Between in a Developing Society: the Case of the Japanese Marriage Arranger," *Human Organization*, **20**: 112–120.

───── *Japan's New Middle Class: The Salary Man and His Family in a Tokyo Suburb*. Berkeley: University of California Press, 1963.

Wagatsuma, Hiroshi, and George DeVos. "Attitudes Toward Arranged Marriage in Rural Japan," *Human Organization* (1962), **21**: 187–200.

Waller, Willard. *The Family: A Dynamic Interpretation.* New York: Holt, 1938.

Whyte, William H., Jr. *The Organization Man.* New York: Simon and Schuster, 1956.

Young, Michael and Peter Willmott. *Family and Kinship in East London.* Glencoe: The Free Press, 1957.

AUTHOR INDEX

SUBJECT INDEX

263